MW00651649

ECCLESIAL ENDORSEMENTS FOR THE
ENGLISH TRANSLATION OF
CUM CLAMORE VALIDO

"It has been by God's loving Providence that I came to know about the most extraordinary private revelations as recorded in the book *Cum Clamore Valido* to an anonymous contemplative nun in France in the late 1930's. and that I succeeded in obtaining a copy of the book in English with the title "The Redeemer's Call to Consecrated Souls" from Logos Institute in the USA.

"I must say that while reading and after I finished reading this book I felt overwhelmed by Our Lord's 'APPEAL' as revealed to this contemplative French nun. All that Our Redeemer wanted to reveal to this anonymous nun could be summed up in the recorded revelation to her on All Saints Day 1940 (p. 199): 'CONSECRATED SOULS, BE SAINTS.'

"I highly recommend this book to consecrated souls and to the lay faithful in general. I am convinced that they would willingly agree to heed the 'Appeal' from Our Lord to be saints. This is because the Call for Holiness is Universal. How many lay persons from among the Church's faithful along with so many consecrated souls have been officially raised to the honors of the Altar!

"TOLLE ET LEGE! Yes, take up the book and read!"

+ *Francis Adeodatus Micallef, OCD, Emeritus Bishop of Kuwait*

"I am so thankful for having this instructive classic in an English translation placed into my hands. It is spiritual reading at its best.. I gave a copy of the book to a consecrated woman and she told me she 'couldn't put it down.' I cannot recommend strongly enough its promulgation. It is a gift to the Church. If you are a consecrated soul, a very great treasure has fallen into your hands. Dedicate yourself in diligence as you are instructed by The Teacher Himself."

—*Rev. John Olin Brown, hermit priest, Archdiocese of Trani-Barletta-Biseglie-Nazareth*

THE REDEEMER'S CALL TO CONSECRATED SOULS

CUM
CLAMORE
VALIDO

THE REDEEMER'S CALL
TO
CONSECRATED SOULS

TRANSLATED FROM THE ORIGINAL
1943 FRENCH PUBLICATION

CUM CLAMORE VALIDO

"with loud cries and tears"

(Heb 5:7)

HENRI MONIER-VINARD, S.J., EDITOR

(1877-1961)

LOGOS INSTITUTE PRESS

The original, 1943 French publication of this work, under the title *Cum Clamore Valido*, bore the *Nihil Obstat* of Jos. du Bouchet, S.J., and the *Imprimatur* of A. LeClerc, Vicar General.

PUBLISHED BY LOGOS INSTITUTE PRESS

Tarpon Springs, FL 34689

http://logosinstitute.org

Editor's Note in the Original French Edition

This "appeal" (on p. i) was made by Our Lord on March 29, 1936 to one who was to perfectly understand and respond to it, with the charge and urgent request that she propagate it and make it known to all the consecrated souls (priests and religious) whom it especially concerns. Inclusive and practical, the "appeal" would be one of the means the Sacred Heart makes use of in the present times to save the world.

Translator's Note

The original French publication of *Cum Clamore Valido*, with subtitle *The Redeemer's Call to Consecrated Souls*, appeared in 1943 at a time of great turmoil in the world. It is being re-issued here in translation in the belief that Our Lord's words are no less directed to consecrated souls today, souls seeking to live consecrated lives in today's unsettling times. In this "appeal" we learn what it is Our Lord asks of all souls who have given themselves to Him.

—*B. E. Scott*

Logos Institute

MY URGENT, PRESSING APPEAL FOR LOVE, ADDRESSED TO CONSECRATED SOULS.

TO SAVE THE WORLD
I NEED CONSECRATED SOULS
WHO ARE TRUE,
REDEMPTIVE SPOUSES OF MINE.
I DON'T HAVE ENOUGH OF THEM, THEY ARE WHAT I LACK.
GIVE ME THESE SOULS.
BE THESE SOULS FOR ME.
MY HEART AWAITS YOU.
MY HEART BEGS YOU.
BUT KNOW THIS WELL:
I ESPOUSE A CRUCIFIED SOUL BY CRUCIFYING.
A TRUE SPOUSE'S HEART IS THE VICTIM OF HER SPOUSE;
IT BEATS IN UNISON WITH THE HEART OF HER SPOUSE,
LOVING ALL THAT HE LOVES.
CONSECRATED SOULS THUS MUST LOSE
THEMSELVES IN ME,
ALLOW THEMSELVES TO BE TAKEN AND CONSUMED
BY ME AND FOR ME.
LIKE ME, THEY MUST HAVE AN ARDENT THIRST
FOR THE SALVATION OF SOULS AND FOR THE GLORY
OF MY FATHER;
LIKE ME, THEY MUST LOVE THE CROSS AND
REDEMPTIVE SUFFERING.
DO YOU NOT ALL WISH TO BE AMONG THEIR NUMBER?
CAN I SHOW MORE LOVE THAN BY ASKING THIS OF YOU?
FOR YOUR SAKE I MADE MYSELF HOST;
BE WHOLLY CONSECRATED HOSTS FOR ME.

TABLE OF CONTENTS

OUR LORD'S COMMENTARY

PREFACE

FROM THESE AUTHORIZED TESTIMONIES, readers will become acquainted with the message that has been transmitted to them, the soul to whom it was confided, the end that this message lays out, and the path it traces for them. After these testimonies, is a preface really necessary? Certainly not. And yet, since I have had the honor of being asked for help, how can I refuse. The "appeal" has touched me greatly, as has the commentary. Many of the readers will be affected, more deeply than I, by these sentiments of humble gratitude and by this generous offering. In their names as well as in my own, I would like simply to express the stirrings that these pages have aroused in our hearts.

But first of all we must acknowledge our shortcomings. If we whom the Lord has called to his service and guarded by his graces would have responded completely to his call and made fruitful all his gifts, our apostolic work would have spread throughout the world and made it more Christian, and preserved it from the plagues that overwhelm it. The "appeal" makes this quite clear. "Religious souls, if you had been more abandoned, more espoused, the world would not be as it is."

The commentary emphasizes this. It denounces the egoism of those who see in the sacerdotal or religious life a shelter in which they take refuge rather than a spring whose waters they must spread, the egoism also of those who by their actions only seek to radiate their own thoughts and life, and not the thoughts and life of Christ.

In the face of these miseries and failings, we contemplate the unfathomable greatness of this love: "God so loved the world that He gave to it his only Son."[1] "The Son of God loved me and gave himself up for me."[2]

God so loved this dishonored and condemned humanity that, to save it, He willed that his Son become man and die for us on the cross.

---

[1] *Jn 3:16*
[2] *Gal 2:30*

But this gift of divine love will only bear fruit if human love understands it and responds to it.

God has chosen witnesses; He reveals his love to them, He wants them to witness to it. The gifts they are showered with are not for them alone, but for all their brothers.

This Divine Will honors us infinitely but it also engages us. "Christ's love impels us; one died for all and as a consequence all have died; one died for all so that those who live no longer live for themselves but for the One who died for them and was raised up."[3] The Apostle's words here spell out for us the mystery that the message is calling us back to, a mystery whose unfathomable richness neither our contemplation nor our lives will ever exhaust.

This love that we marvel at we must also respond to; this love of Christ that we contemplate we must also reproduce in ourselves. We wish to spread his life; we can only do this by uniting ourselves with our Lord's death and resurrection. "Unless the grain of wheat falls to the earth and dies, it remains alone."[4] How often have we not experienced this! If our actions have been sterile, if our voices have not given rise to an echo, if we have remained alone, is it not because we have not died? This is what these pages ceaselessly call us back to.

The host is "alive" only through a perpetual act of giving, of immolation, or, in other words, of death. It perpetuates its "consecration" only as it is consumed over and over again through an ever-renewed sacrifice. . . . "The darker your being of nothingness and sin, the more triumphant my Being of purity and love. And each time I triumph more profoundly over you by your annihilation, the more I advance my triumph in the immense family of souls that my love has entrusted you with."

This transforming, life-giving death is never entirely consummated here below; to each effort of the soul Christ responds with a stronger light that reveals in the soul a new misery it had not been aware of, and in Him demands of love that the soul had never suspected. This inexorable law of ceaseless improvement is recalled again and again by the Lord: "Once I start asking, I cannot stop, so avid am I to be able to

---

[3] *II Cor 5:14-15*
[4] *Jn 12:24*

give more." "To give everything, one has always to give more."

When egoism begins to get a presentiment of these demands, it becomes frightened; once it has had an experience of them, love rejoices: "To live with great desire is to live by rising, into the realm of true love. . . . How my Heart thirsts for these quickenings of love, that a blazing barrier might hold back the furious onslaught of hatred. This is why, with all imploring tenderness, I beg for this tremendous desire that will only be satisfied as it grows increasingly acute, that finds its repose only in the ardor of its agony."

To understand better these insatiable demands, we can recall the first lessons that Jesus gave to his apostles: "Whoever loves his father or his mother more than Me is not worthy of Me; whoever does not take up his cross and follow Me is not worthy of Me; whoever wants to preserve his life will lose it; whoever loses it for my sake will find it."[5] The most cherished affections and life itself must be sacrificed to Christ. And even more than these demands, the goal that they propose to our efforts frightens us. The more the Lord reveals himself to us, the better we grasp the inaccessible nobility of this ideal: *to be worthy of Christ*. We would never be able to claim such a thing if He himself did not call us to it, and did not raise us to it by his example, by his death, by his Eucharistic presence, by the gift of the Holy Spirit, by the merciful assistance of Our Lady, his Mother and ours.

Several stages in this ascent to which we aspire, including the highest, are described in this message. In the course of the years which preceded the war (1936-1939), the Master related to his faithful servant the principal requirements of the perfect life: contempt for the world, the interior life, the gentleness, peace and delicacy of love. The soul rises up in total fidelity and confidence to the ends to which the Lord is drawing it. All of a sudden, one hears the crash of great catastrophes, the sounds of hateful cries. Now love has become more sorrowful and more urgent: to the fury of hatred one must now oppose the folly of love. Then, little by little, on the dark horizon there spreads a celestial light (1940-1941); the Lord does not relax his demands but He makes more vivid the savor of their fruit. In the appeal one senses less agony, more admiration and joy. The message is a promise: "Yes, the highest happiness, giving immediate access to beatitude, is to die in Me, after

---

[5] *Matt 10:37-39*

having generously spent one's life dying to self. . . . Blessed little deaths of your terrestrial life, each time bringing you further into my Heart and preparing you, at the moment of your last breath, to enter on the same footing as I into the bosom of my Father. Oh blessed death!

It is well to contemplate from afar these heights, in order afterwards to pursue the slow ascent with more energy.

P.S. Since this book appeared, a document of supreme authority, the Encyclical *Mystici Corporis Christi*,[6] sheds new light on the central theme developed in the course of these pages. We eagerly reproduce from it here the most explicit passage, encouraging our readers to meditate attentively on the teaching that it offers:

"It is quite evident that the faithful absolutely need the help of the Divine Redeemer, since He himself said, 'Without Me you can do nothing.' Still, it is necessary to state, astonishing as this may seem, our Lord needs the help of his members. This is not due though to any poverty or weakness on his part, but rather because He himself has disposed it thus for the greater honor of his Spotless Spouse. As He was dying on the Cross, He communicated to his Church, without any contribution on her part, the limitless treasure of Redemption but when it came to the distribution of this treasure, He not only shares with his Immaculate Spouse the work of sanctification of souls, but He wills that in some way it be due to her action. A tremendous mystery indeed, about which we can never meditate enough: the salvation of great numbers of souls depends upon prayers and voluntary mortifications suffered for this purpose by the members of the Mystical Body of Christ and on the collaborative work that the pastors and the faithful, in particular the fathers and mothers of families, must bring to Our Lord."[7]

—*Jules Lebreton, S.J.*

---

[6] *Pius XII*
[7] *Édition de la Bonne Presse, p. 24.*

INTRODUCTION

THE PRIVILEGED SOUL TO WHOM GOD has communicated this "appeal" with the mission of spreading it has recently ceased to suffer by ceasing to live. A holy and very painful death has ended her saintly life. Her ardent wish, ratified by Our Lord, was that she remain completely unknown and we only know her by the name Jesus gave her: "The little victim of his Heart."

"Your name will no longer be anything for my Heart but "my little victim" (16 March 1936).

Out of obedience to the same concern for discretion, the religious community she belonged to also wishes to remain unknown. It was they who entrusted me with the editing of these pages.

The priest who was her spiritual director would not have been able to sign these pages without lifting the veil at least in part. He too insisted that my name alone figure at the beginning of this book that he inspired and approved, for a signature was needed. When a message, so ardent, so insistent, so demanding and so anonymous is conveyed, those to whom it is addressed have the right of some particulars. They need to know they are not confronted with a pious fiction. They want there to be someone who can attest to the reality of the person and the facts, who can function as a witness, and, when the occasion offers, make his own the words of St. John's, "The one who recounts these things saw them and we know that his testimony is true."[8]

I have been a humble passer-by in this life so rich in fidelity and grace, but in the course of those last years I saw the "little victim of the Sacred Heart" on many occasions. For three years she asked me herself to proceed with the publication that she knew Our Lord wanted. And when the "appeal" came out, after delays due to the legitimate hesitations of her superiors, she related Our Lord's no less pressing

---

[8] *Jn 19:35*

1

request that the moving commentaries which follow it also be published.

It was difficult and delicate to do this during her lifetime. God removed the difficulty Himself by her death, placing on this life the definitive seal of grace. Henceforth, apart from her name, one can make known certain details that will suffice, I believe, to make her creditable to the readers.

Here are two documents, one of which comes directly from her, the other had been written by her superiors shortly after her death. They speak for themselves well enough; they clearly reveal a "graced soul" as was said of Blessed Columbière.

FIRST DOCUMENT

TWO STATEMENTS MADE TO HER DIRECTOR,

THE FIRST IN SEPTEMBER, 1935

Six years ago, during a retreat, my soul was so overwhelmed by the purity and holiness of Infinite Love, and so pierced with horror at my own lack of worthiness that a powerful seizing took possession of my soul and has not left it since but has only strengthened.

At first this extraordinary seizing was more this painfully agonizing impression of being repelled by the very One who drew me. . . . According to the direction I received at the time, a redoubling of humble but absolute confidence was the proper attitude for the soul. . . . An impression that lasted three years, with more or less violent ups and downs.

It took place at a time when the grip of love which was somehow investing me with purifying fire, little by little, more and more freed me interiorly from a taste for all created things. I was gradually being freed from the human and increasingly held by the divine, all this most often in painful ways.

Fifteen days ago (the First Friday of September, 1935) at the close of my retreat, the Heart of Our Lord, during Holy Communion, had so penetrated my heart that, in a moment of inexpressible happiness, He substituted his own pain for mine, wanting only that in some way it be me who suffers the weight of his crucified love, but that it be Him in me who suffers, having become Himself this me, or at least seeking to become so entirely.

Now, after several years of purifying pain, I feel that He wants to purify this pain itself. It isn't that the pain is less real, quite to the contrary, but it feels more pure. It is no longer mine but his pain in me, pain of his pierced and crucified Heart, of his Love wounded by the thoughtlessness of souls that are nevertheless consecrated to Him.

This is no longer the pain coming from a love that has been rejected, crushed, cut off, but from a compenetrating love that wants to continue the redemptive work in other Itselves, in my unworthy soul.

Also, since this communion, there has been a continual resonance of suffering for all the suffering that souls cause His Heart, a wound so open that nothing — I know this well — will ever close it.

A state of soul not only during pious exercises of personally painful contemplation and compenetration, but that also secretly pursued me throughout the day and night. Most often and almost entirely at such times, the soul experiences an agony that seems to capture all the suffering that lack of love caused Our Lord to experience, and which by his mercy He wishes to have me share a little, in order to console Him.

As He said to me, "Allow me to torment you that I may be relieved. The more you become my victim, the more you will be my joy."

And with all my soul I could only answer, "Yes, and thank you! No more, no less, nothing other than what you wish, desire, prefer."

Daily communion restores the courage that seems to fail after these long hours of resonating pain, and gives the strength needed to free myself as much as possible from this consuming grip at those times when duties of state called for activity and work; but this never without excruciating effort.

The repercussion of this on the soul's deepest feelings heightened the need to humble myself, to obey, and with the help of grace to suffer still more, for the consolation of Him who, despite my unworthiness, pursues me with such love by his confounding and crucifying mercies.

SECOND STATEMENT, MARCH, 1936

Since Christmas the all-merciful action of Our Lord has continued and become more pronounced both in its intimacy and sharpness, while the attacks of the demon have become more and more violent and frequent; a double influence which though opposing each other, nevertheless are both progressively leading to the same total, profound destruction of the human me that wants nothing more now than to disappear and give free and sovereign place to divine life.

The keenness and intimacy of this direct action by Our Lord manifests itself by an increasingly unbroken communion that participates in all the sufferings of the Passion, and this in a particularly painful way since Lent, when the soul is no longer able to leave this abyss of bloody, crucified, outraged love, a love that looks for relief and consolation in loving consent to keep Him company.

And this Heart so wounded has extended his incomprehensible Goodness to the point of wanting to drive a blade into me, opening a burning wound into which He keeps penetrating further and further all the while having me enter more deeply into his own.

Even mercifully painful participation in his Crown of Thorns, in the Chalice of his agony, in his Crucifixion. Physical sufferings but even more, moral, with the sole intention of consoling his Heart which never ceases to beg me for "love, love. I thirst for love, above all the love of my spouses. . . . Consecrated priests and religious are not giving Me enough and thus they constrict my Heart that would overflow into them and through them save the world." And He wants to show me these souls in order to move me to make reparations, pointing them out to me at times, especially this one or that one, or several of them.

But the more pressing and penetrating this direct action of Our Lord becomes, the more frequent and violent also is it attacked by the demon's assaults, entering into me and furiously trying to destroy what Our Lord has done soon as He does it.

Most painful, agonizing, humiliating times during which the true life of the soul seems paralyzed, enchained by a hateful force. And in this distress, prayer is no longer possible, the feeling of having been completely abandoned by heaven.

But I am helped by a single, assured turning to my superiors, whose repeated benedictions succeed in delivering me.

Our Lord more and more drove me to this humble, total, simple, confident dependence so costly to my nature, it being the most profound denial of my egoistic, independent, proud personality that I could give Him, a personality that never wanted to see itself as dependent.

By this humility of profound detachment that He asked of me, and helped me with, He made me see in a horrible vision the abyss of misery and iniquity I was in, which filled me with confusion and indignation towards myself, and desolation for Him, while at the same time, and in due proportion, his Heart, in an excess of tender mercies, drew me more and more to boundless, unconditional trust, abandoned to whatever action He wished to effect in my soul at that moment for his consolation.

On the Feast of the Holy Wounds (which fell that year on Friday, the 20th of March) this action was most especially profound, deep within me, having me participate all during communion in his suffering love, as consuming as it was consumed.

SECOND DOCUMENT

STATEMENT OF HER SUPERIORS

"Your name will no longer be for my Heart anything but 'little victim'" (March 16, 1936). Little victim consumed in a holocaust of complete self-annihilation in order to fulfill the mission laid out in August 1936: "Mission that is nothing less than a transmission, yes, transmission of my Heart's supreme effort to appeal to consecrated souls, to obtain from them the consoling, compensating, reparating love that It awaits in order to save the world so infernally shaken and inundated by acts of hatred and paroxysms of violence. Give yourself completely to the waves of suffering and humiliations that it pleases Me to sweep over you. This is the price if my revelations are to be efficacious."

Faithful "transmitting echo," this was her role.

Day after day, she will have to give up her most intimate secrets, and this transparency of soul, this dependence, vowed without reservation and practiced to perfection, entailed a baring of self most costly for a nature so delicate and reserved as this.

Her mission! At what price did its realization cost her? Nature before long would have had to shatter by the amount of suffering that accumulated over the span of six years, heroically veiled beneath the communal life of a simple religious to the point where those around her, except for her superiors, had no idea of the divine communications that she was receiving or of the terrible tortures and martyrdom that only a supernatural force could account for.

First, physical suffering, due to frequent, often acute headaches and to her fragile health. Later, sufferings of a supernatural order, participating in the pains of the Heart of Jesus, sharing body and soul in the sufferings of the Passion, the crown of thorns, the invisible marks of the nails, and above all the piercing of the heart, the interior wound forever open, always deepening, a suffering whose acuteness will keep growing until her final days.

And besides this, diabolical assaults in all its forms, alternating with divine attraction in transports of love, assaults whose violence grew in proportion to the divine favors. These favors completely ceased, when, in September 1937, the request to publish the "appeal" was rejected. Then this became a "rejection by the Father that would last until the Lord obtained satisfaction for what He wanted," rejection all the more excruciating because the divine union had been so deep, and the action of the devil thereupon grew in frequency and violence. It took all forms, even the most perfidious, and I can add, the most disconcerting and repugnant.

Speaking of the tortures, she described them in part: "dreadful or-

6

deals from hell, curses, damnations, abyss of sufferings of all kinds."
It seemed to her to be dragging souls with her into hell.

No respite, no rest, never any sleep over the years, frequent holy
night vigils marked by a further outbreak of suffering. Only the benedictions of her Superior drove the demons off. This recourse, wanted
by the Lord and always effective, was all the more painful to her for
she was afraid of becoming a heavy burden.

In this agonizing, interior condition, she carried out to perfection
all the work called for by the duties of her state. One saw in her only
sweetness, patience, serenity, charity always ready to oblige. Truly
humble, she considered herself the least lovable of all, seeing herself
in God's light.

On the 21st of November, 1936, she bound herself to Our Lord by
a vow most loving, ever more loving, which is to say ever more generous in accepting and in choosing of her own volition that she be
wholly at his service.

The demon fought furiously against this vow; the Lord was ada-
mant. "The success of your mission has this as its price." The faithful
keeping of this vow never cost her any loss of peace.

The publication of the "appeal" in June, 1939, only occasioned a
brief respite; the success of its distribution and the profound effect it
had on souls called for further sacrifices.

This diabolical action, which had become daily during the last
year, only ended several weeks before her death. Then all she knew
was a state of painful dryness borne with the most peaceful abandon.

After nine days of acute suffering, spoken of moreover by the Lord as
"the final preparations for her coming," she died the death of a saint.

The One who more than once offered her the choice either of
seeing the Father right away, or a prolonged sharing in his suffering
so that to live was further sacrifice, found the work accomplished.

He came like an abductor to carry off "his little victim."

These two documents, so eloquent in their brevity, complement and confirm one another. They show us the worth and quality of the soul who received the message. She is certainly in the lineage of saints and belongs especially close to St. Margaret Mary, as much for her mission as for her sufferings and the heroism with which they were borne.

I will add that the Lord confirmed his direct action on her by a double sign:

1. *Secrecy.* She herself never spoke of anything except to her superiors and two or three priests; and in her community God disposed of matters in such a way that everything happened without attracting attention. Her Superior has testified that during the sometimes quite protracted sessions during which she sought to disengage this religious from diabolic action in order to free her for communion, no other sister ever needed to come speak with the Superior.

2. *Supernatural endurance.* She was of precarious health needing considerable care and attention. She had an assignment that called for demanding physical and intellectual activity. Now, for five years, she only had rare moments of sleep; her nights being but a sequence of dreadful sufferings most of the time under demonic attack, without her duties of state ever being affected by it.

The "appeal" was communicated to her in 1936. Its purpose was the salvation of a world more compromised than ever; the forces of evil now seemed triumphant and threatened to destroy everything.

The hour is grave for all of mankind, but the Heart of Jesus is standing watch; He points to the danger and its causes; He tells us from whence help will come (*vide* the beginning of her Superior's statement).

This "appeal" which seems personal, rather hurried,[9] Our Lord wishes be made known to the consecrated souls (priests and religious) to whom it is really being addressed.

But how? For this it would have to be published and the superiors refuse to do so; they are able to attest to the great virtue of the messenger, they dare not do the same for the authenticity of the message. Happily the spiritual director is there to reassure and work through the many steps. Authorization is finally given and in July 1939, after a wait of three years and interior martyrdom of the "little victim of the Sacred Heart," the little book that the document cited above tells us of appears in print.

And very quickly the blessing of the Sacred Heart accompanies it. The "appeal" appeared in December, 1939: the great events unfolding just then should have prevented any attention from being paid to it.

Just the opposite happens.

Without any advertising, the first edition is sold out in a few months, and two years later, more than thirty thousand copies are distributed in every direction, touching, enlightening and stimulating a good many souls.

Since then, Our Lord has also asked for the publication of the commentaries to the "appeal" that He often made to his "little victim." They form 18 small notebooks, written on occasions immediately after and sometimes during the teaching of the divine lesson. In order to facilitate their publication at the time Our Lord considered opportune, something she knew her sufferings would achieve, she herself assembled them under special titles according to their principal ideas, grouping all the teachings of Our Lord on a given subject.

If one were ever to publish these commentaries as an independent work, it would no doubt be better to preserve their order by date, in accordance with the daily lessons, to see how they fit into the tragic moments that we are living through.

---

[9] *March 29, 1936: "Write down my 'appeal' of love and the message that I charge you with for souls; hasten to deliver it. Why do you wait? My Heart cannot wait."*

And it would perhaps come as a surprise for some to notice that Our Lord makes no predictions regarding events, that He is content with expressing and explaining over and over his love for France, whose protection, despite her faults, He wants very much to take over, adding that the test or the chastisement — they are one and the same — could have been spared our country if consecrated souls (priests and men and women religious) had all done their duty, and that it could be cut short if they did this with all their hearts.

This is more sound and more reassuring than all the prophesies and messages being transmitted so often these days by souls who, though no doubt of good will, for the most part are more or less deluded.

The 55 titles under which the "little victim of the Sacred Heart" has reproduced the commentaries still do not give us all of them. In all they made up a collection of approximately three or four hundred pages from which selections had to be made.

We will preserve her ordering of the material, taking care simply to date each fragment. One will easily be able to place it back into its historical setting, and the various dates, by highlighting the repetitions, will let us see the significance that Our Lord himself attaches to this or that teaching.

DOCTRINE OF THE APPEAL

THIS DOCTRINE REVEALS TO US the Heart of Christ the Redeemer, of Christ impassioned for the glory of his Father and the salvation of souls because the Father loves these souls with an infinite love. He created them in the image of his Well-Beloved Son for the glory of divine adoption. But by the sin of Adam this image had become deformed and sullied, the children of love became children of rage, demeaned and depraved, sitting forlornly in darkness in the shadow of death.

They are fully culpable and most unhappy and the Mercy of the Father is moved. With love He bent down over these miserable ingrates who had become his enemies. By the act of Incarnation He sent them his Son to enter into the corrupt human family, with the mission of recovering lost souls for Him and freeing them from the bondage that held them captive, of purifying them and, by incorporating them into Himself, bringing them into the divine Family, all at the price of his bloody Passion.

This redemptive work that was his mission, his duty of state (*propterea veni in horam hanc*[10]), and which gave the Father so much glory and joy, Jesus embraces with all his Heart. He consecrates himself to it entirely and sacrifices everything for it. His mortal life was nothing more than a suffering that was going to increase until the horrific death on the Cross, but a death He wanted all his life, called for by his own desire. He hastened the steps that brought Him to it because this death consummated the work of redemption. Everything He was supposed to do, and more, Jesus did. Henceforth an easy means of salvation is available to everyone born into this world:

Available everywhere is the Blood that is to cleanse and expiate our faults; the treasure that is to pay off our debts and enrich us is piled up beside us; the charter of reconciliation between God and us is here, signed by God.

---

[10] *Jn 12:27* — "... *for this purpose I have come to this hour.*"

But for all that everything is still not finished.

This salvation that we obtain at so huge a price each of us must still appropriate to himself. For as St. Augustine said, "He who made us without us cannot save us without us." *Qui te fecit sine te non te justificat sine te.*[11]

By a free adherence to Christ, one must become "one" with Him as He has made Himself "one" with us in order to ransom us, taking upon Himself our faults.

Through contrition and penance, we have to draw to ourselves the Blood of Redemption.

We have to take out the charter from the treasure that lies open before us and place our signature on it next to God's.

And now, a sorrowful yet poignant observation! Nineteen centuries after the death of Jesus Christ, only a third of the world is Christian and among Christians themselves, how many fail to profit from this Redemption that was so sorrowfully made and so lovingly offered!

The Sacred Heart complains about it in this "appeal";

He points out the causes and the remedy.

The primary, principal, most hidden and also the most active cause is the furious efforts of the demon, in his obstinate hatred towards Jesus Christ, to block the blessed effects of Redemption.

He employs all his powers to snatch away souls from Christ Who loves them, and drag them with him down into hell. How many times Our Lord alludes to this in the "commentaries"!

The second cause is the malice of the wicked, those who have allowed themselves to be perverted by the demon.

His power notwithstanding, Satan by himself could do little to us here if we did not allow ourselves to be seduced. He gets his strength

---

[11] *Sermon 170. M. 38.923*

from human wills that give themselves over to him or that give in to him to be held at his mercy.

He has his creatures here, those upon whom he can count, who belong to him. They constitute numerous powerful groups in various nations, French Masons, Bolsheviks and others, everywhere seeking to lay hold of the levers of power in order to have souls at their mercy and by all the means of seduction or violence to turn them from God. They have the gold, the strength, the power; they are ever more and ever better organized for the material conquest of the world. They have their false prophets, their false evangelists. They understand the art of domination and seduction. In order to have heaven and the divine law scorned and forgotten, they seek to bring heaven to earth by the intensification of material well-being. And the world is in great danger, because in addition to these two causes two others are joined to it:

— the negligence and indifference of ordinary Christians who like their well-being and comfort. Never dreaming of struggling against those who procure these things, they are even tempted to see the demands of the divine law as too hard. Carelessly, they give in to easy pleasures, thereby losing all combative strength. And there is no one to help their torpor, because:

— the last cause of evil and the most important: consecrated souls are also, themselves, negligent and lax. And more than anything the "appeal" holds them responsible.

The consecrated! Those whom the Sacred Heart has chosen to be his Own, the priests, the men and women religious! Those whose mission and duty of state here below is to stir up the flame of divine love, those who are the mediating advocates of the Father and of Him, to intercede on behalf of sinners, to express to God the prayers and repentance of the guilty, and drawing upon all the blessings and the pardons from on high to put them in efficacious contact with the Blood of Redemption. If these fail in their essential duty, if they fail to understand their obligations and only see in their sacerdotal or religious vocation a security shelter where they are safeguarded against damnation, contenting themselves with a small, sweet, tranquil life spoiled with well-being, then the world is lost!

But perhaps one will say, "Isn't God more powerful than men and demons all united together? Can't He, by Himself without any human help, triumph over all these obstacles?"

No doubt He could, but his Providence has disposed it otherwise. Christ has ascended to heaven where He lives in his glory, just as Satan lives in his hell. It is true, mysteriously true, that He remains present and hidden in the Holy Eucharist and mysteriously in his living members who are Christians in a state of grace, but from there where He resides nevertheless with all his power, He only works through the instrumentality of humans who give themselves over to his action, just as Satan can only act through perverse humans who have turned their freedom over to him.

Thus the entire struggle between Christ and Satan is pursued here below in the inner life of souls. Of the two, the one who will carry the day is the one who has the best and most devoted combatants; I do not say the most numerous.

A small number would suffice through whom the divine force would pass, provided this force can indeed pass through and be used!

This divine force can only act if these, the consecrated, are what they are supposed to be, so fully given over to supple cooperation with its action that they pose no obstacle to its work. On the other hand, if there are personal interests, infidelities, refusal to cooperate in a practical way, then to the extent that these obstacles exist, Christ's hands are tied and his actions without effect.

Here then is the great cause of the evil that Christ laments in his "appeal": that the perverse apply themselves to their ruinous work with more ardor than do the good to Christ's work. They are more stimulated by the fear of Satan and his seductive lures and promises of worldly goods, goods that for the most part he doesn't even deliver, than are the consecrated by the love of Christ and the goods of eternity. This is a disgrace and affront to his dignity.

And Our Lord calls to mind what He did for the salvation of the world. He reminds us what the Co-Redeemer par excellence did, the Holy Virgin. He revisits the essential obligations of the consecrated and details them at great length.

They are His, chosen and preferred, "privileged among the privileged." Loved by Him with a special love, they should return a special love to Him, entire and exclusive.

This love creates between Our Lord and them an intimacy of back-and-forth communication of all that one is and all that one has to say.

And that is why love ends in conformity, in a deep-reaching resemblance, imprinting on hearts and souls the effigy of Christ's Heart and Soul, identifying them with Him to the point of their becoming another Himself.

In virtue of this love and the conformity that it asks, all of Christ's sentiments should be the sentiments of the consecrated. Jesus relives in them, manifests Himself in them, acts through them.

Now, Christ the Redeemer to whom they are so closely tied burns with ardor for the salvation of souls, for their purification, their divinization, and because this great work by the Father's designs is only achievable by the Passion of the Cross, Christ has longed all his mortal life for what He called *his time*, the time when his Blood shall be shed, the time of liberation and salvation, the time of his sufferings.

This love of suffering and of the cross is necessary for consecrated souls as well, not because these are lovable in themselves, but because they alone can effect redemption and thus give glory to the Father in heaven. It should mark their lives. The road to Calvary being the only path to Redemption, consecrated souls have to pass resolutely by this same road, however difficult it may seem, generously accepting its rough patches.

They have to be both victims and apostles, and victims under the double titles of apostles and consecrated souls; consecration calling for this identification, and the apostolate, which is to say the salvation of one's neighbor, only being possible by the cross. Apostles pay a great price for souls, just as Christ paid a great price for them. And each consecrated soul is responsible for a certain number of souls who will not be saved without them and who will be saved because of them.

The Sacred Heart says that if all had fulfilled their office, the world would not be as it is. It isn't because the number of consecrated souls is insufficient, but those who are presently in the world are not doing their duty, that if they did what they should, the world would come back to life.

And in the commentaries to the "appeal," the Heart of Jesus urges this of them in most moving terms.

There is nothing new in all of this, as Our Lord Himself says. One has only to call to mind familiar but all too often forgotten truths. Certain of them however stand out most especially, such as Our Lord's desire for suffering during his mortal life to consummate the work of redemption. Truly one discovers a Christ panting for suffering, a Christ that lets no occasion for it to slip by, seeing in each an opportunity to be more helpful to us and to glorify his Father more.

Just as all Christians, and all consecrated souls most especially, are supposed to cooperate in the work of redemption. They can do this because they are mystical members of Christ and all of Christ therefore belongs to them. They are Christ. And that being the case, they are indebted to Him and are responsible for certain souls whose salvation depends upon their faithfulness.

One also sees the providential role of suffering by consecrated souls. In the measure that God wills, they are called to be apostles and victims, little hosts who must be changed into the one great redemptive Host and offered with Him in communal Sacrifice; a Sacrifice whose redemptive value will be that much greater the more perfectly that little hosts will have been transformed into the great Host. And acting only as one with It, through their free and total oblation, they will cause It to spread until It covers the world.

One knew all that, but to hear Our Lord repeat it Himself again and again touches us deeply and to see it practiced so perfectly by a soul like us places it more within reach of our weakness.

"The more I cause you to suffer," Our Lord had said to her, "the more you should endeavor to smile, smile out of gratitude and love.

"The more I cause you to feel the rigors of love, the gentler ought your *Fiat* be.

"Smiles and gentleness are like delicate flowers and without them

16

something is lacking in the gifts of my consecrated souls, gifts so costly given.

"The more I associate you with my suffering, the deeper I reach into the capacity of your soul. And the more you embrace this suffering with love, the more I fill this capacity to overflowing so that you spill Me out upon those souls whom I confide to you.

"I am helping you; you help Me. Let us help one another to carry the Cross of Redemption."

Thus was this "little victim" made, silently, heroically. Is it any wonder that, with such excellent and austere schooling, she arrived at sanctity so quickly?

For indeed, while recalling dogmatic truths, the "appeal" and its commentaries at the same time offer a complete lesson in lofty perfection. Here one sees practice of the highest virtues: humility, obedience, sacrifice, self-denial, virtue therefore in all its forms, virtues that are unfailing and never on display.

We are given new insights of a most profound kind into religious poverty and obedience.

Here one sees the power of prayer and how by it things can be done which seem impossible.

Do not these words shed good and salutary light, "Ask of Me what I ask of you," showing clearly that whatever Our Lord asks of us we can accomplish through prayer.

And as the job of the interior life, the necessity of prayer for discipleship is striking! How practical too are its means of atoning for infidelities in performing acts that cost us something. And how instructive is this lesson about charity towards our neighbor which is only real, true charity when it is made at our expense. Any act of charity that costs nothing is but simulacra. Sacrifice and self-immolation are the foundations of Christ's charity and of his disciples' as well.

Conformity to the gentle, humble Heart of Jesus consists in the practice of these genuine, solid virtues. One feels oneself breathing air of truth and clarity, nothing vague or sentimental, everything here encouraging genuine, disinterested, efficacious love, neither lazy, bored, nor affected.

These pages should be read slowly, dwelling on one subject alone, and letting it penetrate the soul. Reading too much or too quickly risks leading to fatigue, over-stimulation, or nervous tension.

A final, important question poses itself. Do we have here a genuine, direct communication from Our Lord? Are these the very words He pronounced?

God speaks to the soul in multiple ways — *multifarie, multisque modis*, as St. Paul says.[12]

At times Our Lord appears visibly in human form and his words are heard by both the interior and exterior senses. Such was probably the case when Our Lord showed His Heart exposed to Margaret Mary, saying to her: "Here is the Heart that has loved mankind so much."

Or the Holy Virgin when she revealed herself to Bernadette and said, "I am the Immaculate Conception."

But generally God speaks by means of interior lights. And sometimes, He infuses himself through a supernatural light that dazzles the soul, transporting it outside of itself into an unknown world that the soul, when it returns to itself, can neither speak of nor recover. Anything the soul says would seem a falsehood: "I blaspheme," St. Angèle de Foligno wrote of herself when coming out of her ecstasies.

Sometimes, with the help of ideas or images conformed to our intelligence, but which He selects and which He himself infuses according to the need, Our Lord speaks to the interior of our soul, and the soul then has the distinct impression that God is speaking to it, even that He sometimes is dictating to it. Thus, as was often the case

---

[12] *Heb. 1:*

in the life of Margaret Mary, we are told of resolutions and consecrations as dictated by Our Lord.

Most often God conveys what He wants understood through illumination, and the soul then translates this into its own personal language. God having placed this illumination within its understanding, the soul knows, feels that it is translating exactly the divine thought. Often, the soul is not even aware that it is translating. It seems to the soul that it has but received the divine thought, that the soul itself has been purely passive.

Still — and here is a sign of the soul's activity — if upon reflection a different formulation would seem to express better the intended understanding, the soul does not hesitate to adopt it so as to conform more exactly to what it has received.

In the present case it would seem that this third way is the one that applies.

God has spoken to this soul in all these ways, but the particular wording of the message, especially in the commentaries, belongs to the "little victim."

In it one readily recognizes her style. A clear, precise, methodic mind, she delights in a word play that makes the distinct idea spring out. She likes repetitions that, by striking the intelligence, engrave things in the mind. This is how she very naturally translates the divine teaching without falsifying it in any way.

We must add moreover that every saint who receives a revelation acts in more or less the same way, always leaving his or her own mark such that it is always possible to distinguish between what is uniquely divine and what is human and personal.

Here the divine origin of the message is assured us by the heroism of a life far removed from human weakness, where virtue so simple and genuine is so clearly in view. Moreover, the message is guaranteed by its doctrinal unity and profundity, its theological exactitude, its supernatural robustness, its transparent purity.

To be sure, one can't attribute equal authority to every little detail, but one can very legitimately believe that the message as a whole comes from God.

In any case, the message comes at just the right moment and if it is well received it can do much to bring about the climate of peace and charity on earth, which the Sovereign Pontiff and all the faithful with him so fervently desire. It can even be the world's salvation, in which all Christians are invited to cooperate.

—Henri Monier-Vinard, S. J.

CHAPTER ONE

THE APPEAL

I. MEANING OF THE APPEAL

My "appeal" is intended to bring about a great stirring that will free the many souls still held bound to the earth — to what is purely human — by weights that press down on their egoistic *me*, and to draw them into the great currents of Redemption. For my need of you, O consecrated souls, is more urgent now than ever, if only you would understand and answer it.

November 18, 1938

My "appeal" is a searing superabundance which burns to overflow in consecrated souls in graces of co-redemptive partnership. For, alas, satanic hatred abounds and superabounds at this moment in the world, robbing Me of souls that it plunges into icy death. And my vast and merciful tenderness as Savior-Host cannot but come to beg for consolation, compensation, partnership with my faithful, consecrated ones in order to arouse their love to overflow and superabound in "co-redeeming spirit"!

For, alas, in too many hearts this love is still asleep, mixed as it is with "egoistic apathy"!

The purpose of my "appeal," through the superabundance of graces that it contains, is to draw these hearts out of their slumber, to

21

seize their benumbed and lukewarm souls, to awaken love in them and have them burn because of it!

March 17, 1937

The great drama of my redemptive Passion is perpetually being renewed in the world, and with what intensity at this particular moment! . . . Learn to recognize in this the sublime workings of infinite love, abyss of marvelous mysteries, of justice and pity, of mercy and holiness.

In this working, in this drama where all of you are like reclaimed sinners, never be unmindful of it so that your contrition and humble, faith-filled gratitude may always be aroused. But listen to my supplication as well!

Enter into it, all of you, as co-redemptive spouses and with your generosity give yourself, lose yourself so that you may be seized by love as "victims"! This is the great wish of my "appeal."

Hear the Heart of your Savior searching for, appealing for reinforcements for the camp of love, multiplying his calls for help from his faithful spouses, from his friends, his priests, asking them for help in the great work of redemptive conquest. Oh, yes, for help, for love's help, souls so very much loved by my Heart! For by my Father's wise plan of mercy, I am not able — I, all powerful Lord — I am not able to save the world alone by Myself. I need partners, collaborators. "I need help!"

Meditate deeply in the depths of your hearts on this need for love, this need for love! . . . And search with fervent industry for all the little helps you can give Me, multiply for Me, without excepting here your very breath.

Help Me to pour Myself out in you and through you.

The hour is grave at this moment. I say it again to you. And on whom should I count if not my consecrated ones, on the faithful generosity of each to ascend his or her co-redemptive way of the Cross. For they are Savior with Me, charged with the world, charged with all of it.

When, as at present, hatred speeds up its ravaging movements, must not love also accelerate its movements to conquer it? In order to seize the "initiative" everywhere and maintain it at all costs. The hour has arrived where not to press forward is to lose ground and let oneself be overcome. It is the hour for endless speeding up, the hour where every heart that is a real heart has to battle in ever-rising tempo under the impulse of its love, of my ever more supplicating love.

In the mercy-laden thoughts of my Heart, my "appeal" is a powerful "stimulus" to this speeding-up of love in your hearts. But for that to happen, isn't it necessary that it be revealed, known, and meditated upon by as great a number as possible?

In the light of this "appeal" you will understand that for you to "quicken your step" is to "adopt my step." It is to follow my race of love in the redemptive ascent to Calvary where I was led by my Father's Will. For this Will is what gives the measure. By its daily more crucifying and thus more animated petitions, It takes command of this accelerated movement to love on the part of every generous heart that is ready with unreserved *fiat* to answer the incessant calls of this adorable Will!

"This is what it means to be in the footsteps of Love."

Not always quick and lively, but like the *Magnificat,* all the more so if one gives one's *fiat* promptly, responding with all one's heart and being. My cause will not triumph without these accelerations of love.

March 15, 1940

Yes, it is true, my "appeal" is a "complaint," but a complaint of love. The complaint of great "desire" let down and unfulfilled . . . yet unflaggingly passionate and supplicating.

Indeed, if I complain, it is because I do not have you. I want you and if I want you doesn't that mean that I love you? Then recognize in this "appeal" further evidence of my love for you, this immense love I have for my consecrated ones, as tender as it is strong. And come to see in it also a precious sign of trust. For how would it serve Me to beg of you this way if, knowing your hearts, I was not sure to find response? All-merciful trust that itself is touching proof of love.

And then always remember that "every sign of trust" should be for your souls a "grounds for trust."

Each time my love says to you by its requests, "I am counting on you," understand that it is at the same time telling you, "Count on Me."

Indeed, could I who know your poverty trust to ask something of you if I Myself did not have the willingness and the ability to give it to you? Never forget then that the more I ask of you the more I crave to give you.

My Heart is a begging love because it is an overflowing love. Is there a truth more able to melt all the dreadings of your heart into one immense and courageous trust?

Learn to make use of my grace so that you may serve my glory! Know that my "appeal"— despite its grave tone — is not meant to dishearten or frighten you, but much to the contrary, to encourage you and stimulate you.

Yes, my wounds, particularly those of my Heart, are springs end-lessly pouring out even as they are no less an ever-imploring thirst. And it is by drawing from them that you water them. Come then and with generous trust, draw out this spirit of holocaust that you must have if you are to respond to my imploring wish. That you may all be:

— wholly consecrated hosts,

— totally consumed victims,

— crucified spouses,

— auxiliaries of my Redemption,

— little, co-redemptive continuators (*survies*).

For if the life of every Christian is to be marked by the stamp of "sacrifice," the life of every consecrated soul is to be marked by the stamp of "holocaust." Do you understand the difference?

Sacrifice can have degrees in both the matter and form of the gift. . . . For holocaust there is only one measure which is the measureless *usque ad finem.*[13] There is only one degree which is totality in a crescendo of love and self-oblation.

Now, without this holocaust spirit, there are no true religious virtues, and it is precisely this spirit that distinguishes between holy priests and religious and those, alas, who are but ordinary priests and religious.

January 12, 1940

— Burden and responsibility for the salvation of the world,

— Burden and responsibility for the eternal fate of souls,

— Burden and responsibility for the application of my Blood,

— Burden and responsibility for the expansion of my redemptive Host!

Here, consecrated souls of my priests and men and women religious, is what confers upon you your title of spouse, if you truly take it seriously in the way my "appeal" asks it of you.

But understand well the meaning of this charge and this responsibility: this responsibility of love, if it be so, entails:

— privileged burden of my "grace," no less than

— privileged burden of my "Cross."

The fervor and zeal of love's responsibility is such that it is able to be a fly in the ointment without being disquieting, having to be stimulating without being overbearing.

For if my redemptive Cross, that I beg you to love as I do, which is to say, to carry as I do, if that Cross is a painfully pressing weight, a frightening burden of all of men's crimes, ingratitudes, and egoistic mediocrities, then my Grace, which always accompanies this Cross, is a "weight-lifter" whose all-powerful efficaciousness is measured by the confidence and vitality of your prayer.

---

[13] *Jn 13:1 — until the end*

Yes, this grace must be begged for most ardently by a fervent *Fiat* of appealing, for without it the *Fiat* by which support is received is not truly plenary. In effect, without my grace being invoked, the cross, with all its sufferings can only be dragged, not carried, and then it does not "carry Me." Without the Crucified One, it is but naked wood. It is not the Crucifix and therefore cannot be a "co-redemptive cross"!

Understand also, as your part, the ardent prayerful trust that my "supplication" asks of you in correspondence, the two-fold *Fiat* contained in the *Fiat* that effects the consecrating action of the Host:

Reception of love — Appeal for love!

Transform into supplicating invocations all my supplicating requests. Repeat to Me often:

"Jesus Redeemer, make of us true co-redemptive souls";

"Jesus-Host, make of us all wholly consecrated hosts."

Love to say to Me: "You charge me with this, now I charge You."

I love this confidence, because, in charging Me thus with what I charge you, you unburden my Heart, you relieve its weight of treasures and graces that I long to pour out, and it is with immense joy that my Heart responds.

II. THE REQUIREMENTS OF THE "APPEAL"

CO-REDEMPTIVE SUFFERING

1938

To be co-redeemers is to continue my excesses of love; excesses that led Me to Calvary. It means to perpetuate in some way these excesses on earth, by a life crucified like Mine, so that love may never fail to exceed hatred.

Now is the hour of excesses, the hour to oppose the relentless, predatory excesses of hatred in order to surpass them, excesses of love without measure or end.

In the light of my Heart, in the light of my Mother, let each search for those excesses that ought to be present in the life of his or her consecrated soul:

— Sacrifice (*holocaust*) in giving;

— Praise in sacrifice (*holocaust*);

— *Magnificat* in the *Fiat*.

For I Myself look after these souls of Mine, to make the cross more crucifying, more sacrificial, the sacrificial offering (*hostie*) of my Good Pleasure.

Thank Me when I cause you to feel more the weight of your cross. "I am the great hungerer after love." May each hear Me tell him in the depths of his heart:

"I so hunger for you, little victim of my Mercy, that I come, I want to enter you to the point of taking your place so that my Father and my brothers see only Me in you. So that you take my place, continuing Me, prolonging Me close to them.

Coming and exchanging places means to give up one's place in order to take one's place. And in order to make place for Me, must I not banish and drive away all the rest, substituting my thoughts, my Heart, my volition for yours, so that there is no longer anything left of yourself, only of Me.

You who are replaced by Me, take My place, continue Me, perpetuate Me.

"Take My place on the Cross of Redemption,"

"Continue Me in the Host,"

"Perpetuate Me in my saving excesses."

Now if I can no longer suffer, I need the sufferings of other Myselves all the more, in order to make my redemptive sufferings fruitful. And who can these be if not consecrated souls?

This mutual exchange of places in love, is it not the ideal of union, of "being only One," the ideal from a perspective that has no limit.

For as total as this unifying substitution is at any one instant, in that very instant it can and must grow greater.

Isn't this the policy of my holy Will, the policy of love in its entirety? To take my place more and more completely in the soul by hollowing out, by my divine means, a deep and ever-increasing capacity in it for various kinds of suffering. If my consecrated ones only knew the ascents that I arrange in their hearts, the extent of growth that I dream of attaining in each of them for the satisfaction of my Father, with what affectionate and grateful eagerness would they respond to the slightest sign and nuance of my divine preferences, even if they be crucifying.

"Crucified spouse, I espouse you by crucifying."

That is the entire meaning of co-redemptive suffering. Believe in the cross, in my Cross, in its absolute necessity, in the supreme efficacy of suffering for the triumph of my redemptive work.

In my divine thoughts of love, the mission and purpose of all suffering is that of annunciation, to be a prelude to Incarnation and Redemption. Indeed, suffering is always (because I never fail) an announcement proposed to the soul, an appeal inviting it to be open to my redemptive coming. For ever since Calvary the cross has never been naked, the Crucified One remains fixed upon it. Every cross is a Crucifix. But this announcement only becomes a true Annunciation, which is to say the realization of this redemptive coming, when, following the example of Mary, the soul pronounces its *Fiat* of consent and acceptance.

Each truly accepting acceptance of each cross, making for a deeper coming of the Crucified Savior, therefore effects a precious advance of my redemptive work. This is what truly constitutes the work of co-redemption.

1937

Write this in order that my true spouses, desirous to be my co-redeemers, may meditate on it, understand it, and live by it more and more.

Does the espousing of my Cross mean to contemplate, admire, and bless my sufferings? Oh no! That is already something too little on your part, far too little to provide Me any consolation. Contemplation may be necessary to allow for sympathy but it is not enough for love.

Then would it be to suffer from my sufferings with a sincere, heart-felt, affectionate compassion? That is already something more and much better that touches my Heart and begins to console it. But even this is too little. To fully espouse my Heart, there has to be a participation that is deeper still, more complete, still more intimate.

One has to suffer my sufferings with a compassion that is crucifying in its effect. Here is the compenetrating transfixion of the heart, of the soul, of one's entire being.

Between these two compassions, alone worthy of consecrated souls, there is an entire world of love, of intimacy, and of union. Do you understand this, consecrated souls, all of whom I would want in this second category? But alas, there are still too few of you in this number.

To suffer from my sufferings by feeling its repercussions, yes, there are many of you who do that, even with a degree of purity and intensity, and I thank you!

But to suffer my sufferings themselves, to experience them truly and completely, how many are there of you?

See the small minority of these victim (*hostie*) souls made crimson by my Blood, these are the ones wholly consecrated, wholly consoling, wholly glorifying, the true co-redeemers whose number my "appeal" seeks to augment.

Beg my Heart, so desirous of satisfying you, to grant you understanding of this two-fold aspect of love: on the one hand of resembling each other, of coming together, of being in contact, and on the other of compenetrating union, identification, of being made one.

Is there not a profound abyss of intimacy separating the two? Only the second responds fully to my "appeal."

February 2, 1939

Celebration, mystery of revelation: *lumen ad revelationem genti-um,*[14] revelation of the true redemptive meaning of Love Incarnate. The sacrificial victim meaning of my mission as Savior is explicitly revealed for the first time in the forecast of suffering that accompanied my presentation to the Father.

This child shall be subject to contradiction.[15] Was not the Cross already rearing up then? And with how much love was the *Fiat* in my Heart at the *Ecce* of this offering!

And also the first revelation of the co-redemptive suffering of my Mother: *A sword shall pierce your soul. . . .*[16] And, by that, the revelation of the merciful need of my redemptive love for collaborators, helpers, companions in accomplishing the work of my Father.

How much was I thinking then of my "appeal" when from the depths of my Heart I pronounced these words:

**"To save the world I need true spouses, spouses
who are co-redeemers."**

1939

"My joy is to help you help Me." I do this in the measure that you ask it of Me. And your prayer is all the more helpful to Me the more it is penetrated with a spirit of sacrifice in order that the widest portals in the world of souls may open to Me.

Recognize therefore in the sufferings that I multiply for you the most precious help that I can possibly give, in order that, by your *Fiat* in fully welcoming love, you yourselves are able to give Me a little more helpful aid.

I am going to teach you a way of the Cross, beseeching those who would be most pleasing to my Heart.

---

[14] *Luke 2:32 — a light for revelation to the gentiles.*
[15] *Ibid 2:34*
[16] *Ibid 2:35*

Say at each station:

"Holy Redeemer Spouse, You Whom I adore and Whom I love from the most intimate depths of my soul, in your infinite, redemptive Goodness, by the virtues of your Blood which the sorrows endured especially at this station caused you to shed, make of us true co-redemptive spouses, in accordance with your merciful, supplicating desire, fully consecrated as sacrificial hosts (*hosties*) in communion with You, working for the salvation of the world and the triumph of your Holy Church.

"I ask this of You, humbly, confidently, ardently supplicating, giving myself to You totally, through the mediation of the Co-Redemptive Virgin, Mother of Sorrows, that the Goodness and Infinite Sovereignty of the Father of Mercies may be glorified."

Ecce ! Fiat ! Magnificat!

It was not at a low price, nor at the price of gold, but at the price of Blood, at the price of all my Blood who am the Incarnate Word, that I brought forth my Church, that I bought and redeemed the souls of these children. Would you associate yourself with my work at a lesser price? Would you have the heart for it? For if the Spouse for his part has already been superabundant (giving to the last drop), nevertheless, to gain the Father's cause completely, He still needs the free and generous contribution of love and blood from his consecrated ones. The time has come and is pressing now for the ample payment of this contribution.

For love that is in the process of proving itself, there is no true service without sacrifice. Here is the full meaning of your vocation in its truest sense.

Let us attend together, as one heart and soul, the great, redemptive vigil of prayer and blood of Infinite Charity, a vigil that is to be prolonged in and by the Host until the end of time, thanks to the association of living hosts formed by the souls of those consecrated to Me.

But they must not forget that to live as "host," they can only do so by an unceasing and ever-increasing series of exceedingly pure sacrificial acts (*actes d'hostie*). Now, the host only remains "alive" by perpetual acts of self-giving, of immolation, which is to say by one's death. One remains "consecrated" only by being unceasingly consumed by constantly renewed sacrifices.

Believe Me and write this for all my consecrated ones: the *Fiat* of a single moment wherein one becomes host has more value for the consolation of my Heart and the furthering of my redemptive work than long hours of sweet and peaceful prayer spent before the Host.

The darker the nothingness and sinfulness of your being and the viler (to Me) your humanity, the greater the triumph of my Being of purity and love, of my sublime, divine "Me." And every time, by your destruction, I thus triumph more profoundly in you, I further at the same time my triumph in the immense family of souls my love has conferred to you (oh how marvelous is this redemptive solidarity!). For each of my spouses is to be seen as charged with a family, with the family of their Spouse, as Mother of the family of my Father's children — and this represents all his creatures that He would want as children. Satanic hatred rages against this family, and what great need I have for compensatory love, for sacrifice even unto death (*holocaust*).

Suffering, true co-redemptive suffering, is not some vague, sentimental notion but an action that is truly sacrificial, a profoundly distressing sorrow. One cannot suffer without suffering.

THE KINGDOM OF HEAVEN
SUFFERS VIOLENCE

1938

The Kingdom of Heaven suffers violence.
It is the violent who bear it away.[17]

When but at the present time are these words most being realized? The Kingdom of my Father in the world is being unjustly attacked by

---

[17] *Matt 11:12*

32

this furious, persecuting violence that hates with a vengeance the all-powerful virtue of my redemptive Blood that perseveres in the Host.

Can this Kingdom be defended in any other way than by the restorative violence of love, by a burning eagerness to make amends that atone and glorify?

It is the violent, the most violent who carry it off.[18]

Oh, all you consecrated souls, the hour has come, the time is pressing to do Me violence! To place powerful pressure on my Heart in order that It may finally realize its grand, salvific desire which is to make of you a generous present, to generously gift the world through you with the fruits of my redemptive Blood.

To do Me the violence of love, first of all, is to render Me a humble, faithful and contrite confession of your cowardice and failures in loving. . . . To see yourself sincerely as guilty of egoism and therefore as responsible for the trials presently afflicting the world. For do not forget, if you would have been better spouses, things would not be as they are.

To do Me the violence of love is also to place your complete and absolute trust in Me throughout all the mysteries of the present course and the course to come, having invincible faith in the paternal Goodness of my Providence which watches with an infinite tenderness over each of its children, even those that It chastises. *My Father works without ceasing*[19] and He always acts as a Father. And even now, everywhere and at every moment, his Goodness is pouring forth.

Believe with assured faith in this incessant action of the Father's Goodness, bless It with a trust redoubled in times of great suffering — this is the filial homage most fitting to glorify his Holiness, appease his Justice, and above all to touch his merciful Compassion.

Multiply unceasingly therefore these benedictions to my Goodness, multiply them as co-redeemers and thus as "mediators," hearts stretched to feel as your divine Lord feels. And offer them to Me on

---

[18] *In their literal sense these words indicate the violence that one must do to oneself in order to enter the Kingdom of Heaven. They are being used here in an adapted sense.*

[19] *Jn 5:17*

behalf of all hearts — on behalf of all those who know but too often forget to do it or who do it poorly, and on behalf of those who do not know and whom Satan makes use of in his work of hatred.

My Heart acts ceaselessly in a superabundant outpouring of Charity, always acting and loving as "Savior," for can this Heart do otherwise than love? My Redemptive Blood therefore is pouring Itself out every moment everywhere. Would that you too might ceaselessly assist It with outpourings, with an invincible faith in the final triumph of this Redemptive Love.

To do Me the violence of love is to make total oblation of one's self, to the complete sacrifice of every fiber of one's being and every drop of blood, in this spirit of co-redemption which is at the heart of my "appeal:"

"Crucified spouse, I espouse by crucifying."

Let yourselves become little hosts therefore, for the Host alone has the divine ability as well as the profound desire to transform into little hosts souls that are wholly given over to Him.

For do not forget, *I am the Lamb of God,*[20] the Spotless Lamb of the Father's merciful Justice! Calvary's bloodied Lamb who remains *immolated*[21] in the Sacred Host for the salvation of the world and Who *in bearing all of man's sins erases them,*[22] bearing them by the humiliation of my "Victim" state wherein the abysmal humiliation of my Passion is carried on.

O my consecrated ones, in this time of great turmoil, listen to the voice of my supplication: "Help Me to bear the sins of the world." This will help Me "wash away" these sins by the "application of my redemptive Blood" . . . and for this allow Me to associate you ever more closely with all the pain, all the humiliations of my Cross and of my Host.

— To do Me the violence of love finally is to beg Me unceasingly,

---

[20] *Jn 1:29*
[21] *II Cor 5:7*
[22] *Jn 1:29*

believing on behalf of souls, praying to the Father of Mercies in union with Me, offering Me to Him in a perpetual Mass: *Suscipe sancte Pater . . . hanc Immaculatam Hostiam.*[23]

Plead also by praying to Me in union with Mary, offering Me the Immaculate Heart of this most Virgin host. And pray this along with all men.

You need to know what it means "to be served by Me in order to serve the cause of my Father," "to be served by my Mother in order to serve my redemptive Cause."

— To do Me the violence of love that longs for my tender sovereignty is to do all these things together: "confession," "trust," "sacrifice," "pleadings," doing all with a heart that is ever more loving, on behalf of all hearts.

SERVE ME AS RAMPART

1936

Oh, yes, consecrated souls, conceal yourself within my Heart in total security. But at the same time:

"Serve Me as rampart!"

as a rampart burning with love raised against the hatred that furiously assails Me, and the egoism that like a coward avoids Me and leaves Me chilled to the bone.

For it would be a terribly perfidious, egoistic illusion, unworthy of souls capable of even a modicum of love and generosity, to claim in times of such great turmoil to find shelter, refuge and rest in my Heart if I Myself am unable to find shelter, refuge and rest in your hearts, my consecrated souls!

Remember that love in its essence is reciprocal. If, in order to

---

[23] *From the canon of the Holy Mass: "Receive Holy Father . . . this spotless Host."*

defend you and give you asylum, my Heart had been wounded and pierced, consumed to its last fiber, emptied out of its last drop, then, to defend Me and give Me asylum, what should your heart be like and what should it do? I will let you draw the conclusion. . . .

If my Cross is the invulnerable "rampart" of fire drawn up against hell in order to save and protect you, what protective rampart have I not the right to expect from my consecrated ones?

May your hearts, your lives hasten to respond to Me with a generous *Fiat*, in fervent echo of the *Fiat* spoken by my sorrowful Mother, itself an echo of my own.

With all my Heart I beg this of you: Raise up again and again without ever ceasing this rampart of love, burning ever more brightly, sustained by the utter holocaust of your sacerdotal or religious consecration lived out in truth and fullness.

Yes, this is the hour when all is to be thrown into the fire, when you yourselves are to be thrown into the great furnace of love, to enkindle your ardor so that you may come to master and vanquish hatred's fury. . . . For you know, do you not, that when it comes to love, "it is only in giving more that one can give back."

"Just enough" does not satisfy love! It needs superabundance, surplus, excesses. It needs luxury, the luxury of gifts, the luxury of suffering.

Look upon your crucified Savior. Remember reciprocity!

Oh, I implore this of you, seek, beg this luxury of love for Me. I need it! I need it to put an end to the infernal fury. And who but my spouses will give Me this?

May each of you search within his or her heart for those little excesses of love that could be added to one's daily life in order that the great excesses of my love may find response.

There are times, and now is one of them, when "giving everything" is not enough, is already too little, and when instead one has to give "more, always more." Love is only alive when it goes beyond itself, each day anew, in fresh demonstrations, fresh gifts.

Don't forget that these little "surpluses" that I ask of you have more to do with the "manner" than with the "matter" of the gift. How many nuances and shades can be found in the way one gives Me "everything," nuances and delicacies that make up the "more," the "better," an increase defined only by "always more," "always better"!

If "giving everything that is required" satisfies justice, "giving more than is strictly required" alone satisfies love. Particularly when it is an avenging love.

Understand well that giving one's "more" is the most certain means of giving one's "everything," but at the same time don't forget that in order to give one's "more," one starts by giving "everything."

Without perfect, scrupulous fidelity, there can be none of the genuine generosity I beg for in order to raise the ramparts of love.

Would that the life of my consecrated ones be nothing but a great clamor of love, ever more vibrant, burning, rising, so as to drown out, to subdue the roaring hubbub of hatred. Here is the rampart of fire I await. Clamor of love through the great sacerdotal prayer gushing forth from a victim soul (*âme-hostie*) in perpetual celebration of the Holy Mass. From love that makes reparation, from love that compensates. Oh, consecrated souls, give Me all this!

1939

See the terrible ravages occurring in this moment of hatred in the world. But always bear this in mind: it would not have been thus if you had not, by your ego-centric reservations, made "breeches" in the rampart of love, in this rampart where I had given you the care of a privileged post, care for raising the rampart high, for making it strong, for ceaselessly moving it forward by your offering which held nothing back.

Yes, each egocentric glance, desire, wish on the part of souls dedicated to a vocation of love forms a fissure in this rampart, at least if no wholehearted reparation attends it, and these fissures multiplied produce real breeches that open passage for the assaults of hatred. Move quickly to repair these breeches!

For I still want to save this poor world, I always want to. Is that not the reason why my Father sent Me to the Cross, and why each day He sends Me back into the Host?

But I need helpers!

And I call each and every one of my consecrated ones to this choice post for the defense of my rampart, the "rampart of my Father's Kingdom." May each of you, at every moment, by courageous fidelity and loving generosity, work ceaselessly to erect it, to widen the surrounding wall and repair the breeches! Each breech closed to the devastating assaults of hatred is an opening for the saving torrents of love.

"GIVE ME TO DRINK!"

1936

Ah, if you only knew! . . . Consecrated souls, if you only knew Who it is that says to you, "Give Me to drink."[24] If only you grasped God's gift to you,[25] the gift of predilection which is my desire that you would serve Me as co-redemptive helpers . . . the gift of my "appeal."

Yes, when wearied of my apostolic journey I uttered these Gospel words, my Heart was thinking of you, seeing you in a special way, thinking of my "appeal."

Meditate on this, pray for the light to understand this scene, these words, then perhaps you will understand all this a little better, so that the copious blessings of tender love eternally gushing forth will wash over you. *It will become a fountain of living water, welling up to eternal life.*[26]

Hear some of my thirsting cries, all variations of the same, immense love:

---

[24] *Jn 4:8*
[25] *Ibid 4:10*
[26] *Ibid 4:14*

"When then will the love of Love prevail over the hatred of Love?

"When will the burning ardors of charity overcome icy half-heartedness and the frigidity of hatred and egoism?

"When, O my consecrated ones, will you love Me as spouses, passionate in love with my Glory, with my interests alone?

"When then will you demonstrate this to Me, by a life wholly bent on reciprocating the gift, even to the point of martyrdom, the shedding of blood both of heart and will. When, then? When?"

"My Heart is waiting for you."

When hatred stirs up violence, as at present, must not Love stir up its own excesses, and from whom have I the right to be loved to the point of folly if not by my consecrated ones that I Myself love to excess?

You know that to love to the point of folly is to love by sacrificing everything. Few actually understand this. And know that:

"The folly of the Cross is the supreme wisdom of the heart."

1938

In my Father's bosom, my celestial home, I am always in a state of blessed contentment. In my Host, my earthly home, I live in a state both of pain and hunger, the pain of unsatisfiable hunger, hunger to devour and be devoured.

As long as my Love is unsatisfied, It will never be able to cease begging for bread. What is this bread? You know the answer. I hunger for the bread of little hosts.

May your faith enlivened by the loving supplication of my "appeal" ever call you back to the full, paternal plan of my Father.

In each tiny fragment of my great redemptive Host, a "little co-redemptive host" must be incorporated so that the saving fruits of my

Blood can be applied to souls. And these little hosts are formed, particle by particle, by the "sacrificial acts" that are to make up the lives of my consecrated ones.

Suffering is the crucible wherein I form my hosts. The most perfect sacrificial act therefore is the *Fiat*, filled with love, to my crucifying, divinely transforming action in whatever form it may take, and shortly will take.

Do not forget that "without end" is the name of Love. No, It never has enough of loving and therefore of begging, insatiably, of tirelessly pouring Itself out. For to love is to communicate, to communicate oneself in order to commune with others in a mutual, perpetual effusion of life. And you know that Love's surest and most direct channels of communication are these two: the Host, and Mary.

I love you too much to be able to hold Myself back, to desist from pursuing this drive of Mine to save, or to back off in the face of even the strongest reasons for doing so. Love has no familiarity with perfidy like that!

I love you too much, my consecrated ones, to quiet down the supplicating cries of my "appeal," pleading for you as co-redemptive partners. Do not be put off by my wanting you so ardently. My divine demands conceal so much tenderness and mercy.

I love you so very much, poor little unworthy one that you are (and I speak to all my spouses through you), I love you too much to stop even for an instant the crucifying operations by which I, the Crucified Spouse, prepare for the triumph of my Savior's Blood.

And you, would you not have enough love in your heart to acknowledge and recognize in this ceaseless redoubling of suffering a major reason for the redoubling of hope? Have I not already said that once I began asking I could no longer hold Myself back, so eager am I to "give still more."

And you, are you able to hold yourself back from giving to Me and asking of Me? Look, hear all the plots that are being hatched in this time of diabolic hatred, deadly plots against Me, in souls, in my Church.

And in the face of all this, what does love do? Is it also vehement, ardent to hatch plots of life, of triumph for my Heart? How many take counsel to seize all the means for vanquishing my enemies and giving Me total victory?

You, my consecrated ones, do you do this as much as you are able? Don't you want this to be the way things are in the future? Do you not sense that the time has come to "give one's all, one's *maximum*, one's *crescendo* for the cause of Love"?

1939

I have been wounded in the house of those who love me.[27]

May these words from my Scripture carry light into your hearts, my consecrated souls, to stir up every fiber in them, to wound them with a love that destroys and expels egoism, and so causes to spurt back to my Heart the blood of a most pure and fervent "co-redemptive charity."

Only a wound of love can allay and heal the wound of hatred.

Of all the bitterness that I suffered in the chalice of my Passion, if the cowardly egoism of my "supposed" spouses was the most bitter — oh, what pain for my Heart! — then the sweetest of the consoling "reparations" that I experienced came from, and can only come from, the fervent charity of my true spouses, which is to say from those who have understood their vocation as co-redeemers, those who, as called for by my "appeal," espouse all that is dear to my Heart.

Each battle of their hearts has been a drop of sweetness falling into the "chalice of comfort" borne by my Angel in the terrible hour of my Agony in Gethsemane.

Ought not this assurance be for you the sweetest of consolations, the strongest of stimulants to respond to my supplicating appeal: *Give Me to drink.*

---

[27] *Zach 13:6*

41

I NEED OUTLETS

1938

Listen. . . . Write this down again. . . .

In order that my "redemptive graces" be able to spread in torrents across this poor world so terribly shaken by satanic fury, "I need outlets."

I need more outlets, that is, more pierced hearts that allow free passage to the outflow of my saving Blood, mixing theirs with It and thereby permitting It to run back to the Father. Hearts letting themselves be pierced as the Heart of Mary, the Mother of Sorrows, was pierced, by the sword of co-redemptive love, freely accepted by a *Fiat* that offers up everything and consents to everything in an overflowing *Magnificat* of love.

These pierced hearts, hearts which are more than merely wounded (which can have a personal basis, some hidden egoism unthinkable in Mary), where will I find them, of whom shall I ask these things if not my consecrated ones? Is not the entire supplicating request of my costly "appeal" to find its response here?

You understand, do you not, how this "transfixion" is the precondition to redemptive "transmission" as well as the "transfusion that makes us one."

Wearied more and more as sorrowfully It waits for souls and yet tireless in desire and confidence, my Heart comes to you seeking a little "rest for love." To give Me rest is to permit Me to pour Myself out, empty Myself into hearts that are completely open, fully alive, so that I may spread Myself out among you and by an immense effusion of loving graces, increase your contentment.

Oh, happy lot of my consecrated ones to be called to serve in this outpouring of love! And this:

— By participating in the cost of the Cross, by a generous spirit of co-redemptive crucifixion, allowing themselves to be crucified by their crucified Spouse.

— By relieving the cost of these graces, fruit of the Cross; by the wholly free receptivity of a soul who through its heartfelt *Fiat of acceptance* has become opened to my divine wishes.

— And by the perpetual state of transmissibility of a soul pierced right through, for it is wholly given over to the interests of redemption, serving as an outlet, as a living passageway for the outflowing of my graces onto and into souls.

Such is the desire of my "loving appeal."

Pentecost, 1939

Like a great cry of thirsting desire, my "appeal" is a torrent of blazing flames shooting forth from its "supreme source," its divine Outlet Who is my Spirit of fire, Spirit of Truth and Love. "Heart of my Heart."

Contemplate this divine origin:

Only a divine end is appropriate to it.

This torrent only spurts out in order to spurt back.

Gushing forth waves of grace so that waves of praise gush back to the glory of Love.

Here is the sublime end of my "appeal."

But by what means?

To be able to gush back, the torrent needs to gain entry into living soil that it can inundate and fecundate. My supplication needs to gain access to loving hearts to embrace them, fecundate and divinely transform them into co-redemptive hosts, to open in them a vast outlet of love.

To Love, on Love's behalf. . . .

Then, every benediction of praise will rise to the Source from Whom this merciful benediction has come. And all this transpires by means of souls. The continual back-and-forth flow of love. Isn't this the life secret of apostolic union?

Oh, do not close the outlets to this torrent. Open wide the floodgates, and to that end, let my "appeal" be known — respond to it.

December 8

So full of the Love that consumes It, my Heart burns to pour Itself into souls in torrents and there to overflow and gush back to my Father in glowing praise. Filled Myself to overflowing, I want you too to be filled to overflowing with "my great redemptive Charity," so that in ever more intimate communion with Me, the diffusion might be wider and more radiant, and that the wound of your hearts might serve as outlets.

Contemplate then with eyes of love this overflowing superabundance, from the mystery of the Trinity to the mystery of the Host, emanating through the mysteries of the Crèche and the Cross.

Carry out this contemplation yourselves, and take from it into your hearts all its loving, practical implications.

"Serve Me as outlets, no less than as ramparts!"

CHAPTER TWO

THE HOLY VIRGIN

*Co-Redemptrix par excellence, by her intimate union
with the Heart of Jesus, the Redeemer, throughout her life
and particularly at the moment of the Passion.
Exalted Model for co-redemptive souls.*

MARY CO-REDEMPTRIX

March 6, 1937

Contemplate the immaculate purity of the sorrows of the Virgin Mary, ideal Co-Redemptrix! Not even in her suffering was She sullied by any form of egoism.

Her entire capacity for feeling was only to feel what I feel. Nothing touched my Heart or caused It to be stirred that did not find in her Heart a vibrant echo, a profound counter-beat in perfect union.

Co-redemptive sharing means much more than simply partaking of the sorrows of the Savior. It means participating in them intimately, which is to say, not only having a part in them, but taking part totally, associating with them completely, espousing the entirety of my Passion. It means not merely to suffer "some" of my sufferings, but to suffer "all" my sufferings.

It was when the Heart of Mary was most desolated that I was most consoled, for this was the hour of greatest love, of the heroic *Magnificat*,

45

of the greatest "co-redemptive help." Desolation becoming transfixion, the highest point of communion with my Crucifixion!

Ideal that I have chosen for you and for each and every consecrated soul. My consolation in you and through you will be in the measure that your heart is completely, spiritually transfixed.

Console the Virgin Mary, console Me by abandoning yourself like Her to the piercing, two-edged sword of redemptive Love that begs for the last drop of your heart's blood. Draining that has to take place drop by drop through the gift of each moment, the drop from your present duty in its entirety, which is to say, by the total self-denial that complete adherence to my Will asks of the present moment.

My Will is this two-edged sword burning with love that pierces the heart so as to permit the transfusion of hearts.

Do you not believe that it would have been sweet for my Heart and that of my Mother for Us to die together, to mingle our last sighs? Yes, very sweet, provided this had been the Father's Will, but that was not to be. The earthly mission of Mary was not finished. After my death, for many years She had to be my continuator (*survie*) as it were, continuing and perpetuating Me as "Co-Redemptrix." This was my Father's plan, otherwise would I have had the courage not to have taken Her along with Me? And what was her response? How pure and ardent were her *Fiat* and her *Magnificat*!

She lived her life most simply nevertheless, appearing humble and charitable; but her soul could only live on after Me in sacrificial bearing as host, as a sublime invention of love. I had chosen to live on in Myself in the Eucharist, until the end of the ages. This in order to completely implement and consummate the redemptive work entrusted by the Father. Just as you too, by the example and with the help of Mary, are to be "my little co-redemptive continuators," closely united with my great "redemptive Continuation in the Host."

That you may more and more become for Me the true co-redemptive souls that I ask you to be, do not forget the sweet and powerful means obtained by looking to Mary, to Mary's love, by recourse to Mary, model of the perfect spouse.

Her secret in this is to be at one and the same time:

Spouse-Virgin – Spouse-Mother – Spouse-Martyr.

Spouse-Virgin, furnace of purity, loving exclusively in a Heart overcome by love, caring only for the Beloved's contentment, a life entirely woven with the fine filaments of fidelity, trust, the gift of abandonment, of detachment, of total disengagement from Herself.

Spouse-Mother, apostle, furnace of zeal, love expansive, a Heart wholly devoted to the glory of her divine Son, a life given over completely to the work of Co-Redemption!

Spouse-Martyr, because it was through her association with Calvary that Mary became Mother of souls, stricken by the desire to spread as widely as possible the Reign of Love.

Spouse: Virgin, Mother, Martyr, espousing until consummated in unity, her whole life one of Love, such is Mary, the ideal and perfect model that I would like so much to see you imitate.

By whom will my Heart most willingly be captured, by whom will my Mercy be most prevailed upon and touched if not by the Heart of my Mother, She who offers Me, purified and embraced, the offerings and supplications of my consecrated ones for the salvation of the world?

There is raging at this time a great and terrible duel between Satan and Mary, between hatred's infernal fury and the celestial passion of divine Love.

Thousands of souls are at stake!

See the souls of all these poor sinners engulfed in hatred, gripped on the one side by the claws of Satan who would capture them and furiously drag them into his abyss, and on the other, held back and supported by the virginal hand of their Immaculate Mother, so very eager to plunge them into my Heart. But as powerful as She is, She needs help, help from the sacrificial prayers of her faithful children, and most especially from consecrated souls, my priests and religious.

See how wide open her virginal hand is to receive this swelling wave of apostolic love. The more this hand is filled, the more her other hand is empowered to raise souls up from the abyss and snatch them away from Satan. But if prayer is lacking, then hell emerges to carry them off. What greater incentive to redouble the fervor of your co-redemptive supplications!

Spend time in tender contemplation of the martyred Heart of the Mother of Sorrows, and know that the moment I see any resemblance to my Mother I am pleased and delighted.

Probe deeply into the three words of life that gushed forth from her Immaculate Heart, beating in unison with the embrace of my Heart:

Ecce, word signifying immersion into the abyss of love.

Fiat, word signifying inundation by the waves of love.

Magnificat, word signifying a surging back to the source of love.

MOTHER – VIRGIN – MARTYR

1940

If Mary was so incomparably Mother, and Mother so mercifully Co-Redemptive, it was because She had so marvelously realized in Herself the ideal of the Virgin-Martyr. Yes, the secret of the admirable fecundity of her maternity is that She was all at once:

Mother Virgin of the Immaculate Heart.

Mother Martyr of the pierced Heart.

And as such, She is the perfect Queen of the Apostles, master-piece, model, incomparable mistress of the apostolic workforce — because "every apostle must be mother."

An apostle is only apostle, conquering by Christ and for Christ, in the measure that he or she is "mother."

To renew your apostolic fervor, go deeper into the school of Mary for these two marks that characterize the maternity of souls!

Mother Martyr: Mary was so by virtue of her sublime mission as Mother of the Infant-God,

Jesus was Mary's martyrdom, her sole tormenting martyrdom, her tormenting but most beloved martyrdom. How can this be?

Couldn't an infant martyr be a martyrdom for the heart of its mother, in proportion even to the depths of tenderness of her maternal heart?

Now, what child was ever more martyr than Jesus? And what mother's heart was ever more tender than Mary's?

The Infant-God was the Martyr *par excellence.*

What does "martyrdom" mean if not blood spilled, life given over, sacrifice consummated in testimony of the highest order, in testimony to charity in the highest degree. Now, what was the reason for my Life as Incarnate Word and its climb to Calvary if not to give evidence of my Love for the Father and for men, children of the Father.

There is no greater sign of love than to lay down your life for those you love.[28]

The life that I gave up as soon as it was given to Me, each breath of which was given in suffering (*holocauste*), was a testimony to love at its purest and strongest; life, each breath of which was taken under the sign of the redemptive Cross, was true martyrdom in the most profound sense of the word.

And how would this martyrdom not have had its intimate, deep, martyr-making repercussions in the most tender, the most delicate, the most sensitive Heart of Mary, the Mother of Mothers? Everything that touched my Heart had repercussions in her breast with such vividness that She was truly pierced and martyred by it.

The Mother's first martyrdom was a martyrdom of compassion.

Ought not this also be the martyrdom of my spouses? Jesus, their crucified Spouse, is He not to be their Martyrdom also? A tormenting Martyrdom borne of the most acute convergence of

---

[28] *Jn 15:15*

sufferings; but also a Martyrdom relieving to the heart, as it was for Mary, consoled by her ability to soften a little, by her compassion, the Martyrdom of her Son!

To suffer "along with" Jesus: grief indescribable!

To suffer "for" Jesus: sweetness indescribable!

Here is the testimony that martyrdom gives to love, love's profession of every true co-redeemer.

Mary's second, concurrent martyrdom was that of her co-redemptive maternity. In order to become Mother of the children of God, She had to endure all the sorrows of Calvary. For it was only then, from the height of my Cross, that I let fall the words consecrating Her under this title for all eternity, conferring upon Her and confiding to Her the universal Maternity of souls.

Ecce Mater tua!. . . Ecce filius tuus! [29]

Creative word as are all my words!

At the very moment that I pronounced this word, seeing in a vision of immense tenderness the entire human family in my virgin Apostle, I created in Mary a true Mother's heart for each member of this family, and at the same time created each true child of Mary, child of her co-redemptive sorrows.

Thus each Christian soul can say:

"I was born of Mary's martyrdom! — of Mary's freely offered martyrdom!" For, though her *Fiat* of acquiescence was silent, you cannot doubt its profound, intimate reality, so full of *Magnifcat!* Response that I awaited in order to pronounce the *Consummatum est* of my redemptive work.

And each child of God — child of Mary's martyrdom — being thus a brother of Jesus, another Jesus, "a continuator of Jesus," the repetition of my Life, each child is therefore still Me, Jesus, Who was true martyrdom for Mary, the Mother of the children of God.

---

[29] *Ibid 19:26-27*

Jesus, to be born and grow in souls.

Jesus, to defend and elevate them when exposed to contradiction.

Jesus Savior, to save and exalt them!

And this martyrdom of Mary's maternity with regard to each soul is all the greater when this soul has been called by my Father to closer identification with Me.

I leave it to your heart, consecrated souls, to draw love's conclusions from this: gratitude, trust. You understand that your calling as "privileged children of Mary's martyrdom" entails yet another calling: to be "fervent associates and helpers of this co-redemptive martyrdom."

For you must not forget the signal honor that I conferred upon you to be my Mother's continuators, prolongers therefore of her maternal mission: apostles, mothers, martyrs like Her!

The great heart of my apostle Paul understood this well: *I suffer*, he said to his followers, *I suffer on your behalf the pains of childbirth until Christ be formed in you.*" [30]

Souls live by the martyrdom of the apostle: martyrdom by the absolute gift of suffering (*holocauste*) in witness to love — blood shed in all its ways to the last drop (self-denial, patience, humiliation, mortification).

Just as it was with Mary, it is Jesus in souls who brings about the apostle's martyrdom, martyrdom lovingly agonized by a great maternal thirst to give birth and growth to Christ so as to enlarge more and more the circle of the great, divine, adopted family, to the eternal glory of Infinite Goodness.

As with Mary, the maternity of the apostle must also be a virgin-maternity.

The meaning of this spiritually fecund virginity is found in the Angel's reply to Mary's *quomode fiet istud*:[31]

---

[30] *Gal 4:19*

[31] *Lk 1:34 — How can this be done?*

"The Holy Spirit will come upon you, and the power of the most high will overshadow you; therefore the child to be born will be called holy, the Son of God."[32]

The dwelling, animation, operation of the Holy Spirit in the soul of the apostle is the great secret of all spiritual fecundity:

"That which is born of the Spirit is spirit."[33]

All activity taking form in this holy Flame gives birth to a holy work, producing a fruit which, in truth, can be called Son of God!

Meditate on this marvel: All acts accomplished under the movement and with the cooperation of the Holy Spirit have the power thereby to give birth to Christ, to increase Christ and extend the rays of the Father's complacency over his creation.

And the closer the dependence upon this interior Host (*Hôte*) and Master of the soul, the more pure and more "virgin" and at the same time the more fecund and more "mother" is the apostle's activity.

Marvelous alliance of virginity and maternity that should characterize all my consecrated souls. But let them not forget that this dependence upon the Holy Spirit, "source" of perfect purity of intention, disposition, operation, is itself "fruit" of sacrifice and renunciation of all self-interest, in a word, of total unselfishness, the virtue without which zeal is never perfectly pure, no matter how ardent.

There is no virginity without suffering no more than there is maternity without suffering.

The purity of the Virgin Mary is a purity of fire, of consuming fire so as to be fruitful and espousing!

Thus are joined in love these three inseparable titles and functions:

Mother – Virgin – Martyr.

---

[32] *Ibid v. 35*

[33] *Jn 3:6*

MOTHER OF MERCY

August 15, 1940

My Heart feels the need to speak to you of Mary whose help in Redemption is so perfect it has led the Church justly to invoke Her under the title *Mother of Mercy.*[34]

To assist Me in my great work of mercy, be Mary's continuators, just as Mary was my continuator, "continuators of Mary Co-Redemptrix."

My Mother's mission here below had ended with her glorious Assumption, but her distinctive legacy is the legacy of love that She has conferred in my Name upon all her terrestrial children in these times, and upon you especially, consecrated souls.

Have you never fully understood the honor of this legacy? — the legacy's value? — the responsibility of this legacy? Isn't the theme of my "appeal" all here?

The life of a continuator is no longer its own; it no longer breathes for itself: *It is no longer I who live . . .*

Life whose entire course is to die in order to prolong and expand the life of another, the only life that matters, the life of Christ, of crucified Love: *. . . but Jesus Christ who lives in me.*

The supremely unselfish life of the sacred Host, that can say in all truthfulness: *Vivo jam non ego, vivit vero in me Christus,*[35] and that through Me lives on to pursue its redemptive work.

Life that was Mary's sole life, from my last breath on Calvary until her last breath on earth. Life that She bequeathed, bequeathing to each of you the right and grace to prolong this life during your earthly sojourn.

---

[34] *In the well-known prayer, "Salve Regina."*
[35] *Gal 2:19 — It is no longer I who live, but Christ who lives in me.*

This life of co-redemptive continuation that She lived by the perfect exercise of her two inseparable functions as spouse and mother.

As spouse, with her own quality of "intimacy": a contemplative intimacy that draws breath within.

As mother, with her own quality of "fecundity": a radiating fecundity that bears fruit without.

Learn from Her that love's perfect intimacy cannot be had without identity of loves, without perfect fusion of all the feelings, all the affections, all the desires and wishes of the heart; this is the beating of hearts in unison that my "appeal" speaks of.

Is yours one with Hers, consecrated souls? Is there any dissonance between your heart and Mary's, and thus between your heart and Mine?

In the same way, learn from Her that there can be no fecundity in love unless my love is communicated to souls, a communication which presupposes that your apostolic hearts possess my love to overflowing, and that you therefore renounce your own love.

For, understand this well, fruitful apostolicity is not the gift of self to souls, but the gift of Me — the gift of souls to my Heart through the gift of Me to souls.

How perfectly Mary realized this indispensable condition of spiritual maternity!

Do not forget I have told you that on the day of her Assumption, She bequeathed to you simultaneously the grace, the duty and the model of this maternity. Draw from her Heart and be for Me continuators of Mary Co-Redemptrix.

Through her maternal grace, be for Me spouses that are ever more mothers, mothers that are ever more spouses, with an intimacy ever more intimate, with a fecundity ever more fertile.

For I cannot keep Myself from repeating this to you: "To give souls to Me, you have to give Me to souls."

To give birth spiritually to other Christs, other Me's, true children of my Father, I and not self, not you, am the One who must be given to them. It is my Life, my great Life of Love that must be communicated to them, you being no longer yourselves but my very pure, animated "continuators."

If I insist so much, it's that consecrated souls who claim to be my apostles have not fully understood the true, great and profound meaning of this spiritual maternity of souls. With many, too many, the dominant note being played is their own personal activity. As well as attachments to their own ways of seeing and doing, the egoistic habit of insisting upon their own interests and points of view! Have they never pondered — so as to act on it — the sublime "impersonality" of the sacred "Hosst"?

August 29, 1940

To imitate and touch the Mercy of your heavenly Father and by it to draw Mercy down upon the poor world, be merciful like your heavenly Father, and do not grow weary gazing at the Heart of Mary, the most accessible model I have given.

Mistress as well as Mother of Mercy. Learn from Her to be like Her, each of you, to be merciful mother to souls. Go to her school: She will teach you the great secret of maternal mercy.

See most particularly the child in every soul, a potential Jesus, a Jesus to be realized, a Christ to be engendered so that the circle of the Father's great family may be widened. Work of love that inspires pity and compassion because this potential Jesus in every soul in some way is a Jesus in peril, a Jesus exposed to contradiction, attacked, oppressed by thousands of enemies stirred up by my great enemy, Satan.

A Jesus awaiting deliverance, therefore well-deserving of attracting a mother's compassion, who thus sees in each soul a Jesus to be saved, a Jesus to be freed from the foe's captivity, a Jesus to make flourish in some way, a Jesus to be raised up, as this word so profoundly puts it, an ascension of life rising from the depths of a life created in the divine image. And finally, a Jesus to be offered to the Father.

The art and the secret of the maternal apostolate of Mary is to bring forth souls to the Father by bringing forth Jesus in souls. All the love that She has for her Infant-God She bears to all the children of God, brothers of her Jesus, and especially to consecrated souls, they who are privileged among the privileged.

Aides of her maternal love, meditate and meditate again on the sweet gentleness of charity, goodness, and condescension that you must have for souls that I have given you to defend, souls in which my Life is ever more in peril in this hour of such infernal, satanic contradiction!

THE HEART OF THE HOLY VIRGIN

Feast of the Immaculate Conception, 1936

The Heart of my Mother is at one and the same time:

A "sanctuary" and a "Fount."

Immaculate sanctuary: Cradle of my incarnate, loving tenderness.

Contemplate it that you may admire it, that you may praise Me for it.

Contemplate it that you may enter in and remain there: the drawing-near movement of the *venio!*[36]

Contemplate it that you may imitate it, that each of you may make of your heart a sanctuary: the appealing movement of the *veni!*[37]

Let us be sanctuaries for each other, as my Mother and I were together.

Sanctuary: a sacred place, holy, sanctified, whose center is the altar, whose life is the Host. A place exclusively reserved of the great Eucharistic Mystery: oblation, consecration, communion, consummation, to the glory of the Father and the Redemptive Host.

---

[36] *I come.*

[37] *I came.*

That is what the Heart of Mary was for Me — the first altar of the Incarnate Word, immaculate sanctuary of the Immaculate Host!

I offered myself in Her and She offered herself to Me in perfect oneness of spirit and heart! For that too was what my Heart was for Mary: Immaculate Sanctuary of an immaculate Host!

Infinite Holiness and Purity offering to the infinitely Holy God the Father a completely pure creature in union with the Host. This is the sublime Life that my Heart asks you to strive for, always remembering that in order to become a sanctuary for Me, in order to enter and take up residence in the Sanctuary of my Heart, you have to become a host as I myself was, and as my Mother was also. You, little hosts, impure in and of yourselves, that is true, but being purified by the fire of loving sacrifice.

If her Heart is a sanctuary conducting you to my Sanctuary, it is also a fount. "Immaculate Fount" feeding into the supreme Ocean of Charity that is my Heart, from which waves of divine life gush forth in torrents so that it may become yours!

December 8, 1937

In oneness of heart, let us make a feast to honor our Immaculate Mother!

Masterpiece of my tenderness, Purity most resplendent, radiant in guilelessness, crystal of fire, azure of crimson.

She is all that and more, inexpressibly more, this nameless beauty, heaven's ravishment.

Take my Heart to praise Her!

Take her Heart to praise Me!

Love Us, give to Us, sing to Us, One in the Other, so intimately fused are our two Hearts!

Enter into this double, unique Sanctuary, this incandescent Brazier of love. The more one enters here, the more one discovers precincts that are unifying and irresistibly appealing.

Draw from this unique, double Fount, this overflowing Fountain ablaze with Purity. The more one draws from It, the more one finds in It; the more one imbibes of It, the more one is changed by It, becoming a flame that blazes up to sing love's praises.

Draw from It all the intentions of my Immaculate Mother, intentions that are also Mine.

Honor the Heart of my Mother as immaculate fount, not only to draw from it but to imitate it as well, just as already I have asked you to imitate this immaculate sanctuary. Without this there is no true devotion.

Sanctuary: life of "communion." Fount: life of "diffusion."

The fount-channel has nothing of its own, nothing for itself; its entire function is to empty itself, to pour out waves of living water in the measures that have been opened up for it, water that the fount itself has drawn from the depths of the bottomless Ocean and that must flow back to it.

You will recognize here the completely impersonal, supernatural mission of this apostle of souls, my "fellow Co-Redemptrix": little fount so closely united with the Supreme Fount, so very pure, so very disinterested in order that everything, absolutely everything should rise up again in loving praise to this Fount alone.

My love now wishes to tell you: Let us be founts for each other.

Me for you: Fount inexhaustible, Fount of all graces.

You for Me: little founts faithfully bubbling up where I can come to draw, quench Myself with a little joy and consolation. I am so flooded with outrages and egoistic indelicacies. *Sitio! Sitio!*[38]

You recognize thirst's burning clamor in my "appeal."

---

[38] *Jn 19:28 — I thirst! I thirst!*

THE SECRET OF MARY'S INTERIOR LIFE

October 20, 1940

The secret of Mary's prayerful bearing needs to be written for the benefit of all consecrated souls.

What did Mary do, given her apparent inactivity and exterior lack of mobility?

Hear her reply to you, to make you understand her word of life:

"I listen in my heart where the Heart of my God lives.

"I obey my heart which only wishes to please my God. That is my great and intimate secret, the secret of intimacy, the entire life of my soul.

"I listen to my love: secret of intimate prayer.

"I obey my love: secret of intimate conformity."

Do you listen as She does, consecrated souls, in courageous silence amidst all the voices of egoism? Do you obey Him promptly with this generous gift of your whole being?

Shouldn't you be able to say at any moment, as Mary did, "I listen in my heart to the Heart of my God, of my Father, of my Savior, of my Spouse. Listening only to Him, I hear Him alone, and I hear Him at every moment. And at every moment He tells me the same thing: 'I love you, love Me.'

"Also my one, constant reply is to obey Him, believing in his Love however veiled it may be, proving my love through a ceaseless *Fiat*.

"And in thus obeying the Heart of my God, I am obeying my own true heart, my heart of a child, of a spouse, aspiring only that my heart have its identify in *Cor unum*."[39]

---

[39] *Acts 4:32*

Oh, understand and live, live and revere this secret of Mary's life of love, this secret of your Mother!

THE 1ST SECRET OF INTIMACY: PRAYER

Learn from Mary that prayer — the soul of this renewed fervor that I ask of you — is to be defined thus: a mutual, perpetual pleading and relieving.

Pleading for love and relieving by love, one and the same movement of the heart.

Pleading: movement of an indigent heart, needy but confident, that begs, calls, implores and attracts.

Relieving: movement of a liberal heart, generous and merciful, that lavishes, leaps forward, gives out, that gives itself.

The plea of your hearts calling for the relief of my Heart.

The plea of my Heart calling for the relief of your hearts. For I, the All-Powerful, in my infinite condescension of love, want so ardently to turn to you and find relief in you for the continuation, the accomplishment of my work of Redemption.

Understand this marvel: you can, you must bring relief to Christ, bring relief to God, by the offering of your co-redemptive collaboration; bring perpetual relief to Him by the ceaseless offering of all your heartbeats; serve Him thus as his post-holder, possessing the true co-redemptive spirit that my "appeal" calls for, which is but an appeal for relief.

But, poor indigent hearts that you are, you must turn to my Heart to be able to tender this relief. You must look here, in this infinite source of all Goodness, to find and draw out the relief that my perpetual plea asks of you.

Pleading in order to bring relief.

Plead of Me in order to bring Me relief!

As I Myself plead with you in order to bring you relief; for I only ask in order to give.

Understand and reflect on this well: "To those of whom I ask I give an infinite treasure of love, and I give it to those who ask of Me."

Respond to this liberality of my Heart and let its supplicating, anguished, urgent calls resonate in the depth of yours:

"Bring relief! with the relief of love"

for the triumph of my redemptive work so furiously attacked by Satan. Do not forget that this relief of love is the host's relief. Only the host can save the Host.

THE 2ND SECRET OF INTIMACY: CONFORMITY

Which of your hearts, in imitation of Mary's, will be more intimate if not the one that is most conformed to Mine in all its affections, feelings and inclinations?

This unifying conformity is the second great secret your Mother wishes to confide to you.

Listen and blend your voice in a love duet with my Heart, duet in unison:

"In Cor unum cantemus.[40]

You Yourself pray in me, Jesus, your prayer of love.

Pray together: *Oremus.*[41]

You Yourself perform in me, Jesus, your work of love.

Let us work together: *Collaboremus.*[42]

You Yourself love in me, Jesus, in accord with your divine love.

---

[40] *Let our hearts sing as one.*
[41] *Let us pray.*
[42] *Let us work together.*

Let us love together: *Amemus.* "[43]

Listen again to this from Mary:

"The beloved exists to help her Spouse."

That is her entire function, her only reason for being, her concern, her joy, her sweetness and her glory. In a word, her life.

To help her divine Spouse in what? To fulfill his office of Christ.

To help Jesus in his two-fold service:

> service to the Father: to render thanks for his Glory.

> service to his brothers: to implore grace for their salvation.

To help Jesus by sharing in everything, taking part in all that is His, associating with everything, identified with everything.

Ask Mary Co-Redemptrix for the secret of this.

---

[43] *Let us love.*

CHAPTER THREE

CO-REDEMPTIVE SOULS

Infinite Love which is at the heart of their vocation
demands on their part a response of total love.

THE SOVEREIGNTY OF LOVE

1939

In essence Love is a Sovereignty.

It can only be where It reigns as Master.

It only reigns as Master where It possesses all.

It only possesses all where the heart freely surrenders all to It!

For, marvel of divine delicacy, It does not take by force, even though It wants everything; its infinite gentleness gently solicits; its power to conquer resides in its Goodness.

Sovereignty in liberality no less than in demands.

"I want to have all only because I want to be all."

"I only ask for everything so that I may give everything."

The trial that is afflicting the world at this moment stems from ignorance of this unique, two-fold Sovereignty — and has as its end that all souls in the world, beginning with my consecrated ones, come to a practical understanding of this Sovereignty.

For if consecrated souls do not hasten to respond to this sovereignty of Mine with all their love, the world will keep on its ruinous course. Oh, if they would only take this to heart!

The biggest portion, no matter how big, can never satisfy the Sovereign Love of my Heart! It wants all. Ponder deeply this *all* that my Love so desires.

"Love's *all* has loved men so much that it has spared Itself nothing, pining away to the point of exhaustion."[44] It tells you that Love is all offering, all Sacrificial Victim (*Hostie*), total effusion of mercy!

O, consecrated souls, this *all* that It wants, is it not written on the first page of your duties and obligations, *In capite libri!*[45]

"I want all of your heart."

"I want all your hearts."

"I want you all Mine, all of you."

And that, in light of this two-fold *all*, you reconsider your attitude about love, for I tell you this again:

"If all of you had truly been all Mine, if all my spouses had truly and fully been spouses, the world would not be where it is." So if the world is where it is, it's because it lacks something from this *all*, some reservation, some withholding on your part. Isn't there something still missing? Just one thing would be too much, spoiling the purity of this totality that alone can satisfy my Heart.

Ponder in deep meditation, all of you, this examination of love, and reform yourselves. The hour is so grave and so urgent!

Be each one of you "a fully consecrated host."

I, your Sovereign Master, want to employ you to extend my Sovereignty of love to the entire world.

If the Father in loving the Son has placed all things in his hands,[46] hasn't the Spouse in loving his beloved also given his spouse all things?

---

[44] *Our Lord to St. Margaret Mary.*
[45] *Ps 39:8 — At the beginning of the book!*
[46] *Jn 13:3*

"All things," which is nothing less than my Heart with its infinite treasures of Charity. Treasures with all its virtues, its graces, its loves, its desires, poured out in torrents upon souls who are open, and who come to draw from these Treasures with the two-fold *Fiat* of receiving and appealing.

And by that same token, if the Son in loving the Father has restored all things in his hands, including Himself: *Father, I place my life in your hands,*[47] should not also the beloved who truly loves her Spouse place all things in his hands, giving her soul over to Him totally in this spirit of co-redemptive sacrifice (*holocauste*) that my "appeal" is begging for?

Receiving everything from my hands, placing everything back into my hands, this is the undivided agenda of sovereign love.

In order to realize both of these in your acts, do not forget that you must open your hands and open them wide both to receive and surrender. Such is the gesture of a truly loving heart, a heart that gives "unceasingly, without reservation." The two-sided demand of divine Sovereignty! Yes, any let-up is a limitation, any slackening a pulling back of the gift of self, the gift that is the life of love.

The love that relaxes is but a faint-hearted love! The love that keeps growing alone is true, alone is pure and strong. To give all, one must keep giving more. Meditate on this necessary union between the all and the more.

If growth is the law of all life, how can it not but be so of the life *par excellence*, the life of love? Read what is written in the Book of Life, the Gospel:

"I keep working."[48] *"Jesus grew. . . ."*[49]

In this light you will understand that the infallible route to love's unending growth is simply that of doing always the Will of my Father. For however modest it may seem, each of his divine wishes is an appeal for *more* because it is an appeal for something *better*.

---

[47] *Lk 23:46*
[48] *Jn 5:17*
[49] *Lk 1:80*

More and better in the *Ecce's* boundless offering.

More and better in the *Fiat's* loving fealty.

More and better in the *Magnificat's* hymn of praise.

But there are privileged times when the calls for "more' by the Father's Will are requests for an "all" that is particularly costly, resembling more what had been asked of Me as Redeemer of the world.

The expansion of love in my terrestrial life had as its end the redemptive Cross and its accomplishment.

The hour has come for you, these most precious hours of redemptive collaboration. How are you to live them? Learn to see in the trials that afflict the world one of these calls for "more," one of those *ascensions*[50] arranged by my Heart for your hearts . . . a precious stimulant for you to give Me more love, to give Me a love that is more loving, more pure, more adoring, more zealous, more humble, more trusting, and which turns you more into a host (*hostie*), all in accord with the wish of my "appeal," an appeal for more, so tender and so urgent.

To respond to the Sovereignty of my Love, you must know that "the all, the always, the always more" are inseparable. There is no all without constancy, no constancy without growth. Never again forget that my Heart's All entails such a superabundance of love that its effusions are an Always, always overflowing more and more. And It multiplies its appeals for more only so as to be able to pour out its grace the more.

Yes, my Heart is entirely at the disposal of those who place themselves entirely at my disposal! Serve Me by being served by Me!

Serve the cause of my Glory by being served by the treasures of my grace, for all my appeals for more are at the same time:

Appeals to give more,

Appeals to take more!

Appeals by the merciful Sovereignty of my Love, so urgent, so actual.

---

[50] *Ps 83:6*

HAVE FAITH IN THE WORK OF LOVE

O, my consecrated ones, have faith in the work of Love that cannot help but be interested in you at every moment! Work that is mercifully care-giving in everything, that wants to keep each and every one of you at the breast!

If too many souls do not move forward, do not ascend, or at least do so too slowly, it's because they are focused on themselves and lack lively faith in this tireless, transforming action of Mine in them!

For my Love always works in you to find a place, an ever larger place to the point of absolute sovereignty, whether by dilating your heart through consolations of merciful sweetness, or by hollowing you out through the merciful rigors of suffering!

If souls only knew, only comprehended the grace, the signal favor that I do for them when I work in them through suffering, whatever form it takes, when I burrow in and purify them! For my Love only digs out that It may fill in, that It may pour Itself headlong into the deep hole It has made so as to be able to splash back up higher, to the heights of the Father's house, in waves of praise and most pure, loving gratitude.

"The more I dig out, the more I fill in."

Meditate on this well, my consecrated ones, you about whom I dream so tenderly of filling with Myself.

To let yourself be hollowed out is to let yourself be filled in, by a Love that is as deep as the dug-out hole is deep; the deep attracting the deep.

I choose my mode of action for each soul, burrowing into it as I have just been telling you, or by dilating it so that here too I can fill it with Myself. And if it pleases Me I vary the mode! But whether the phase is more austere or more gentle, on my part it is always a phase of infinite tenderness, for divine Wisdom knows infallibly the best path for each, the best treatment.

Therefore I insist once again:

"Believe in the incessant work of Love": and also, "Believe in the best path that Love has chosen" for each one in accord with its special plan. And to this I add: "Cooperate with the work of Love," for It can only fully act if you allow It to have absolute latitude in all that It wishes.

How is this done? By a spirit of unbroken oblation, of disregard for yourself to the point where you are no longer able to disregard Me! Do they not go together? Can my Love disregard any one of you?

Not being able to get along without each other is the essence of intimacy, of the Spouse's true love for his beloved; this profound love that I beg of you from the depths of my Heart that wants you so much!

For what would my Love be doing if not to make true co-redemptive souls such as my "appeal" so earnestly asks for. And my work of choice, what can it be if not to fashion for Myself souls that are hosts?

Oh, that each consecrated soul would believe and understand this, saying to itself in each little difficulty and most especially in each trial: This is love, the mercifully jealous love of my Savior Who is working on me to make me more His, and thus peacefully, courageously, the soul allows this work in the suppleness and gentleness of a profound attachment of love.

Oh, if only everyone would believe in this incessant work, in all that takes place, in all the things I make happen, if only everyone would surrender to it fully, what dreamed of masterwork would not be accomplished for the glory of my Father?

And those among you who by your apostolate have the most sublime mission of all (do all of you really think about this sublimity?) to be mother of souls, getting souls to know and understand this work of my Love in them, helping them by your counsel to correspond to that work and thus be my faithful and ardent collaborators, for all of this I entreat you.

Would you like to know still more in what my work of redemptive Charity consists?

"Love is an untiring, insatiable quest for reconciliation, contact, union."

O my consecrated ones, when then will you take your duties seriously, your great life of consecration?

The only true way to pursue Love and therefore to attain It is the way of Calvary, and its supreme end is the embrace of the Cross.

Isn't this the place to which love of the Father and love of souls drives and impels Me?

That is why, among my consecrated, souls that are particularly espoused to Me, those of Mine who have been touched by love are closer and are held in crucifying embrace.

Apart from that there is nothing but illusion:

"Crucified spouse, I espouse by crucifying."

Believe in my work of love in you! And believe also in the work of love that I wish to accomplish with you and through you. *Collaboremus!*[51]

ASK OF ME WHAT I ASK OF YOU

1936

The more I beg of you, the more I want you to beg of Me.

To say to you, "Give Me," is also to say, "Ask Me first."

For who knows your poverty better than I, and who wishes to provide for you more when implored? If you cannot give Me what I ask of you, you can always ask Me to give it to you Myself.

Ask Me, then, for all that I ask of you, both personally and apostolically.

This is the first response you are to make to my "appeal" of love.

If you want irresistibly to touch my Heart, address to Me this "appeal" that I address to you, by availing yourself of my own words turned into prayer, thus:

---

[51] *Let us work together!*

69

"Most loving and beloved Spouse, in accordance with your desires, make me, make us true co-redemptive spouses. Make me, make us fully consecrated hosts."

This, in the form of tireless, trusting and adoring supplications passing through the maternal and virginal Heart of the Co-Redemptive Virgin.

Know that love always entails giving and asking. For isn't asking for something really saying: "Give me the means, with your gifts, that in turn will let me give You more."

Thus every petition for love is a gift of love.

The most demanding petitions therefore are the most precious of my gifts as Savior and Spouse. My love would not keep making these petitions if it were not so affectionate and giving.

Would that you would give Me, in the same way, as your first gift, this spirit of humble, trusting petition, filled with humble and confident dependence.

Thus, gift for gift, petition for petition, an exchange of love making our contact ever stronger.

Taking all from my Heart in order to bring all back to It. Yes, taking is the great act of prayer and petition: taking at the source of infinite Charity. And taking from my Heart is not a particularly specific function to the consecrated, e.g., one of their choice offices, not even of the hour of prayer, but a function of every hour.

Besides, for my consecrated ones every hour should be prayer; prayer prayed or prayer lived.

What can gush forth from this spring/furnace that is my Heart if not a shower of fiery sparks? But in order to draw from it, you must first be thirsty, a burning thirst to quench my own thirst for love, and thus to respond to all my wishes, to all my merciful wants.

To be able to draw, able to quench one's thirst, you need to be free and broadly fit. And for that it is absolutely necessary to pour oneself out in total offering, an offering that pours out everything, in full and in detail, to the bottom, to the brim, to the last drop.

Pour out handfuls so as to draw in handfuls. Draw in handfuls using two hands, seeking, taking nothing from the creature, not so much as a taste of anything created.

Draw handfuls by detaching from anything created, and by unshakeable trust. Draw continually from each other's heart the life of mutual love, the admirable exchange of intimacy. *O admirabile commercium!*[52]

And to draw with ever broader hands, implore the intercession of Mary's maternal hands. And then above all, with ardent apostolic charity, don't forget to do the same for all souls. Draw so as to make all things redound to the Glory of my Father.

"Which among you who has a friend and will go to him in the middle of the night and say to him, 'Friend, lend me three loaves. . . .' I say the same to you: Ask and you shall receive."[53]

Do you not hear this word of my Evangelist resonate in the very depths of your hearts, words that I would have souls hear at this moment most particularly?

Am I not the Friend *par excellence*? Who desires, Who waits for you to come and find Him. . . . Doesn't my Heart always heed all cries for help from those who are Mine?

The help is in proportion to the appeal. Help all the more responsive and generous as the appeal is confident, humble and persevering.

1939

Keep in mind the merciful teaching that my Heart loves repeating to you:

The first response you are to make to all my appeals: The "be Me" of infinite Goodness, is a "make me."

"Make me, You Yourself, Jesus, all that You want me to be."

This humble, confident, supplicating, persistent prayer is to Me a

---

[52] *O wondrous exchange!*
[53] *Lk 11:5, 9*

very sweet little "co-redemptive assist" which is all that is possible for you, poor miserable little nothings that you are!

The *Fiat* in the act of appealing is no less dear and agreeable to my Heart than the *Fiat* in the act of receiving: the two actions of love and union.

How I love the little prayer appealing for help that I Myself have inspired in you. Address it to my Heart as often as possible, never forgetting that my Heart is as inexhaustible as it is insatiable.

I am the great Beggar for love!

Learn to recognize in everything that my Will asks an appeal for help from my Heart to your poor little hearts. Mutual appeals for help therefore!

GOD'S WILL

1936

I look for souls bowed down, souls whose will is so identified with my Will that they no longer can do anything but cling to It, submit to It, bowing until they merge and disappear in It. And doing that before the least indication, before any manifestation of my good pleasure, of my divine preference.

If you want to unite yourself intimately with my inmost Life, keep in mind that my Life of intimacy with my Father has always been one of perfect accord with his paternal Will. Will perfectly fulfilled and therefore fully glorified.

Meditate on this deeply so that you yourselves may become part of this in all its intimacy. Understand that "will perfectly fulfilled" means "food devoured and savored with the satisfying hunger and permeating flavor of love." Food devoured with this avidness that takes and consumes all, leaving absolutely nothing.

Food savored with this sweetness and fullness of assent, where the enamored heart entirely takes its stance and from where it draws all its activity. *Totaliter, Libenter, Suaviter.* Totally, Willingly, Sweetly.

Do all of you do this? Do you do it better and better each day?

Remember that the food of my Will becomes divinizing only on condition of being devoured and savored, and that in the very proportion you do this you advance with Me, by Me and in Me into the boundless, fathomless depths of divine intimacy.

These are the utterly crucifying paternal Wishes that my truly consecrated ones devour with utmost ardor, savor most sweetly, for they understand that it is just in the measure that they cause the human *me* to die that these Wishes become divinizing, satisfying, and therefore amiable, loving, utterly adorable.

Here is an effective way to examine how faithfully one adheres to what so pleases my Heart: Nothing more, nothing less, nothing other than what my love wants, desires, prefers:

"Nothing more," because the more is often pride;

"Nothing less," because the less is almost always cowardice;

"Nothing other," because this is always a turning away from mortification and an egoistic attachment to one's own views.

Rather: "All that I want:

nothing but what I want,

such as I desire and prefer it."

1938

The total acquiescence, total abandonment that my love asks consists at one and the same time both of total consenting and total contentment. Consenting of the *Fiat*. Contentment of the *Magnificat*.

The *yes* of consenting. The *thank you* of contentment.

It is impossible therefore for a soul that wants to console Me fully to pronounce its *Fiat* from the bottom of its heart without at the same time singing its *Magnificat*, in a harmonious duet with love.

Learn by contemplating my Mother this secret of the *Fiat* entirely filled with *Magnificat*.

A soul in whom resonates this *Fiat* filled with *Magnificat* is a soul completely in harmony with Mine, in continuous, instantaneous harmony of all its wishes with the least good pleasures, desires and preferences of my adorable Heart. Here is the heart-felt *Fiat* that my earlier commentaries on the "appeal" speak about.

And how could the love of my Heart not be in accord with one so fully in accord with it? How could it resist someone who does not resist it?

What ruins the world, what offends the divine Majesty and merits chastisement and demands reparation is unbridled rush to pleasure, egoistic, sensual, earthly, immediate pleasure. Deceitful pleasure, because in reality this rush to sensual enjoyment is flight from true happiness.

And with you, my consecrated ones, truthfully, is there no act of your life that is ruled by this mortal law of human pleasure?

Would you not want to make reparation both for those of you who are aware of this and for those who have no clue or have forgotten? And wouldn't the best reparation be to form a "bond with the divine Good Pleasure"? A bond intended to bring about the triumph of Love, to raise high its rampart of fire by diminishing egoism; for if the egoistic self above everything else is seeking its own enjoyment, the loving heart is generous and seeks without self-interest to enjoy Me, all of which means to please Me, to give Me pleasure in everything. Its sole refrain is:

"For such is the Good Pleasure of my Father."

And for that, the loving heart knows first of all to accept with joy and full heart all the little personal annoyances that life in the world is littered with in so many different ways and that at present adorn the obligations of one's state, itself an expression of my Good Pleasure. Yes, Pleasure of Infinite Goodness, despite aspects that are frequently hard and crucifying.

In the second place, and this is more and better, the loving heart learns on its own how to roll with little personal annoyances by courageous renunciation, in line with obedience, of the arrogant, sensual egoism of human satisfaction.

In the third place, the loving heart knows full well that living under the sole law of divine Good Pleasure means also to seek my pleasure by giving pleasure to all the Father's children, by the exercise of a cordial, liberally bestowed charity, by multiplying little acts of thoughtfulness, fidelity, and generosity to Me.

"If you want to delight my Heart,

delight your own in my Will!"

"BECAUSE I LOVE . . . I DO."

Christmas, 1936

It is because I love my Father, because I love mankind, my brothers, that I act as I do, that I come as Savior. It is because I love you, my consecrated ones, that I come to claim you as co-redeemers. And isn't it because you love Me that you have given yourself over to Me?

My urgent desire is that the *Quia diligo . . . sic facio*[54] be constantly echoed in religious families, places so beloved of my Heart. Would that each soul might comprehend its true meaning:

The *Quia diligo* is the only truly worthy reason for each movement, for each heartbeat of hearts that are genuine hearts.

My love is the divine reason for all that I am, for all that I do: the reason for my redemptive Cross.

Wasn't it as I left for Gethsemane that I pronounced this word with eternal repercussions?

My love is the reason for my Eucharist, masterwork of my affection, the reason for all my views and ways with each one of you, the reason for my appeals and for my gifts in both the present moment and forever.

---

[54] *Jn 14:31 — But that the world may know that I love (diligo) the Father: and as the Father hath given me commandment, so do (facio) I (Douay Rheims).*

Believe it, recognize it through all the veils with their many shades that surround your life from dawn to dusk, and be clear-sighted, trusting, adoring, fully cognizant of Love!

If the "why" of all that I did (or was allowed, permitted to do), am doing, or will do can only be the *Quia diligo (because I love)*, should not the "why" of all that you are doing or will do also be a fervent *diligo*? Should not all this also be evidence of love on your part, offering of love in other words, or at least love given back?

How my Heart yearns that this "because I love" be the sole response your heart could give Me, if I were to ask you, "Why are you doing this? saying that? thinking this? wanting that, desiring this?"

What marvelous accord, what delightful harmony there would be between your hearts and Mine! What a symphony of love to the glory of my Father! What compensation, what consolation for offended Love! What powerful intercession for the entire world of souls!

This is to be your response to my great Thirst for love's intimacy, to *Manete in delectione me*[55] which follows the *Venite*,[56] and that is always accompanied by the *Ambulate in delectione mea*[57] of the *Crescite in delectione.*[58]

O my consecrated ones, be among the confident, among those who believe in this predilection of love of my Heart, and to that end be courageous, generous in accepting it, in loving it, preferring all its mysteries and rigorous consequences, its often crucifying favors.

Would ordinary, vulgar, second-rate love suffice your heart? And could it suffice Mine at this time most especially? Choice love alone can respond to a choice love like Mine. Crucified love to crucified love.

---

[55] *Jn 15:9 — Abide in my love.*
[56] *O come.*
[57] *Eph 5:2 — Walk in my love.*
[58] *Be fruitful in love.*

1939

Be "specialists in love."

That is what my infinite tenderness invites you to be, wanting each of you to be fully consecrated hosts, just as my "appeal" has said.

"My specialty is love."

Love seeking love, love breathing love. Ought not the hearts of my consecrated ones be able to say the same, by the gift of each heart-beat, without reservation, each engraved more deeply with the divine mark which is the loving gift of self?

By this sign alone will my Father recognize Me in you and have mercy on the world.

Help Me in this saving work by being specialists in love. . . .

Quia diligo . . . Sic facio. . . .

GOODNESS AND PROVIDENCE

1938

"I am the Holy One surpassing in love."

When hatred is redoubled as at present, my Heart increases a hundred-fold with goodness, urgent desires, outpourings, with redemptive outbursts for the re-conquest of souls, to the glory of the Father's Goodness.

My consecrated ones, would that the entire world might know this, above all else:

My Charity burns to overflow into hearts, to conquer with mercy the egoism whether cowardly or malevolent that reigns there so unfortunately. But I have to be allowed to enter, not forgetting that goodness is the key that opens the widest ports for the outpouring of infinite Goodness. For the proper gift of goodness is to open, to open one's own heart and to open the hearts of others, whereas egoism's way is to close.

Goodness is nothing other than the overflowing of love; you will give Me back the goodness that I await from you by putting *Fiat* filled with *Magnificat* into true, life-lived practice.

Would that your lives, like Mine, were all consecrated to the Goodness of the Father in living this program: "Bless this Goodness, appeal to this Goodness, imitate this Goodness."

"Bless this Goodness,"

everywhere and always, in the name of all who are finding It in all things, adoring It, celebrating It.

Fiat to your Goodness! *Magnificat* to your Goodness!

If only you would know how sweet this is to Me, how it touches my Heart! My Heart as Spouse as well as my Heart as Son, that sees in this the most pure praise addressed to the Heart of my Father for whom my Heart beats.

All *Fiat* to his Will can only be plenary and truly transforming to the extent that it is spontaneously followed by the *Magnificat*, by this *Magnificat* which is itself goodness, for all of love's overflowing, love's exalting, is no longer able to hold itself in, and thus exalts infinite Love.

How souls of good will would advance with swifter, lighter strides taking them further along perfection's path if they could always recognize, in the way of my Wishes, the ways of my Goodness.

Being in my Goodness a total effusion of love, I crave to sweep into hearts. I am love's great invader in pursuit of hearts to invade, so that everything there may be for the glory of the Father's Goodness.

O my consecrated ones, give Me the key to your hearts. Give Me the key with the marvelous ability to get everything functioning, the gold key of the "welcoming *yes*," wholly cordial at every moment to all my slightest preferences, my Wishes for love, my Wishes for goodness.

"Welcoming *yes*" that opens an always wider access to my invading love. Invasions that are divinely fulfilling in the measure they are taken in.

"Turn to this paternal Goodness,"

at every moment, for everything and for everyone, in humble and most ardent, trusting supplication.

Draw my redemptive grace from the infinite treasure of my redemptive Goodness, so immeasurably eager to pour itself out, *copiosa apud Deum redemption.*[59] Grace of response to the grace of appealing. My appeal for this redemptive partnership is a mercifully prevenient grace, a grace-help absolutely needed in order to respond to it. Grace which, in the divine plan, in large part is the response to the appeal of supplicating, persistent prayer.

"Imitate this paternal Goodness,"

by contemplating its incarnated reflection in my life as Savior, by conforming yourself without reservation to its gift, to its continual outpouring upon the souls of my brothers, by the exercise of Charity most generous, by the most loving filial Piety in the Bosom of my Father:

I am the Good Shepherd. . . . I give my Life.[60]

I do always that which is pleasing to my Father.[61]

Do likewise. Do this and you will live and you will give your life to Love. Do not be satisfied with daydreaming about your love. Actually do it!

Goodness is love lived out in acts, thus presenting with each heartbeat a freshly offered token, by a diffusion of self that allows ever deeper entry into the dwelling places of my Father's House, for the glorification of his infinite Goodness, by the recovery of souls in accord with the grand desire of my loving "appeal."

"Make amends for the outrages done to the Father's Goodness," . . . for the blasphemies against Providence which, alas, all too often block my Mercy in its immense desire to save the world.

Right there is a proper mission for consecrated souls.

---

[59] Ps 129:7 — *With God there is plentiful redemption (Douay-Rheims).*
[60] Jn 10:11,15
[61] Jn 8:29

Would that they understood and admired the marvelous "clarity/obscurity" of my Providence.

Would that they recognized and blessed the luminous clarity of love's principle, and the loving purposes of a God of Charity's paternal Providence.

That they revered and adored the mysterious obscurity of his divine means, of his diverse ways!

Yes, at this moment from all corners, ardent and confident supplications are mounting to my Heart to touch It and console It, but I would love to see and hear in them another still more adoring note!

That the *Adoro Te* would spring forth from your lips and from your hearts, before all manifestations of my Providence, in this spirit of loving and generous co-redemptive compensation.

"Everything in me adores and blesses You, O Goodness of the Father. Thank You for everything!

"Everything in me implores You, trusts in You, divine Mercy."

The more you thank the paternal Providence from the bottom of your heart, on behalf of all hearts, through the Heart of Mary, the more this Providence of Goodness will bless you and fill you with its merciful benedictions and predilections!

FAITH AND CROSS
THE TWO TERRESTRIAL BEATITUDES OF LOVE

1936

"Believing" and "suffering" on earth are love's two beatitudes! They entail love's strongest trials, but for that very reason they are its strongest tokens.

Open my Gospel:

Blessed are those who have not seen and yet believe.[62]

---

[62] *Jn 20:29*

Blessed are those who are persecuted. . . .[63]

Rejoice therefore over these occasions that keep multiplying, reminding you that

"Faith and sacrifice" are always properly partnered with Love.

— Faith, as trusting as it is adoring;

— Sacrifice, as generous as it is detached;

— Joy, as deep as it is radiant.

June 21, 1940

My consecrated ones, there is no better time than now to remind you that:

"Faith and the Cross are the two terrestrial beatitudes of love."

The time has come through them to increase and intensify actions so that the flame of your hearts may be fed and stirred up.

So that you may be aroused by them, listen to Me as I tell you with my customary tenderness: "My Heart now more than ever wants your security and well-being."

Yes, I am your security, your sole but nevertheless absolute security! in the heartfelt absence of any poor little human security amidst all the insecurities of the earth.

It is as Father, as Spouse, as Savior that I take care of you, of yours, of all those who are Mine.

It is the loving Goodness of my Providence that arranges everything for the greater good of each soul.

Believe this with a grateful, adoring faith, all the more adoring as my ways are more mysterious.

With a faith that is humble yet invincibly trustful and secure. *Nolite timere quia Ego sum vobis.*[64]

---

[63] *Mt 5:10*

[64] *Lk 24:36 — Do not be afraid for I am with you.*

With a faith opening itself to an abandonment that surrenders everything, with a trust that expects everything.

Make your own the sentiments that animated my Heart when, during my mortal Life as Savior, I prayed the Psalm *Dominus regit me*[65] for which the *Ego sum pastor bonus*[66] is but the counterpoint.

And do the same for my France, my poor, dear France, poor lost sheep that I so mercifully run in search of with my rod and crook, that I might place her on my shoulders and rejoice in her penitence.

And may these sentiments fill you with peace and complete security. *I have told you these things that you may have peace in Me.*[67]

"I am your abundance," abundant good that wishes not only to be your storehouse in the midst of all your shortcomings, but also and above all to be your superabundance in the soul's true life of charity, all in the measure of your faith.

Now, for faith to be alive, sincere, beatifying, it must ceaselessly ask for, beseech for nothing less than the gift of confident abandonment.

In the *Adoro Te* you will find expression for all the acts and feelings that make up the beatitude of faith, founded as it is on sacrifice, on renunciation of all human perspectives, on flourishing in hope and charity, the real sources of happiness.

Receive with joy therefore the occasions I am giving you at this moment for multiplying these acts, reminding you that it is only in the measure that faith is put to the test that it can give full testimony of its love to Love.

June 28, 1940

If the heart's beatitude is but the appeasement of its desires in all their force and power, no different than the appeasement of its burning thirst for love, what can the beatitude of My Savior's Heart be if not to pardon and to bestow, to be as I have been saying the security and

---

[65] *Ps 22 — The Lord ruleth me.*
[66] *Jn 10:11— I am the good shepherd.*
[67] *Ibid 16:33*

abundance of the poverty-stricken hearts of my brothers and dearly loved children! This is my joy as Redeemer, for here is the mission conferred upon Me by my Father, to care for souls and fill them with good things.

These souls therefore are my beatitude in the measure that they allow themselves to be cared for by the divine Wisdom of my tenderness. Oh, believe with complete security in my Love's good care whose treatments, no matter how rigorous, have only merciful healing as their end.

Give yourself over with complete security to Love's good care, Love that only chastises in order to pardon, that only knocks down in order to elevate higher.

With complete security bless and invoke Love's good care, whose superabundant Charity is never exhausted and whose pleasure is its ability to fulfill you.

And know that in my Heart you will always be secure, finding there rest, contentment, relief, a bastion of love, a place of refuge against all those who persecute Me with their hatred, an idyllic place where all my pains are forgotten in proportion as you, by your exercise of living faith, find yourself secure in my Heart.

Is there any sweeter beatitude for a loving heart than to be, through its faith, the security of love for my Heart? By the same token, you will be abundance for my Heart in proportion as you find abundance in my Heart by your spirit of sacrifice. Oh, marvel of my merciful Will, together you can be for Me what I am for you,

"substitute" and **"superabundance."**

My substitute as my continuator — my little co-redemptive continuators — achieving what was lacking in my Passion.

My superabundance as instrument of my Kingdom's expansion, serving as outlets for the outpouring of my redemptive graces.

Is there any beatitude sweeter for the heart of a consecrated soul who truly loves than to be able, by its spirit of sacrifice, to be the abundance of love for my Heart? But understand well that the cross only

truly beatifies when it really crucifies, when the soul lets itself be crucified by it, by blessing it, by embracing it with a will filled with love,

O bona Crux![68]

For remember this well: acceptance and support are not enough —
in cases where the cross crushes and overwhelms but does not truly
crucify. For it to really crucify there has to be loving partnership, *Fiat*
with full heart, *Magnificat* full of love; there has to be the *Ecce* of a
heart that willingly, without hesitation, gives itself up to the nails that
must pierce it so that it may really be crucified and thereby unified
with my Heart.

This, because, in crucifying, the cross unites the one who is loving
to the One who is loved and beatifies that soul.

That is why, then, by your more generous cooperation with its action, suffering is crucifying for you and also thus more unifying and
therefore more beatifying as well.

Can there be any greater happiness for your hearts than to be intimately espoused by your crucified Savior, than to be so closely
associated with my redemptive work; than to supply in this way a little
assistance to the expansion of my Kingdom; and thus to be for Me
sweet consolation and genuine joy?

Yes, happiness beyond all happiness, for one who has faith! For
you it means that these two beatitudes are inseparable:

Faith can never be complete without the spirit of sacrifice.

Sacrifice can never be absolute without the spirit of faith.

Oh, from these two points of view, how precious and blessed are
the times we are living at present!

O bona Crux! Salva nos!

---

[68] *O precious Cross!*

CHAPTER FOUR

THE INTERIOR LIFE OF CO-REDEMPTIVE SOULS

*Before co-redemptive souls can be "continuators" and "replace-
ments" of Our Lord here below, they must be alter egos, perfect,
living images of Our Lord.*

*For this they need to conform to the point of identification with
Our Lord, a conformity they have to draw out of a deep interior
life, and this conformity in return will make them (a) hosts and
victims like Our Lord, and (b) apostles.*

SILENCE

December, 1936

Silence is a precursor. A precursor to the coming of my love.

Silence is preparation because it purifies and attracts; at the least,
deep authentic silence forgets the creature and invokes the divine.

Learn from Mary the secret of this attentiveness that draws you into contemplation, a life of prayer as eloquent as it is silent.

In this, be like Her, readily unmindful of the creature, impervious
to the human.

Saturday, June 28, 1937

Learn from Mary's profound Heart what this is: "The silence that calls forth the Word, that draws It into the soul, that makes It listen closely to the soul."

Yes, silence makes room for the word. — This intimate silence coming from the ardent longing of the heart in search of the divine.

Silence that thereby deepens the soul, by freeing it from all human congestion.

All of you, be these silent souls who alone can be deep souls and souls eloquent to my Heart.

Eloquent because silent. For I am the great Captivator of all being and of all life, the Occupant Who is there in the ordinariness of external occupations, the constant Absorbent of the heart.

Oh, how these silent souls console Me in this way, and help Me in my redemptive work.

If these silent souls alone are eloquent to my Heart, they alone also communicate Me to souls, being as they are but faithful resonances of my love as Word.

These true apostolic souls of my Heart, these pure impersonal resonances, yes, I am in them . . . (and they are my helpers and consolers!), but I still have too few of them to lift up and save the world.

It is true, many are good talkers and can even speak abundantly of Me, but for all that are they always eloquent? Do they truly communicate Me to souls?

Truly silent souls alone are able to stay in close communion with Me, and my apostolic diffusion is conditioned by and proportional to the perpetuity of this continuous communion of love.

That is why the most silent souls are at the same time those who best diffuse the profound love of my Heart.

If I come back to this so often, to these two words — "communion and diffusion"— it's because they form one of the principal themes of

86

Love by which I have conveyed to you your mission to be my faithful, little transmitting echo.

June 30, 1937

How is it that silent souls are so eloquent to Me, I would even say in my fondness, so appealing to my Heart?

You have guessed it. It's because they are humble, or bravely strive to be so.

Silence — the profound activity of a love that listens, the ardent longing of a heart smitten by God alone — is both a principle and a source of humility, abolishing words of excuse or vanity, stilling the inner buzzing of various conceits, resentments, of envy born of self-love.

To cultivate silence is to cultivate humility, this deep humility that makes room for Me to enter in, for all such deepness attracts my Heart.

1940

To be instruments of my Love for souls is nothing other than to be most pure resonances of Me, faithful transmitting echoes, free and living passageways of my Word of Life.

But in order to hand down and pass on, one has to receive.

In order to receive, one has to listen.

In order to listen, one has to be silent.

The true apostle is one who is able to make his own that word which I spoke to My Father: "I have given them all the words You have given Me,"[69] and who, for that reason, is always listening to Me, is always at my school. And silence is part of the discipline of love in this divine school.

If too few words truly speak to souls to give them life, it is because this discipline has broken down, because the words are no

---

[69] *Jn 17:8*

87

longer listened to in prayer, in prayer made fruitful by sacrifice. Sacrifice that requires recollection so that silence may be imposed on the dark, confused, unsettling rumblings of egoism, so that I may be heard, Me, the Word of Life, instead of listening to one's self.

LIFE IN SOCIETY WITH MY HEART

July, 1936

To live in society with my Heart is to ever remain and be ever more deeply lost in the ambiance of Love. And for that:

— to have no attraction but to my Heart.

— to be under no influence but that of my Heart.

— to aim only at complacency in my Heart.

"Nothing between us,[70] everything between us," that is the first rule of life in society.

Never anything between us so as never to lose contact. The delicate jealousy of the virgin's love.

Always everything between us so as to always strengthen contact. The avidity of the spouse's union of love.

The society of my Heart is more than simple company, more even than contact or adherence. It's an intimacy of association so strong, so deep and permanent that it becomes true compenetration. Compenetration that is transforming, defining, and rising to the point of consummation in union: the great dream of love.

And how is this ideal to be realized? By strict dependency on my grace which, through the frequency of our relations, leads to their constancy and growth.

One can no longer get by without the other. One gladly gets by without all the rest.

---

[70] *That is, no cloud, no divergence no matter how small, no strange affection slipping in between us.*

88

That is the secret, the ideal of this life in society.

I love you all to this point of tenderness and mercy that I can truly say I can't get along without you. See the Eucharist!

And you all, can you say the same, that you love Me to this point that you can't get along without Me? Yet this is true love:

To be indispensable to each other,

To be inseparable from each other.

My love was not able to get along without suffering — look at the Cross. This was for my Father, for my brothers. Can you get along without yours?

I love you too much, my consecrated ones, to be able to get by without your co-redemptive partnership. I want you all for Myself, no one but Me, in all places, at all times, and always more.

But ponder this well: To be truly all Mine is to be also all for others, to be neighbor to them, to all souls, for my "Me" as Savior contains all the "me's" of all my brothers who are to be saved.

All two, all One,

All for the Father, all for souls.

"Communion and Diffusion" therefore are the two-worded program of life in society with my Heart.

Communion ever more intimate to the point of closest fusion of thought, heart, and will.

Receive all of Me in Communion, and as regards your Crucifix, understand where this leads. To sacrifice, sacrifice to the point of holocaust.

Be like Me;

Totally in the possession of my heavenly Father: *Ecce!*

Totally in the service of his Good Pleasure: *Fiat!*

Totally solicitous for his Glorification: *Magnificat!*

We think in communion: We think together and in the same way.

We love in communion: We love together and in the same way.

We speak in communion: We speak together and in the same way.

We act in communion: We act together and in the same way.

Omnia in unum.[71]

Marvelous and merciful "we" of unity, of the two in one, of the "we" of love, where my "I" longs to expand itself in and through your poor human "I," freely lost in Me, as prey of its unifying flames, repeating to Me truthfully and without ceasing:

Non jam ego, sed Tu solus et amplius, in Te, per Te, ad Patrem.[72]

Diffusion ever wider of the Father's charity that sets my Heart ablaze.

Diffusion by the radiant transparency of my Spirit, of my Life.

Diffusion by the all-consuming agony of zealous souls, by the sacrifice of all their interests, their egos, in order to conquer them for the Father and to extend his Kingdom:

Adveniat![73]

Feast of the Sacred Heart, 1936

In order that you may grow in this life of society with Me, let Me tell you again what my Love is and what yours should be:

My Love is nothing but desire and action for union, and this by an unremitting effusion of prevenient graces, fruit of my redeeming Blood. And if I become so very much yours in this way, it is in order to make you so very much Mine, so that in some way you become another Me that I may offer to my Father in a holocaust of praise.

And your love, what should it be if not desire and action for union, by unremitting response to the constant advances of my Love, a Love which can only anticipate; a response which should be the fruit of sacrifice, the heart's blood shed drop by drop in that share of sacrifice asked of you by your present duties.

---

[71] *All in one.*

[72] *Now not I but Thou alone and more, in Thee, through Thee to the Father.*

[73] *May it come!*

For what does it really mean to love Me? Two things:

— to let yourself be loved by Me, which means to the full, divine extent that I wish, manifested by all the indications of my Will, the circumstances and events, the obediences, and for Me, for the unique pleasure of my Heart.

To lose yourself completely in Me, therefore, and thus allow Me to take you, consume you, crucify you, in order to change you into Me, your Spouse-Host.

Eucharistic life of virginal union.

— to love Me, which is also to get others to love Me, to spread, radiate, diffuse my Love, through your zeal for prayer, for devotion, for suffering.

Make Me loved. This means also to avenge, console my Love, so insulted and neglected, by a reparation that is truly co-redemptive, a reparation which not only compensates but outdoes what Love has lost.

Look upon my Heart and call to mind my "appeal."

PRAYER AND THE INTERIOR LIFE

1936

This is what prayer is:

Looking at each other in love, loving by surrendering oneself in unifying reciprocity.

Communion of glances that never tire of looking at each other.

Communion of hearts that are insatiably in love with each other.

Communion of wills that irresistibly melt into each other.

This is how the interior life of a truly espoused soul should be, through all its exterior occupations, a life that is but a continuation of offered prayer, never watered down or weakened, ever increased and intensified.

To never lose sight of Me is to take my divine perspective on all things, which as you know is the complacency and the glory of my Father.

That is the one and only true communion of glances that is always possible and that assumes and brings together communion of hearts and wills.

This means then that you are to be lost from view yourself, and how rare this is! Already too few of my spouses know how to lose themselves in contemplation of Me! While my eyes as Savior and Spouse never grow weary of fixing on them with such tenderness!

Oh, ask of the Immaculate Virgin that our glances meet each other and intertwine, mingle and intermingle in an ever more fixed and penetrating gaze so that nothing ever interposes itself between us.

Ask Her too to teach you to love Me as She does, with a heart lost in my Heart and completely enamored with It, and thus completely detached from itself and from every creature.

This is what communion of hearts is!

And in order that your glance also remain fixed and your heart be enamored of a communion that more and more adores the sublime greatness of my Father, don't forget that at every moment your will has to melt irresistibly into Mine, totally, merging in Me to the point where you disappear in a continuous act of the most sweet attachment of love. This is what the true life of prayer consists of.

Contemplation is the path to desire[74] just as desire is the path to possession.

No love is profound without profound glances upon the one who is loved.

No life is profoundly loving without profoundly contemplative prayer; and of this there is not enough. Why? Because too many glances are superficial and only lightly touch upon my Heart.

Glances too curious for the trifling curiosities of the earth to be able to fix themselves upon the great divine realities.

---

[74] *That is, in order to possess one must desire, one must contemplate; for one only desires what one knows, and one only knows God through deep contemplation.*

O my spouses, don't you want to compensate Me for love by offering this profound love that I am begging from you? Bring us back to life through the contemplative glance of your prayer.

True prayer is first of all:

A glance that profoundly contemplates my Heart, that penetrates It in order to conform to It and then get lost in It.

But bear in mind that, to do this, you must courageously turn away from all the rest, constantly mortifying all the little, human appeals of curiosity (glances whether exterior or interior) which arise in the course of your day.

Here then is the first step of the interior life, and yet it is one that few of my spouses have the courage to take in earnest, without stopping along the way!

1937

If, as my Precursor has said, *"The friend of the bridegroom . . . greatly rejoices at the bridegroom's voice,"*[75] how would it not be so for the beloved of the Spouse, if she knows how to hear and, in order to be able to hear, practices silence!

Oh, this silence of love for the sake of listening, how it ravishes my Heart and immediately makes resonate my words as Word. But, alas, how rare this is, even among my consecrated ones!

Silence that is the indispensable accompaniment of the contemplative glance and that itself is the essential condition of profound love.

Silence that is an indispensable collaboration therefore in the great transforming work of my Love in souls.

What else does it mean to pray?

It's to spend one's life by spending it in my Life!

Understand well the double meaning of this term:

---

[75] *Jn 3:29*

"To spend one's life," meaning the continuous movement of the unceasing, private activity of the soul, without a breath, a hint of interruption, without a single parenthesis of personal reservation.

"By spending it in my Life," meaning to give up one's own life, to lose it in order to be lost in Mine, in order to take Mine!

Continuous flight from yourself for the sake of an ever more profound immersion into the Ocean of Life, my Heart of fire!

Given over so that my ascendancy may grow!

Dead to everything at every moment to make room for the Life of my Life.

Yes, that's what good prayer is:

It's "to go into the hearts of each other."

To go from the depth of your heart to the depth of my Heart!

from intimacy to intimacy,

without ceasing and without reservation.

Learn the secret of this from the Virgin Mary!

Incomparable Master of prayer!

1937

The life of prayer, the interior life, is a mutual and perpetual outpouring of the soul.

Outpourings that the infinite tenderness of my Heart has merciful need of.

Outpourings that souls have need of, and most especially consecrated souls, the souls of religious.

But where and to whom do they pour themselves out? To what, in this need of the heart, are they chiefly oriented?

One can classify them into four chief categories, in accordance with the purity and fervor of their love.

There are those who are without radiance, who become their own confidants, interiorly soliloquizing all the activity of their egoistic *me*.

Even when they pray, it is to themselves that they speak of Me, rather than speaking to Me of Me. When then will they reorient their center; when will they let themselves be seized by the divine attraction of my Heart?

Others are inclined to pour themselves out into other creatures, to take them as confidants to find relief and sensible satisfaction there.

Superficial souls, turned to the outside, wasting silence in order to unburden themselves into other human hearts, souls that are inevitably more or less pitiful.

When then will they choose Me, choose my Heart as their divine confidant, an infinite reservoir of love that comprehends all?

Under such circumstances, it is with good reason that these souls will feel themselves misunderstood and will suffer because of it.

I am the great Confidant for my genuine spouses, hosts who are purified and who consecrate themselves unceasingly.

Willingly, often, they pour themselves into my Heart, and how willingly, in return, do I pour myself into their heart.

The comings and goings of love that itself has many degrees of life and fervor!

Nevertheless, there are still some fits and starts in their outpouring, in their confidence. Yes, I am the principal, the primary Confidant in their lives, but I am not entirely the Only One. The *me* or the creature still has place in their lives!

Finally, for some, spouses who are wholly spouses, wholly pure, wholly consecrated, radiant, wholly spouse hosts, I am truly their One and Only, perpetual Confidant, and with what joy for my Heart!

There is not a breath of their intimate life that does not rise up into my Heart, in It alone.

Thanks to their spirit of faith, when they pour themselves out to my representatives here below (superiors and confessors), which I Myself inspire them to do, they are pouring themselves out to Me, to Me alone.

Oh, if the preceding souls give Me satisfaction, how much more consoling, refreshing and glorifying are these to Me!

Nothing but Me counts for these souls.

As for the two earlier categories, you understand that they are painful to Me. They disappoint and make Me sad.

Oh, don't be like them!

They do not have genuine trust, which is the virtue *par excellence* of intimates, and thus of spouses.

They have not understood the real heart-to-heart nature of prayer, of the interior life.

And how could they be completely happy?

Prayer is a consuming, divinizing crucible where love works its marvels of union, on condition and in proportion to the soul's courage to plunge into it, to sink into it without reservation, to dwell there without in the least holding back, dressed and ready for all the annihilations that Love will ask of it.

But, alas, the souls are too few who love with enough courage to plunge themselves completely into this crucible of Love.

And yet these are the souls who alone can be totally "consumed" in order to be wholly "consecrated" in the way the "appeal" asks it of them.

Oh, do not forget this supplicating appeal of my Heart. May its present, ever-living memory stimulate your prayers, flashing back to you ever more charged with light and fervor in all of your prayers, to make of your lives lives that are truly "co-redemptive."

Love's plots are woven in the rich counsel of morning prayers and most particularly in the most intimate prayers of Holy Communion!

It is here that the revelations, the outpourings, the ever more intimate solicitations of my Heart render the heart of my spouses more and more resourceful, more ingenious, more delicately audacious and generous in proving its love.

Having no secrets from each other, it is here that we plot together so that the work of the Father may be fully accomplished in all the souls of the world.

These inventions of love, where will they come from if not from my spouses?

And from where will they be drawn, if not from my Heart?

Should It not be their single, constant source of inspiration? Have I not promised you that my Spirit of Love *would teach you all things*[76] if you loved and called upon It?

Right here is the secret of interior souls, of those whose exterior occupations are animated and made fruitful by a principle of divine love.

Quia diligo, sic facio.[77]

To pray is to take:

Not to take for yourself, for the petty benefit of personal enjoyments, but to bear in everything the poverty of souls and through an offering of disinterested love to bring them back to my Heart.

INSEPARABLE

1939

"Inseparable," that is love's word, love's irreducible need! The word that reveals the deepest wish of my Heart for each soul, and in particular for each of my spouses to whom I speak with such tenderness.

"Where I am is where I want you to be!" Echo of my Gospel prayer with which my Eucharistic prayer itself so perfectly resonates!

Being inseparable! Love's merciful ardor, itself inseparable from another need of the heart: "Being alike."

---

[76] *Jn 14:26*
[77] *Ibid 14:31 — I act for the sake of love.*

Because in order to dwell with increasing intimacy in my Heart, to be with Me and to be more and more in Me, isn't it necessary to be like Me?

To be where I am, isn't it necessary to go where I go, by the way that I go? To have the same destination, take the same route!

"Where I am," is the House of my Father, for the contemplation and glorification of his Glory!

"By the way that I go," is the crucifying road to the recovery of souls!

If everything is one between the Spouse and his beloved, isn't it necessary to do in common, feel in common?

The Mother of Sorrows is the most perfect example of this *everything in common*, inseparably!

Sufferings in common with Me! Intentions in common with Me! Dispositions in common with Me!

This *everything in common* comprises the true life of this perpetual communion of love that I so desire between my spouses and Me.

Omnia in communione dilectionis. . . .[78]

Communion of "sweetness" in a communion of "sorrow."

Such was the real, effective, co-redemptive compassion of sorrowful Mary. Inseparable partner in my service as Lamb of God, Lamb meek and humble, bearing with an infinite sweetness of merciful charity and loving loyalty the terrible, humiliating weight of all the world's sins.

Here then is the model that I ask you to contemplate and imitate in these hours when the cry of my "appeal" is more timely than ever.

"In order to save the world I must have true, co-redemptive spouses."

Oremus: Pray! Let us pray together!

---

[78] *All things in the communion of love.*

This is the urgent invitation my Heart addresses to you at all times from the Host of the Tabernacle as from the depths of your souls, where the Host, don't forget, by its grace lives in residence.

May your response be to address this same invitation to Me, so as to pray always with one and the same voice, with one and the same heart.

Pater noster qui es in caelis. . . .[79]

Oremus: first word of infallibly pleasing prayer to my Father; true prayer in my Name.

Oremus: first word to begin a conversation of love, secret start to a prayer of love, of union!

Yes, let us pray in a communion of praise, benediction, adoration, and the action of grace!

Oremus! Adoremus!

Laudemus! Benedicamus![80]

Let us pray, let us pray in a communion of entreaty, of ardent supplications.

Oremus Petamus! Imploremus![81]

Let us pray in a communion of oblation, of dedication, of total surrender!

Oremus! Offeramus! Adhaereamus![82]

You can continue these communions of prayer without end, stressing one or the other, following the urges of your hearts, and of my Heart too!

And whatever these be, we will always begin, continue and conclude and then start over again by saying, "Let us pray, let us pray in a communion of love."

---

[79] *Matt 6:9 — Our Father who art in heaven. . . .*

[80] *Let us pray! Let us adore! Let us praise! Let us bless!*

[81] *Let us pray! Let us ask! Let us appeal!*

[82] *Let us pray! Let us offer! Let us hold fast!*

Oremus!   Amemus!   Amemus et Redamemus![83]
"Let us together return love for love!"

To this plural unity of two-in-one I invite all my consecrated souls, all my spouses. To this life of unity, of the *we* of love where the *you* is lost in the Me, where the Me expands in and through the *you*, I call each spouse of my Heart, most especially for service as my redemptive continuator.

Oremus!

Let us continue therefore to pray together my "appeal" with one and the same heart, with the heart of a host, of a host totally consecrated to the work of the Father, and for that reason constantly consumed by the fire of suffering!

How sweet to Me in these circumstances is this duet of love, of this "appeal" in "unity of heart and soul" . . . "in the unity of the Host."

It is not only in the direct practice of this prayer that this plural love is to be recognized in this manner: in viewpoints, feelings, desires. No, the *Oremus* is to continue at every hour of one's life, in one's labor, in all that one does, in *Laboremus! Operemur!*

"Let us work together, act together."

If it is necessary to speak, let us speak together, inseparably!

If it is necessary to listen, let us listen together, inseparably!

If it is necessary to write, let us write together, inseparably!

Yes, "inseparably," and therefore "similarly, in the same way."

Thus in every kind of activity, a communion of perpetual love.

All in one, all two all one, ever more one.

Omnia in unum!

Me in you, you in Me! Me to you, you to Me! We two in one: for the Father, for my brothers!

Meditate on this unity of life in the light of my Gospel (discourse

---

[83] *Let us pray! Let us love! Let us return love!*

at the Last Supper) in order to unite yourselves intimately with all the acts of my Sacred Heart.

Collaboremus![84]

This word is an entire prayer, an entire "life." Yes, spoken with Me, heard by Me, addressed to Me, this *we* of love should be the life of all the Father's children, and therefore of each of my brothers, and how intimately of each of my spouses, associated by vocation with the great work that has been confided to Me as Saving Word!

Collaboremus — doesn't one find together in this word both work (*labore*) and prayer (*oremus*), each fortifying the other in the service of the same cause?

In effect, work only becomes fruitful when it is praying, when it is offering made to the divine intentions. And by this same token, prayer only becomes fruitful when it is work or suffering, which means sacrifice to the divine intentions, a host of praise, of gratitude, of reparation. Again, this is forever the spirit of my "appeal." The life of my true, co-redemptive spouses should be able to recite these words without ceasing:

Oremus!   Amemus!   Collaboremus!

I CAME! . . . I COME!

December, 1936

Yes, I am all desire for I am all love, all thirst for union.

Ardent, vehement desire, expressed by kind and thoughtful acts no less than by supplicating appeals.

Desire ardently desiring desire in return.

Desire expressed so tenderly in this Gospel passage:

Behold the bridegroom! Come out to meet him.[85]   *Behold, your*

---

[84] *Let us collaborate!*

[85] *Matt: 25:6*

king is coming to you, humble,[86]... in the middle of the night[87] of this poor, anguished world.

I come to each of you, wishing to have this cry of supplicating love resonate deep in your heart. With a silent soul that is wide awake, hear its profound resonance, and then make echo of it.

Ecce venio ... Veni,[88] two-fold rhythm of the same unitive movement of love, having to beat in unison with the heart of the beloved and the Heart of the Spouse.

The *Venio* who approaches, the *Veni* who attracts. *Venio* and *Veni* call to each other, respond to each other in order that there may be an encounter.

Such is the true desire of the soul who approaches, who approaches by calling, calling by approaching, in order to encounter by seeking, with an intimacy always more intimate. An interior spirit that can and should animate the least of all movements, works and exterior actions of your life.

Venio, Veni, per viam Crucis.[89]

You have understood that the true way of love's encounter, of coming together and intermingling, of souls handed over to each other and loving one another, is the way of the cross, the way of sacrifice, for this is the way of great love, the way that has been chosen by the God of Love for his Well-Beloved Son.

I came to you by this way, I return to you by this same way (Host and Calvary are but one).

You yourselves must come to Me by this same route, and just as my Father had Me come to you through Mary, my tender and Immaculate Mother, to soften for Me a little this way of suffering and humiliation, so in like manner I give you this same Mary to soften your way, saying to you: "Come to Me through Mary, with her

---

[86] *Ibid 21:5*

[87] *Ibid 25:6*

[88] *Ps. 39:8; Heb. 10:7-9; Matt. 19:21 — Behold I come ... I came.*

[89] *I come, I came by way of the Cross.*

maternal help. Call Me to you with her voice, or still more, with her Heart."

Veni . . .Venio . . . per Mariam.

Et venimus, in unum, ad Patrem.[90]

If my desire for encounter and union becomes so urgent, so earnestly imploring, it's because my Father's glory is at stake, the triumph of his work, work which is the return of all his children in Me and by Me.

Why, then, these tireless measures of my Heart, these ever more supplicating appeals, why if not to lead his children back to Him in his eternal, paternal dwelling place, transformed as far as possible into the Object of his infinite complacency, into Me, your Jesus, your Spouse, your King!

Thus, ever deeper into one another's hearts, by an irresistible, unending impetus of mutual, compenetrating movements.

These mutual appeals and responses would lack something, indeed would lack much if they never led to truly amalgamating encounters, if apostolic fire in them were lacking.

Isn't this how I come to you, with my immense thirst of love for all souls?

Also, in order to encounter Me, each of you cannot come to Me all alone! You have to come with other souls, with all those whom my Heart has charged you with (and isn't it the entire world), drawing them, carrying them along by example, charity, devotion, prayer, sacrifice.

And then, also, you still have to call Me into these souls, this with a large heart consumed with zeal.

Be assured that the more your *Venio* and your *Veni* are apostolic in this way, the more they will bring us together, the more they will strengthen us in a life of union, so as to rise up to the Father.

Listen to Me again, without growing weary, as I tell you of my

---

[90] *I came, I come . . . through Mary. And let us go as one to the Father.*

Father's great, loving desire for the *Venio* and *Veni*. It relieves Me to reveal my Heart in this way.

In this world, this desire is the path to possession. It prepares for the possession of Heaven, and this in the measure that each step is a new encounter, where each encounter is a fresh, ever more compenetrating embrace.

To live without desire is to mark time in place if not to move backward. To live desiring little, desiring selfishly, what is it if not to live in slow motion? Oh, these religious who are just marking time, these slow ones, how they sadden and hinder Me!

But on the other hand to live with great desire is to live rising upwards, to the realm of true love.

To live with vehement, growing desire is to live in *crescendo*, in fast-forward.

How my Heart thirsts for these accelerations of love, that an impassioned seawall might be opposed to the furious waves of hatred.

That is why, with all supplicating love, I beg for this vehement desire that is only satisfied by being endlessly awakened, that only rests in the ardor of its agony.

Desire that is gift no less than claim.

Desire that attracts in the measure that it rushes forward. *Veni* whose appeal is all the more irresistible as the fervor of the *venio* is more generous. Great desire that is love rushing to an encounter with Love.

Ecce sponsus venit. . . . Exite obviam ei.[91]

On this eve of the feast of the Nativity, I draw near with eager Heart, hastening to renew in each of your souls my mystery of mercy.

Are your hearts also eager, hastening more and more to draw near to Mine?

Oh, this eagerness of love, how pleasing it is to my Heart, how

---

[91] *Matt 25:6 — Behold the bridegroom comes. . . . Come out to meet him!*

well it describes my true spouses, the fervent ones who alone give repose, glory, consolation. Yes, these are the eager ones, thirsty for prayer, sacrifice, charity, for everything that makes up the gift of self.

Do you wish to please my Heart? Make an examination of your eagerness.

Do you have any? Are you not souls that are apathetic, dulled by egoism, living in slow motion?

What are they like? Pure and ardent, like the ones I spoke of earlier? Or rather are they self-centered, pleasure-loving, eager for the merely curious and purely natural?

Search by my light and confront your souls with my Heart, with Mary's Heart, and tell Me what will you be from this point forward? Nothing less than loving impatience responding to my impatient love.

HOST

July, 1939

As Christ-Redeemer, my being on earth was a way.

I am the Way.[92]

And my way is Host. There alone am I, but I am there always, and being there I am everywhere, with a redemptive Presence that only aspires to spread Itself so that It may encompass, overrun, win over the entire universe of souls!

To serve this spreading of my redemptive Host is the sublime mission my "appeal" of love confers upon consecrated souls.

My Heart cannot help but repeat this to you in every way possible, so desirous is It of co-redemptive help from its consecrated ones.

There is such an outburst of satanic hatred in the world that to ward off its ravages nothing less will suffice than a torrential overflowing of love by way of the outspread Host, by the Host expanded

---

[92] *Jn 14:6*

each day more and more through the liberal cooperation of Christian souls, and above all of consecrated souls: priests, men and women religious.

That is the great design of my Savior Love, in them and through them.

So that the Father, no longer seeing the world except as covered over by the redemptive Host of the Well-Beloved Son of his complacency, might pour down mercy on it for the glory of his infinite Charity.

Become host, more and more, in order to ever enlarge my Host.

Serve the advancing of my Host of love by the advance in you of my host spirit. Can there be any program of love more beautiful, more urgent than this? This is the one I confer upon you. Be truly faithful to it.

There is no true, unifying communion without this encounter and fusion of two hosts, the one vanishing into the other, the little host into the Great Host (Mine), so that the reach of its redemptive activity may expand.

Tollite hostias et introite in altria Domini.[93]

Meditate on these words of my Scripture. Does it not tell you that to enter into the intimacy of my dwelling place, to penetrate the enclosure ever more deeply, as right of entrance you have to bring hosts, the deeds of hosts, you have to be hosts yourselves.

If Eucharistic Communion does not produce fruit in souls (alas!), it's because It is not sufficiently understood.

Many come to It as "source," but not enough as "sacrifice."

Yet, It is both one and the other, or rather one by virtue of the other, that is, source of unifying union, sacrifice of egoism to the point of selflessness.

What indeed is my Host if not the on-going life of the Crucified Savior, a life that is truly synonymous with sacrifice, sacrifice and source of Life.

---

[93] *Ps 95:8 — Bring up sacrifices and enter into the courts of the Lord (RSV).*

That is why I can say to your heart in all truthfulness, "Love has given you the Host."

The thoughtful, considerate Love of my Father, of my Heart, and of my Mother as well (did She not by her *Fiat* contribute to the total work of redemption?). "May love give you to the Host," that is, "may the return of love by your hearts transform you into hosts," so that it can be said, "the Host is giving you love," so that with each new communion It may be for you a source of growth in a life of charity, not only Eucharistic Communion but also spiritual communion with my Will.

September, 1939

"Love for love," "Host for host."

That is the entire spirit of my "appeal."

> *O salutaris Hostia*
>
> *Quae caeli pandis ostium,*
>
> *Bela premunt hostilia*
>
> *Da robur fer auxilium.*[94]

Yes, my spouse, the Church says it well and you cannot chant it and meditate on it more opportunely than now in these present hours of terrible conflict. "I am the Host of salvation."

Host of redemption for my brothers,

Host of my Father's glorification.

No salvation without the Host.

Salvation assured in the Host.

It is the Host that, after having given strength and help against the assaults of the infernal enemy on earth, opens "the doors of the

---

[94] *O saving Victim, opening wide*
The gate of Heaven to us below;
Our foes press hard on every side;
Your aid supply; Your strength bestow.

107

Father's House" in heaven to all who call upon Him and receive Him with love, above all to all those who give themselves as food for his all-consuming hunger, that it may be fulfilled.

Adveniat Hostia.[95]

Nourish yourselves on the Host, and nourish the Host. That is the program of salvation.

Every beat of your heart, if it is total gift, contributes a tiny bit to its expansion. Think about it, beloved spouses, understand that this host life is synonymous with a life of holocaust, of absolute, plenary sacrifice without the least reservation or holding back of the gift's entirety. Are you taking your part here?

Answer Me, or better, listen to the reply my most Holy Love Itself makes to you: "If you were truly taking part here, would the world be where it is at this moment?" Oh, you well know it wouldn't be!

What is my "appeal" if not an urgent request to have you hasten to take part here, in this life of host.

For why does it surprise you that all the souls about you do not better understand the language of the trial: merciful chastisement.

How can you hope they make a serious examination of their conduct in order that they might be converted to a truthfully Christian life, if you yourselves do not review your love stance so as to be converted to a life that is truthfully religious.

Without this profound, interior conversion of all my spouses, I cannot help but repeat to you: *The world will not be saved!*

Oh, do not fail my merciful hopes.

June 18, 1936

The life of a true religious ought to be a perpetual celebration of Holy Mass, or rather, a continual participation in my Eucharistic sacrifice.

Understand how:

---

[95] *Come O Victim (Host).*

108

"A perpetual offering,"

in a spirit of total oblation; always more "my victim," more completely given up to the Good Pleasure of my most Holy Will: *Ecce.*

"A perpetual consecration,"

in a spirit of loving compliance: my victim always more "host" by burning deeds embracing the devouring fire of my great love: *Fiat.*

"A perpetual communion,"

in a spirit of close identification: my host becoming always more "my spouse" in the compenetrating intimacy of consummating union.

"A perpetual action of grace,"

in a spirit of zeal and praise: my spouse becoming always more "my apostle," my co-redemptive partner through the most pure agony of soul.

My co-redemptive spouse becoming always more with Me and in Me, true "child" of my heavenly Father; all in the service of his great work.

Reparation and exaltation of the glory of Love.

Magnificat!

On earth the true love of the spouse has to be both, and in the same proportion:

"Repose" and "Agony"!

Repose without agony would lack zeal; agony without repose would lack trust.

One without the other therefore would lack love.

In heaven, I am a glorious Spouse about whom my faithful spouses sing in bright light. On earth, I perpetuate myself in the Host. I am and I remain a Spouse-Host who can only espouse souls by changing them into hosts.

These spouse-hosts, "hosts" ever more so, these are the "true co-redemptive spouses" that my Heart ever more begs of you.

I, Immaculate Host, can only be nourished by hosts that are totally pure, by consecrated hosts, which is to say by hosts that have burned away the human *me* in order to be consummated in the union of a life of love.

Virginal purity of a supreme exclusiveness where all the heart's vibrations ask for Me alone and nothing else.

Too few of my spouses understand that complete consecration must be without reservation. This "without reservation" is not only in gift without ceasing, but also entails a *crescendo* of oblation, that is, where each vibration of one's entire being ever asks for more in an ever-increasing mutuality of giving, a becoming that unites one to the other until unity is consummated.

One form of co-redemptive collaboration that I desire of my true spouses is participation in my office as Mediator.

Mediation is a "priestly duty," a duty consisting of:

"Offering the host by a Priest-Host; Host that is offering and Host that is offered."

Isn't this what I accomplished on Calvary, what I perpetually do in the Eucharist, and what, in union with Me, you yourselves should do?

If my Father has loved you so much that He gave Me to you under the form of the Host, it was so that you may offer Me to Him as a Host of praise, of supplication for expiation, of substitution for all your shortcomings.

But remember that in order to be qualified for this office:

The Host can only be offered by a soul-host: a priest-host!

For nothing can please the Father that is not conformed to his Well-Beloved Son!

July 1, 1937

Is not co-redemption a mixing of human blood with divine Blood?

A poor, little drop of human suffering (no matter how hard it might seem, that's all it is in comparison to Mine), lost, all at sea in the immense waves of Christ's suffering.

Little drop, nothing in itself, a bit of water destined to vanish as it is poured out but whose absence hampers all the work.

Oh, what marvel is my Mercy!

Oh, what responsibility this little drop of water has!

Meditate well on this triple role of the Host:

The Host alone "receives" my presence.

The Host alone "preserves" my presence.

The Host alone "communicates" my presence.

Therefore it's in virtue of these acts as host, of its host life, that:

The soul who is consumed is imbued with my presence,

The soul who is consecrated is taken over by my presence,

The soul who is consummated is radiation of my presence.

But do not forget that it is a host's life, forged by continual, loving acts, that lets the Divine Will take the place of the human will.

Non mea sed Tua Voluntas.[96]

In this hour when hatred strikes at my Heart with so many blows, may the love of my spouses console Me by knocking on the door of my Heart with redoubled confidence, for it is in opening that It finds relief.

Knock on my Heart as true co-redemptive spouses, a Heart agonized by my burning Thirst, asking of Me everything I ask of you, for the eternal interests of my Father's Love and his great family of souls.

And by knocking in this way, be aware that together you are opening yourself to Me and you are opening Me to you.

Divine marvel of my Wisdom, these reciprocities and merciful connections.

Let us knock on each other's door.

Let us open ourselves to one another

---

[96] *Lk 22:42 — Not mine but Thy Will.*

CHAPTER FIVE

THE APOSTOLIC SPIRIT OF CO-REDEMPTIVE SOULS

brought to life by their loving identification with Our Lord: He loved souls at the price of his Blood. They should do the same, through conformity, and also because it is impossible to save souls without suffering unto death for them.

APOSTOLIC SPIRIT

1940

You are "the light of the world"[97] by the design of my eternal Wisdom. You must be so in fact, by your active and loving "cooperation."

For it is to all consecrated souls, apostles by their very consecration to my service, that this evangelical word is addressed; and in a very special, urgent way to those on whom I have conferred a privileged share in my "mission as teacher."

In choosing them, I illuminated them as "living lamps," destined to give light to all those whom I want to draw to my Father's House.

---

[97] *Matt 5:12*

"Nor do men light a lamp and put it under a bushel, but on a stand and it gives light to all in the house."[98]

For it is through light that life is transmitted.

"Light of truth for life of charity."

"And this is life eternal that they may know thee, Father."[99]

Make resolution to have accented in your souls with the greatest urgency my great apostolic command, *Go and Teach! Go therefore and make disciples of all nations. . . .[100]*

And understand, by the choice my Father made for Me during my life on earth, the "loftiness" of this apostolate!

Given Satan's unrelenting determination to oppose it, come to appreciate how exceptionally effective and timely this apostolate is for the "real life of the world."

Now is the time for you to "give new life" to this apostolate, doing so with all your resources and strength.

Do it as Redemption's zealous helpers, just as my "appeal" asks of you, generously audacious and courageous in making all the sacrifices necessary on its behalf; with limitless trust in the grace that this wish and this reminder contain regarding the form of your service of love.

But bear in mind that, more than anything else, the Master has to start out by being "disciple." Before pronouncing the *Ite et docete*[101] didn't I say, *Venite et discite*[102] — Come and learn from Me. Go and teach Me.

Intimacy and zeal are the two complementary sides of love. And I cannot address a *veni* to a soul without accompanying it with a *vade . . . et dicite fratribus meis.*[103] Remember Magdalene.

---

[98] *Ibid 5:15*

[99] *Jn 17:3*

[100] *Matt 28:19*

[101] *Ibid — Go and teach.*

[102] *Matt 11:29 — Take up my yoke upon you and learn from Me. . . .*

[103] *Jn 20:17 — go . . . and say to my brethren. . . .*

Yes, the more I call to intimacy in the sanctuary of my Heart, the more I call to broad openness in the field of my apostolate.

The more I want you as "spouses" the more I want you as "apostles."

The more I want you as "apostles" the more I want you as "spouses."

That's why my "appeal" is no less a most urgent call to more intimacy than an earnest request for more ardent zeal. To implore you as I do to intensify your apostolic life is at the same time to implore you to intensify your interior life.

For there is no genuine spiritual fertility without "intimacy" with Me. My Heart wants to stress this great truth, for It has a burning thirst for your efficacious help in the "salvation of the world."

As my Father has sent me, so I send you.[104]

How had I been sent into the world in order to "save" it?

I made your Name known to them.[105]

For I have given them the words which You gave me.[106]

Meditate on these words of life and understand that it was as pure echo and perfect transparency of my Father that I had been sent by Him, to enlighten the world in order to return it to life.

Therefore I was sent as "Master" of men and as "Disciple" of the Father, or rather as his Logos, his Word, radiation of his superabundant Charity!

And the Word became flesh.[107]

You realize, don't you, that in sending Me in this way, my Father did not leave Me alone, I still remained in Him!

Ineffable realization of the "we" of oneness.

My Father and I are One.[108]

---

[104] *Ibid 20:21*
[105] *Ibid 17:6*
[106] *Ibid 17:8*
[107] *Jn 1:14*

114

Recall also that it was not until after my Crucifixion that the world was truly enlightened by the radiance of this transparency, by the echo of this divine resonance.

Ad lucem per crucem.[109]

Light of life given to souls by the "death" of the Cross.

And now, aided by my grace, I leave it to your heart to make practical application in your teaching mission.

Shouldn't all you priests and religious be instruments of my Love among souls, and to that end, shouldn't you be to Me "most pure echoes and transparencies"?

Be faithful transmitting echoes of Me, free and living conduits of my light and word of Life!

In order to transmit and have it get through, one has to "receive," and in order to receive, one has to "listen"!

In order to resonate, one has to "vibrate in unison," to "be in complete accord in order to be completely resonant."

The true apostle is one who can truly appropriate Christ's word:

For I have given them the words which You gave me.[110]

And who for that purpose are always listening to Me, always in my school.

So in telling you, *Go and teach*, I am also saying to you *Remain in my Love.*[111] As I Myself remain in you: *And lo, I am with you always.*[112] And you know I cannot fail but be faithful!

But is it so on your part?

Are you faithful to remain with Me, in Me, to listen to Me, to be in accord with all my feelings?

---

[108] *Ibid 10:30*

[109] *To the light through the cross.*

[110] *Ibid 17:8*

[111] *Ibid 15:9*

[112] *Matt 28:19*

In order to have souls "vibrate" with my Love, don't they themselves have to vibrate there, "beating in unison" with my Heart, just as my "appeal" has been asking of you?

How I love this little, wonderfully expressive prayer:

"May my silence make room for Your Word, my death for Your Life!" And all this in Me as spouse and by Me as apostle, in souls to whom it has been confided.

With Love I say to you once again:

"The more you are spouse to Me, the more you will be my apostle!

"The more you are my apostle, the more you will be my spouse."

Blessed cycle of love and union.

A TWO-FOLD LIFE

1936

Genuine love of a co-redemptive spouse is a love both "exclusive" and "out-going" at the same time, both "one to one," and "all to all"!

Intimacy can only be transformative when joined to a courageous, "apostolic" charity!

I dream of these wholly "supernatural" souls in whose life all "influence" is from Me alone, and all "effluence" is towards Me alone. . . .

From these alone am I able to shine forth, for their self-effacement gives free passage to the unbounded outpouring of my divine Life!

It's by growing rich in Me that you give Me to souls.

The more one gives Me to them, the more one gives Me to Myself.

Giving Me to Myself is to give Myself to others.

Understand this well, consecrated souls, if you want to appease a little my immense craving for love.

Be those who give out love, who spread my great love!

Radiate Me by the steadfast serenity that comes from having a supernatural full tank, remembering that in order to be able to give Me to others, you yourselves have to be filled with my love to the point of overflowing.

Do not forget that I have entrusted to each of you a certain number of souls for whom you are particularly responsible.

It is to the intimacy of my Life in "total intimacy" with the Father that I ask you to unite and unify your life. Now, the twofold rhythm of this life of intimacy, as you know, follows from the twofold rhythm of my Heart.

It's a life of "adoring communion" and of "unbounded diffusion."

Meditate on it, on its mysteries and marvelous depths.

A life of adoring communion with the sublime Greatness of my Father through profound, deeply felt contemplation, full of praise, compliance, reverence and gratitude.

Confiteor Tibi Pater.[113]

A life of adoring communion with the all-wise Will of my Father, through total, unceasing dependence, most sweet and profound conformance, most supple, fully trusting abandonment: *Ita Pater, quoniam sic fuit placitum ante te.*[114]

A life of unbounded diffusion, of expansion by an all-consuming zeal for the interests of my Father: to avenge and exalt his Glory; to win back souls for Him!

Unbounded diffusion by ardent, ceaseless supplication before my Father, supplication of prayer, of work, of suffering. *Father, I pray for those whom You have given me . . . and for their sake I consecrate myself.*[115]

Unbounded diffusion by transmitting to souls the secrets of my Father: *Holy Father, I have manifested your Name to the men whom You gave me. . . .*[116]

---

[113] *Matt 11:25 — I confess to You, Father.*
[114] *Ibid 11.26 — Yea, Father, for such was Your gracious will.*
[115] *Jn 17:9, 19*

117

"Communion" and "diffusion," the twofold movement of a fervor that burns for love alone, for love's reciprocity.

1937

The conquering power of "radiance" is only as great as "contemplation" is deep!

For radiance can only emanate from contemplation.

From this contemplation comes a "convergence of views," fixed, happy convictions of the heart whose very strength is their radiance.

From this contemplation comes an "atmosphere of peace and purity" that irresistibly attracts my grace!

Contemplation therefore that is a "flooding penetration" by the divine which alone can give rise to an overflowing.

Understand this about prayer:

The more you are recollected and therefore invaded by the divine, the more you will radiate Me and therefore conquer!

1939

Pay heed and live this program of love:

"Make room for the Host in your consecrated souls, by espousing all my filial and fraternal affections, for my Father, for my Mother, for my brothers, by letting yourself be espoused in accordance with my divine tastes of poverty, humility, suffering.

"Crucified Spouse, I espouse by crucifying."

Make the Host pass from your hearts as co-redemptive spouses into the souls given to each of you by my Father, bearing in mind that in all the world there is not one of them for whom you, though in various ways, do not have a real role of spiritual maternity to fulfill.

Oh, understand and rejoice in this beautiful "role" that has been

[116] *Ibid 17:6*

chosen for you, my consecrated souls, in the great drama of the world's Redemption. . . .

How?

By a growing, productive apostolic "agony" that tears out "everything" egoistic in your life forever.

This, as you now know, is the cry of my "appeal," of this merciful "manifesto" of love from my Heart, meant to signify a "loving embrace" of your hearts, stirring you to total sacrifice, to become thereby a source that expands the reign of my Host of fire, for the saving, divinizing embrace of the whole world.

Here's another love program:

Be for Me at once both "a dwelling place," and "a conduit."

Staying and going out: isn't this the whole life of the Eucharistic Host, its sublime purpose?

Be therefore:

"Christ's dwelling place and Christ's conduit!"

Place of rest for your Christ-Spouse! Rest, as you know by now, that He finds when you are filled with Him, with his divinizing superabundance, all "place" that is made for Him, that is "offered" and "open" to Him.

Yes, my Heart takes its rest in a soul as long as my Heart can be active there as gift, as effusion of its superabundant Goodness.

Conduit of your Spouse-Savior's redemptive Charity, so that It may be poured out into souls and that their praise may splash back up to the Father!

Yes, to allow Me to go out is to:

Let Me come down that I may spread out, so that I may ascend carrying others along with Me and thereby satisfy and exalt the thirst of infinite Goodness.

And marvel of divine Wisdom:

The more you will be a resting place for Me, the wider it is!

119

The more you will be a conduit for Me, the more open it is!

And vice versa.

"THE FATHER SEEKS. . . ."

"I CAME TO SEEK. . . ."

"WHOM DO YOU SEEK?"

December 15, 1939

The Father seeks. . . .

Would the One who is satisfied with the infinite plenitude of his divinity ever need anything? Would He lack anything? Believe in my Gospel's loving word, when my Heart mercifully revealed to you the mystery of my Thirst by asking you to give Me to drink. . . .

Yes, the Father seeks. . . .

No one has thirst like the Wellspring.

"Thirst of the Creator's richness," infinitely surpassing the indigent thirst of the creature.

The Father seeks those worshippers *who worship Him in spirit and in truth,*[117] like his Well-Beloved Son on Whom alone his eyes can rest and by Whom alone can his complacency be satisfied.[118] Above all He seeks the radiance of the One who is his Word, his own infinite Splendor.[119]

Only on earth does the Father seek those among his children who are "on the way," for in heaven He already possesses and finds all that his love can wish for.

The Blessed who make up his court are all "those worshippers," each "radiating the glory of his Son," each another Christ.

On earth it is only in the Host that He can "find what He seeks," since it is only there that his Well-Beloved Son resides in truth and in spirit:

---

[117] *Jn 4:23*

[118] cf. *Matt 3:14, 17; Ibid 17:5, etc.*

[119] *Heb 1:3*

120

"Perfect Worshipper, for He is perfect Redeemer."

Also, the Father's "seeking" is a "search for hosts," "co-redemptive" hosts, hosts that prolong, expand, spread out the "one redemptive Host" of the Savior Word.

And where on earth can the Father wish for and hope to find such "co-redemptive and co-worshipping hosts" if not first and foremost among consecrated souls, each and every one of whom He calls to this so noble and so sublime a vocation?

At the heart of the Blessed Trinity, my Father perpetually resides in Me, his *Eternal Splendor,*[120] to the satisfaction of his infinite complacency.

My Father seeks Me in souls all over the world, and it was in order to find Me here that He sent Me. *Exivi a Patre et veni,*[121] — that He had Me live here in the Host; *Et Verbum caro factum est,* [122] — that He ceaselessly sends Me here, giving to Me the "mission of seeking," to find for Him what He is seeking, to find it for Him by saving his children lost through Satan's hateful machinations. *The Son of Man has come to seek and save that which was lost.*[123] The mission to save them by giving Myself over for them, by changing them into Me, by giving them my life, by divinizing them.

In these times of terrible battle between heaven and earth, with souls in such extreme peril, think about the true meaning of my mission as Savior, in order that you may take your share in it:

"Seek in order to save;

Save in order to divinize."

Divinize in order to widen the Father's Glory, the great circle of his divine, adoptive family.

But in order to take effective part as "true co-redeemers" in the spirit of my "appeal," do not forget the way this is to be done:

---

[120] *Wis 7:26*

[121] *Jn 16:28 — I came from the Father and have come. . . .*

[122] *Ibid 1:14 — And the Word was made flesh.*

[123] *Lk 19:10*

"The Way of the Cross — The Way of the Host."

What are you seeking?

"And you, consecrated souls, what are you seeking?" Everything, happiness . . . but what happiness? That's the issue.

Happiness and consolation in giving, or rather, happiness and consolation in receiving?

Which amounts to saying: Do you seek to demonstrate love or do you seek to satisfy ego?

For there are no other alternatives.

With your heart looking at Mine, answer Me in all honesty.

That your answer may be heartfelt, listen to my merciful assertion and my infallible promise:

"Every search for love is an encounter with love."

"He who seeks Me has already found Me."

"He who seeks Me finds Me more and more."

Echo of my Gospel words: *Seek (love) and you shall find (love).*[124]

Another question:

How are you seeking?

Is it as a strolling amateur, wandering about aimlessly at the whim of a thousand moods and desires? Would that be real searching? Do none of you consecrated souls recognize yourselves here?

What then does true searching consist of?

It's a single-minded, fast-paced pursuit conducted by a heart impassioned with singular and insatiable eagerness to glorify and satisfy

---

[124] *Matt 7:7; Lk 11:9*

Love, by a will that has been handed over in perpetual acts of oblation in order that this purpose might be achieved.

Are these the qualities of your search?

"Purity and fervor; actions and eagerness?"

May your examination always be done in the light of my Gospel.

Are your actions for love buoyant, unceasing, without holding anything back?

"Where" and "When" do you seek Me?

Must this not be "everywhere" and "always"?

In truth, do I not reside "in all places" through my loving Immensity as Creator of all being, and "at all times" through the unchanging Eternity of my acts of Love?

And what is it to you, this "everywhere and always," if not:

"the now of each instant"

"the dwelling place of the present moment."

For keep this in mind:

I am only present in the present moment, in this "active" presence that is given life by love — in the loving present that is "my Will incarnate in your duties at this very moment, right where you are." Physically you are bound to be there, but are you there in spirit, with your heart, your will, your soul?

Still another question to stir the fervor of your searching:

Do you think, do you believe that it is "Me," my own Heart that makes the first overtures?

That the main Seeker is Me?

The One who searches for, who pursues your souls?

That you would not be seeking Me if I Myself were not first seeking you?

That each one of you has been insatiably searched for, insatiably pursued in this present time?

Ask Mary to make you understand that being among Love's chosen ones, you are by that very token "pursued," and moreover, you are all the more pursued the more completely you have given yourselves up to Love.

"Mutual searching, mutual pursuit, precondition for transforming encounter."

And see in my "appeal" an evident, touching expression of my Heart's merciful searching. Meditate on it in this light, that you may live it in the fire of this vast divine Charity.

THE AGONY OF LOVE

1937

Consecrated souls, I would like to have you "share" in my great "agony of love," in the agony of my all-consuming thirst for the Glory of my Father, for the salvation of souls. You know that when you "share in my thirst," you "satisfy" it a little.

A heart without "agony" is a heart without "fervor." And is a heart without "fervor" a living heart? Is it a "loving" heart? Is it a heart of one who is "consecrated," the heart of a spouse of my Heart, Heart so tormented by love, by the most acute fervor of measureless charity!

Of my Heart that will only find "rest" when all the desires of the Father in Heaven are fulfilled, all the vows of his redeeming Mercy!

A continual love-sharing in this interior agony of my Heart then is the little "co-redemptive help" that I am asking you to give Me "with all your hearts". . . and my choicest "thanks" for this help will be to increase every day the intimacy of your participation in this great "agony" of my Heart.

A religious soul, a consecrated soul, whose heart is not "agonized" by love's great thirst is a soul agonizing to my Heart.

124

But by the same token, the soul who is most "agonized" by this thirst is the most "restful" to Me, my best "collaborator."

For this great agony to take possession of a soul, it has to replace all of egoism's petty little agonies, the little worries and preoccupations of this world, so that great fervor might consume it!

Was there ever a heart more agonized by love than the pierced Heart of my Mother, the Queen of Martyrs? And at the same time was there ever a heart more "at rest in love" than this Immaculate Heart of the Queen of Peace?

Learn from Her, that true love cannot find rest here below except in the "agony" of zeal, an "all-consuming" agony which is the supreme gift of a heart impassioned for its Only Love.

Supreme gift that brings to the heart its own true "rest," a rest that is called "peace."

"Peace that on earth has the name joy!"

July 6

Any "failure to love" is serious in a consecrated soul, in the soul of a religious, and how heavily these omissions distress my Heart! For these omissions are the sticking mud of egoism, of a stagnated life struggling along without passion, gravitating around itself, seeking only "tranquility" and "pleasure" under the unhappy slogan:

"Be safe! Be comfortable!"

Oh, aren't you ashamed of this life "without passion," where you let yourself be surpassed by so many of "love's rank and file warriors" who though they be "in" the world are so much less "of" the world than you, religious souls who are supposedly "separated" from it.

Therefore, I beg it of you, be soldiers "on active duty for love," be love's fervent ones, be love's militants burning with the "agony" that makes you fulfill, in the grand manner of a religious, all the acts of virtue asked of you by your rules or by the inspiration of grace that the least details of your daily life give rise to, whatever your occupation may be — acts of silence, of charity, of humility, of obedience, (never forgetting that these are other-worldly).

It is by means of this burning "fervor" in response to Mine that my Heart thirsts to be part of your hearts. Agonized as It is by its all-consuming zeal, It must have souls "passionate, fervent" for love, who alone are able to overcome hatred's violent, infuriated fervor.

This is the "fervor" that leads to "passion." Now, only hearts that are "impassioned" in this holy way are able to serve Me as "partners" in the redemptive work entrusted to Me by my Father. Love is only genuine when it is "impassioned," and in both senses of the word:

"burning fervor," and "crucifying suffering."

A heart that is truly "impassioned" — just as a truly consecrated heart should be — is at one and the same time:

an "enamored" heart and a "crucified" heart.

No, this is not loving. It's an indignity for a consecrated soul to be content with living "without passion," like someone half-dead in slow motion, withdrawn into egoistic apathy!

Oh, how these "tepid ones" chill my impassioned Heart! There isn't enough there for even a few weak, intermittent sparks.

"What I need are white-hot furnaces," souls from which ever more blazing sparks shoot out without end!

"My Heart must have souls that are alive and on fire!"

This "passion," which is the most pure and ardent "agony" of love, is in my own Heart a passionate "furnace" of Charity.[125] One must ask for it with great confidence.

Ask for it from Mary also, Mother of Sorrows, "wellspring of love":

Eia Mater, fons amoris
Fac ut ardeat cor meum
In amando Christum Deum
Ut sibi complaceam![126]

---

[125] *Litany of the Sacred Heart.*

[126] *Stabat Mater: O thou Mother! fount of love! Make me feel as thou hast felt; make my soul to glow and melt with the love of Christ my Lord.*

1938

Strive with all your heart to dwell, to always believe, in the

"Peace of Agony."

The "agony" of love's mysteries!

Mysteries of "faith" and the "cross"!

The "peace of love's luminosity"!

Luminosity of "life" and of "union"!

This is how you will give rest to my agonized Heart!

"I HAVE COMPASSION ON THE CROWD"[127]

December, 1940

In this lead-up to my redemptive reappearance, be a faithful "echo" of my *Misereor super turbam,*[128] *super mundum.*

Listen, write how this passage of my Gospel is current today:

convocatis discipulis suis dixit. [129]

Consecrated souls, you who are my privileged disciples, I call all of you near Me that you may receive the outpourings of my Heart.

Yes, I have Great Pity for the great hunger of souls!

Pity for this immense crowd that now "complains of hunger," reduced in the worst way to begging. For whether they know it or not, whether they believe it or not, they are seeking Me in their want, Me Who "alone" am able to gratify them. Their sufferings arouse Me, their miseries draw Me to them.

Misereor![130]

---

[127] *Misereor super Turbam.*

[128] *Matt 15:32 — I have compassion on the crowd . . . on the world.*

[129] *Ibid — He called his disciples and said. . . .*

[130] *I have compassion . . . .*

THE REDEEMER'S CALL TO CONSECRATED SOULS

All their cries of distress, of deprivation rise up in torrents straight to my Heart!

For my Savior's Heart is "full of Compassion." It cannot see you suffer without Itself suffering and wanting to relieve you. *Misereor!*

In its divine pity, my Heart "sees everything." It knows the weakness of human nature in pursuing the course of its life on its own; *deficient in via.*[131] It knows that divine relief alone is able to put it right!

My Heart is "All-Powerful," filled with "Riches," full of "Generosity"! Even more, "being" what It is, It has made itself the Bread of Life.

Oh, my consecrated ones, understand, partake of, assist in this divine pity, for as rich, as powerful, as overflowing as It is, Goodness is moved to want you as "helping benefactors, helping dispensers of this divine generosity!"

Afferte Mihi illos.[132]

Bring them to Me. Bring back to the plenitude of my Heart, where you got them, all the strengths of your love, all the works of your talents.

Unite them to Mine by a living *Ecce!*

Lose them in Mine by a most heartfelt *Fiat!* Without any reservation borne of egoism or sensuality!

Then, under "my divinizing benediction" they will become "bread of life," they will serve to "multiply my Bread of Life"! — Divine Bread that I charge precisely you to distribute with generosity to the great multitude of the poor and the famished of the earth.

. . . dabat discipulis ut apponerent turbae.[133]

Distribute them widely to all those around you. Then faithfully "gather" the "rest" that could not be consumed, never forgetting to

---

[131] *Mk 8:3 — They will faint on the way.*
[132] *Matt 14:18 — Bring them here to Me.*
[133] *Mk 8:6 — He gave them to his disciples to set before the people.*

distribute them to all without any exception, *so that nothing is lost*[134] of my merciful generosity.

Yes, learn how in your prayers to make wide, apostolic distribution to the souls of my brothers, my Father's children, throughout the whole world. In this way you will be "helpful" spouses, true co-redeemers in accord with my "appeal." For you know:

How hungry I am to satisfy,

How I pity the great hunger of souls!

Misereor super turbam!

But do not forget that my Love's "great Pity" had Me come down into the "barrenness" of the crib, go up to Calvary, immolate Myself on the altar. . . .

That in order to become "Bread of Life," I had to make Myself "Bread of the Host" and to remain there.

If your heart understands this, may your life respond and imitate it! For alas, if so many of love's graces remain awaiting delivery, awaiting distributors, it's for lack of spouse-souls who truly live "as wholly consecrated hosts." Oh! be these souls for Me! Help Me, assist my divine pity. *Misereor!*

In this pursuit of bodily nourishment, this restless, anxious pursuit that at this moment obsesses the greater part of humanity:

Who thinks about the great, divine Hunger?

Who suffers because of the great, divine Hunger?

Who is relieving the great, divine Hunger?

Who is sensitive to the Need of God?

Who is in the Need of God?

Who meets the Need of God?

Recall the words of my Gospel:

---

[134] *Jn 6:12*

Do not labor for the food which perishes, but for the food which endures to eternal life.[135]

God's Hunger! The Need of God! In both senses of the word:

"God hungry for the soul." — "The soul hungry for God."

Infinite Love's mysterious need of "opulence": to be nourished by souls so that they may be nourished by Him!

Need arising from the "poverty" of souls. To satisfy hunger with infinite Love and thus give Love satisfaction!

Yes, if the soul needs God it is because God needs the soul!

If God has need of the soul, it's because the soul has need of God!

Marvelous correlation of love's "unitive" course!

From the depths of your hearts, hear Me cry "famine" in a new, never-ending, imploring cry for "co-redemptive help":

"Stoke my fire! Fan my flames! Stir up my inferno! Set my furnace ablaze!"

Isn't it the spouse's responsibility to take care of the family's fire, to always maintain its "warmth," to always make the ambiance of intimacy even warmer! Here is the spouse's loving help: "helping Love to love!"

"helping Love to spread love,"

"to relieve its merciful pity,"

"to create an active echo of its *Misereor.*"

Such is the proper function of a genuine "auxiliary of Redemption"! And remember the solemn words of my "appeal." There's no middle ground. "Not to be an auxiliary is to be an obstacle."

But what is needed then to become an "aide and auxiliary" if not to "surrender one's self to Love as food," as food for its flames, flames which set ablaze, purify, transform, consummate only in the measure

---

[135] *Jn 6:27*

that they are consuming, that is to say, in the measure that they destroy everything that is not them!

In short, the destroying sacrifice of the egoistic *me* is the "inflammable matter" *par excellence*, making the soul "satisfying prey" of its Crucified Spouse, and thus his little, truly helping, refreshing, glorifying auxiliary.

Oh, yes! So that you may satisfy my great, divine Hunger, "serve Me food" by helping yourself to Me who Alone am food for your souls. To each of you I say:

"I pity you! Have pity on Me!"

"I pity your hunger! Have pity on my hunger!"

Misereor!

I pity the "multitude" of your needs, of your miseries, your sufferings, your trials. Have pity on the "multitude" of my needs, of my imploring desires!

Misereor super turbam!

"FOR THE CHARITY OF CHRIST IMPELS ME!"

September, 1940

You must write for all my consecrated souls these watchwords regarding the renewal of fervor that my "appeal" so ardently implores of them:

Caritas Christi urget me![136]

Would that each of you might make "his or her own" this cry of love that gushed forth from the fiery heart of my apostle Paul, echoing the burning cry of my Savior's Heart: *I have come to bring fire on the earth and would that it were already kindled!*[137]

---

[136] *II Cor 5:14 — The charity of Christ impels me.*
[137] *Lk 12:49*

Yes, I Myself am "driven" by the infinite Charity of the Father's Goodness. I have come into the world as the great "igniter of fire," the fire of divine love!

And for that same reason I remain here and ceaselessly return here in the Eucharistic Host, burning to set all hearts on fire, that they may transform the world into a vast blaze of fire, to the praise and glory of my Father.

Caritas Patris urget me![138]

Would that each of you, in approaching the altar each day for the great Sacrifice, might hear this same cry of Mine resonate from the depths of your own heart, ever as vibrant, as ardent, as urgent.

For on earth it is always and only from the Host that my Heart "beats."

It is from the Host that It "burns."

It is from the Host that It wants to "set fires."

— "I am the great Host of fire" that wants to spread in you and through you, making you "Little hosts of fire wholly ablaze and that set ablaze."

— But in order to be "set ablaze," in order that the fire may catch on, the material has to be "inflammable" so as to be entirely consumed without resisting combustion!

Now, who will be like that? Who should be if not consecrated souls, each of whom by definition is a soul given over to Love and destined therefore for fire, reserved for fire as fuel for its flames!

Who among you is like that? The way to know, the great, infallible, irreplaceable sign of this, you realize, is the "warmth of love" of your *Fiat* to the divine Good Pleasure's game of love. Each call of my Will — and there is no moment that It does not summon you by the voice of your "present duties" to its agenda for love — is a burning spark flashing out from the great furnace of infinite Charity

---

[138] *The love of the Father impels me.*

and destined to fall upon your souls so that it might enkindle and stir up in them the fire of my grace.

But any resistance of your own will — as you might well know — is retardant matter preventing the fire from "catching on" in your hearts, the spark from fulfilling love's destiny!

Now, can you say that there has never been in you the least resistance, the least dissatisfaction with my Will, no retardation whatsoever to my grace? Would that your heart might answer in complete honesty.

To allow yourself to be caught hold of and consumed by Me, as my "appeal" is asking of you, is "to allow the fire to catch on in you" by renouncing the love and desires that are "your own."

When fire catches on, it "catches on" to everything in order that it may transform everything into itself. Indeed, to be set ablaze is to be "transformed into an inferno," into a little host, joined to the great Host that is my Heart, for the praise and glory of the Father!

That's how I wish the living host of a consecrated soul to be — setting fires — for such a soul by definition is a "co-redemptive spouse." May you never forget this! Doesn't this ask you to be a "fire-setter" like Me, one who enkindles fire in the souls I have confided to you?

Caritas Christi urget me![139]

Yes, be at the same time both "guardians" and "propagators" of my "sacred fire."

"Faithful" and "fervent" guardians looking after its flame by the combustible love of your total "yes" at every moment to the calls of my Will. For any fire dies out if one does not look after it!

"Zealots" and "ardent propagators," spreading "my flames" through an ever more combustible generosity: putting into action the *Amplius*[140] of this generosity and the passion of *Adveniat,*[141] a passion

---

[139] *The charity of Christ impels me.*

[140] *More, larger amount.*

[141] *May (it) come.*

that includes within it passion for the Glory of my Father and that of souls! and, necessarily, by way of means, the passion of sacrifice.

He who speaks "with fire" therefore is exuberant and all-consuming. Fire alone can give off fire.

To be able to "propagate" the sacred fire of my Love that it may be enkindled in souls, one has to be "consumed by it." Filled with fire, one has to become an "inferno." The poor world is so "cold."

Would that a burning spark might spring from your heart to rekindle this fire! — How might that be done? — Consecrated souls, what would be needed is for all your petty, little personal interests to slip away before the "divine interests" of my Heart, that you might be "filled" with them and become fervently passionate souls.

It's from this perspective that I ask you today to make an examination of your love. That each of you would pose the following questions:

What was it that I took such interest in before? Why did I feel that attraction, that curiosity, that interest? All too often wasn't it for empty things of this world that gave some sort of private, egoistic pleasure?

What interests me "at present"? What excites my desires, urges me to action? Is it only what is able to contribute to the spreading of Love's divine Kingdom? Shouldn't a real co-redeemer take an interest in everything that interests my Heart as Savior?

Now, is "that" what I really find "interesting"? Do I bravely sacrifice all my petty human curiosities, my unmortified passions, to it and for it? What do I want and to what am I going to direct my interest, exclusively and fervently, "from now on"?

The secret to "renewing fervor" is to renew the "spirit of sacrifice" symbolized by the "sacred fire" that consumes and devours with Charity.

But there is no renewing the spirit of sacrifice without renewing the "spirit of prayer" which is an essential element of this fervor.

Actually, it's in prayer before its crucified Savior that the truly loving soul "becomes inflamed" with an ardent and generous desire to sacrifice itself and suffer with Him, like Him, to help Him save the world!

It's a great pity and much to my sorrow if there are consecrated souls who have cooled off rather than become inflamed, for whom the taste of my Heart has become dull rather than exciting, who have become lax in their prayers, both in quantity and quality. Now, when one speaks of "laxity" does one mean "cowardice"? And this cowardice, is it fervor?

Isn't it in fact rather a case of "tepidness" or even "coolness"? Oh, do you think about this? Isn't it "cruel thoughtlessness" towards my Heart, if not even offensive ingratitude, towards a Heart that burns with love so tirelessly?

Reflect well on this, and draw from my Heart that asks of you the "science of prayer, the love of prayer, the courage to pray."

If you wish to be "fervent souls," be above all "praying souls," souls for whom prayer in fact is a "contemplation" of love, a "conversation" of love, a "communion of love."

A contemplation of love: exchange and fusion of looks on fire for each other!

A conversation of love: exchange and fusion of hearts conferring and abandoning themselves to each other!

A communion of love: exchange and fusion of lives consuming and being consumed in each other!

O admirabile commercium![142]

---

[142] *O wondrous exchange!*

"SHOW ME CHARITY! ASK ME FOR CHARITY!"

January, February, 1941

Consecrated souls, my Heart urgently calls to you in the name of Charity that you help It in carrying out its great redemptive work.

For I have to tell you, "If you had all been more filled to overflowing with the Charity of my Heart, the world would not be where it is now! It would not be at this point of distress and sorrow that egoism and hatred have brought it to."

If the world of souls (much more so than that of the body) suffers from cold and hunger, it's because it lacked "fire setters" and "suppliers of bread!"

Because it lacked "distributors of my charities" in the name of my infinite Charity. Because I lacked helpers, spouses with "ardent" hearts, "generous" hearts, hearts that are truly "charitable."

And that is why my "appeal" begs so fervently for you to "renew the fervor of charity."

True Charity is to "take joy in giving joy!" Delight in giving Charity, which is the way of my all-giving Heart, should also be the way for my consecrated ones.

Oh, show Me charity by giving Me the joy of "showing Charity!"

Yes, if I have made Myself the poorest and most beseeching of "beggars," it's so that I might be the most compassionate and the most liberal of "benefactors."

Only my merciful tenderness, wanting infinitely to "gratify," enabled Me to bring down my Wealth to this state of imploring poverty in my Word-Host, and reduce Me to asking for charity from you, poor nothings who are and have nothing of yourselves and who, in fact, have your being only by the Charity of God!

My love needs you to repeat it: "to show charity" is the great joy of God's Heart, whose burning hearth of love can only be sustained by what It gives, satisfied by the gift that is the beatifying life of my Holy Trinity, just as it is also my work as Creator and Redeemer.

Therefore, "to give joy to God's Heart":

— 1) Allow Him to show charity!

— 2) Ask Him to show charity!

— 3) Help Him to show charity!

And you will taste the ineffable happiness that comes from being able, yourselves, to "show charity!"

1. "Allow Me to show charity!"

Offer Me a fully open soul so that I can show charity by pouring my graces into it to the point of overflowing.

For as desirous as I am to gratify, I cannot and do not want to do this by force. Doing violence is not divine conduct! Love is unacquainted with pressure!

Understand this well that one must "be open in order to receive" (that's an entire program):

"be open in order that you may receive,"

"give of yourself in order that you may be open,"

"suffer in order that you may be open."

"Be open" that you may "allow entrance," open yourself freely to Me in order that you may receive Me in yourselves, open yourselves freely, totally, continually in order that you may catch the fragrance of charity! And to that end, banish, remove everything that shuts Me out, that denies Me access to your soul, everything that can screen off or form a barrier between your heart and Mine, in short, egoism in all its forms.

Now, egoism which "takes everything for itself," which stands "at the center of everything," cannot be vanquished except by the divine "Me" being at the center of everything, and by "putting every me-myself back into this divine Me." And this "total putting-back of the self," this "absolute surrender," this lowering of every drawbridge of the soul, is nothing other than the "*Ecce* of the offering, the *Suscipe* of the offertory, the *Omnia Trado* of full oblation!"[143]

Self-offering therefore is the very necessary condition to "being open." "An offering heart is an open heart." Look at Mine and understand what It still teaches you: In order to be open and to "stay open," to what did It offer itself?"— to the piercing of the lance! Heart wounded with wounds that are always open and never heal so that, in one respect, bloody streams of its redemptive Charity might flow down continually upon the world; and in another, so that It might receive from souls of "co-redemptive" charity the balm of consolation from their offering, through the "inner transfixion" [piercing] of their hearts following the example of my Mother!

From this comes the need to "suffer" in order to truly "offer oneself," through an offering that "opens everything" by surrendering "everything." It's by showing Me the charity of your offering, by giving "joy" to my Heart, that you permit Me to show you My Charity.

"Let us then always show charity in mutual joy, through a continual exchange of love!"

2. "Ask Me for charity!"

This again shows Me charity, for this gives Me the joy of being able to more generously show charity and to further relieve the immense pity of my Love!

The more you ask of Me, the more I give and make happy, and "the more I make happy, the happier I become," because being what I am, I can only give Myself, and in giving Myself I expand, extend, I spread the Kingdom of my Father. The whole point of my "appeal" is to spread my great Redemptive Host over this poor world.

Yes, this "all Love" that I am can only give love, can only show charity through love, through love that is divine!

---

[143] *Behold, Receive, I give all.*

Also, dear consecrated souls, if you want to give Me pleasure, then broaden, heighten, intensify the desires of your own hearts so that the object of your asking be "nothing less than Me," nothing less than my Heart.

Be "beggars for God," beggars for the infinite, "beggars for my grand Life of love," for I can and I wish to give alms to you only and entirely for this.

In the plan of incomprehensible paternal Goodness, the human heart, created and limited as it is, can only be satisfied by my divine Heart!

And my divine Heart, as infinite as It is, can only be satisfied when It has filled Itself, laden Itself with the poor human heart! Understand and make these wonders known, and make a sincere examination of your own desires, your aspirations, in order to then make your requests.

Are you begging "only for God"? And do you do this with a great cry of burning desire that springs from the heart? To satisfy your soul, is there nothing human, nothing of this world in your searching? Does this soul truly have no other desire but for Me?

And do you beg for "all of God," with supplications that are ardent, tireless, insatiable? Are your longings for the infinite never limited by egoistic apathy?

Am I really not just the "Only" but the "All," the "Always," the "Always More" of your basic needs?

Answer Me by asking Me to "purify" and "enkindle" the flame of your desires, to make you true, fervent "men and women of prayer." Such alone are "truly helping collaborators" who truly show Me "charity" by asking Me to do the same for them!

May this spirit of most pure and fervent asking find expression in the habit of always having "recourse" to my Heart, put into practice by the *Fiat* of the Call, in various ways that accord with the soul's present needs.

"My Jesus, Charity!

— show me charity by your lights!

— show me charity by your power!

— show me charity by your gentleness!

— show me charity by your humility!

— show me charity by your patience!

— show me charity by your zeal!"

Charity "from You," Jesus! Charity "for You."

The alms of your grace for the praise of your Glory!

"Show us charity through charity for You!"

3. "Help Me to show charity!"

Most beloved souls, if you want to give Me still more joy, through charity help Me to show charity!

It's true that asking Me for charity already helps Me to show it, most especially, as I was saying to you, when the apostolic "show charity to us" accompanies the "show charity to me"!

But all the more would my Heart wish for a more direct help, the greater help of a "fervent assistant."

How so?

You help Me truly and directly to "show charity" by showing it "with Me," by showing charity as I show it, by showing it "from Me" to "all those who are Mine"! Weigh all these words well.

It means to have the soul full and overflowing with "my" divine and merciful Charity.

Search my Gospel — how often I tell you this — and understand that:

To truly live a "life of charity" is to have in your heart the "same" fervor, the "same" zeal that the Heart of Jesus has, to have the "same" burning love, source of all loves "like unto It."

Hoc sentite in vobis quod est in Christo Jesu.[144]

It's to love Me with such a love that "all that I love, all those that I love may be picked up and taken into this divine love." The Spouse and the true beloved do not have things that are "just mine," but in the affectionate *we* of oneness, they call them "ours."

It's to have "at heart" the Heart of Jesus Christ, in an intimacy of union that has become "one," in a communion so close that it is "consummation." *That they may become one.*[145]

This is the *Cor Unum, Cor Christi, Cor flagrans amore.*[146]

How well the "spirit" of Charity is summed up in this one word, "Heart."

February 11, 1941

Penitence! Penitence! Penitence!

Isn't it time to hear resonating in the depths of your souls this imploring call of my Virgin of Lourdes, my Virgin of France! Grasp its striking timeliness so that you do not suffer the harsh inevitability of these times like a captive, so that you do not content yourself with accepting this call in a spirit of submission, but that you may actually do so with a fervent heart. *If you do not repent you will all perish.*[147]

Hear it resounding from my Heart like an echo, "Charity! Charity! Charity!" *Repent, for the Kingdom of God is at hand,*[148] the kingdom of my merciful love.

If the penance that this moment of time imposes on men is due to a lack of charity on their part, to a virtually universal absence of true charity, on my part to the contrary it is the "mark of my Heart's infinite Charity" that does not want the death of the sinner, but rather that he convert and live.

---

[144] *Phil 2:5* — *Have this mind among yourselves, which was in Christ Jesus.*
[145] *Jn 17:23*
[146] *One Heart, Heart of Christ, Heart on fire with love.*
[147] *Lk 13:5*
[148] *Matt 3:2*

My Heart charges my Mother to remind the world of this, to remind it that "penitence" under whatever form of suffering it takes, is truly "only expiatory when filled with charity," only when it is reparation, "love's payback." Also, in repeating to men in the voice of Mary, *Bear fruit that befits repentance,*[149] I ardently implore them to make, initiate, to multiply fervent acts of charity. Such acts alone are "worthy" to touch the merciful Heart of my Father. In order to show the world the charity of his Forgiveness and through that the charity of his Peace, you have to oppose the ice-cold waves of egoism with a sea-wall on fire with charity. His Forgiveness awaits that from you.

Charity is "the heart in action," the heart "as total gift," as total effusion of love. It's a heart "in love with another heart," in love to the point of "breaking" so that, without holding anything back, it may pour itself out and merge with Him as one life! It's a mutual, unending, unifying intimacy "Heart to heart," intimacy of an everlasting exchange of oblation.

On the other hand, a heart without charity is a heart "without heart" for it is a heart "without life," without the exercise of love, and thus a "dead heart."

O you, my consecrated ones, reflect seriously, deeply on this exercise of the heart that is charity. If you are not on fire with an "active" charity, one that is productive of "acts of giving," it's because your heart lacks heart! And then all the qualifications in which you take such pride are nothing but vain pretenses, so hurtful to my Heart!

The form of this charity is two-fold: charity of good will, charity of good deeds.

Charity of Good Will

It consists of "seeing" and "wanting" the "good," to see it and want it everywhere.

"To see the good" is to see with my eyes, to see with the two

---

[149] *Ibid 8:3*

lenses of divine light that everywhere sees only the radiance of the Father, through his works, that only sees in souls the more or less formed image of the Son of his complacency!

Seeing the good everywhere therefore is to see Me, Jesus, the Incarnate Splendor of the supreme Good. And in order that you may see Me everywhere, think only of Me. For bear in mind, if you only hear in the direction you are listening, you will only see in the direction you are looking! And this is the direction the heart leans as well!

Blessed are the pure of heart for they shall see God.[150]

Not only will they see God face to face in eternity but they already see Him on earth through all his "transparencies." "Purity of heart" comes from looking in the right direction.

While egoism is blurred vision turned toward the self, focused on the self, charity is a most pure look turned toward Me with the *eyes of the heart enlightened.*[151]

Purity and charity therefore are closely tied.

This perfect "purity of charity," thus understood, practiced, carries with it the boundless expansion of charity!

Am I not "latent" in "every soul," without exception, longing to be brought forth so that the family of God might blossom? Wasn't it for "all" of them that I shed my Blood?

Isn't "each" of them some part of Myself, whom I cannot and will not do without?

And as "latent" in every soul, I am also held there "more or less in suspension," "exposed to contradiction" by my enemy and yours.

Right here is the meaning of the mercy, the indulgence, the good will that I ask you to have for each of your "neighbors."

Blessed are the merciful for they shall obtain mercy.[152]

In the school of my burning Heart, learn that the charity of good

---

[150] *Matt 5:8*
[151] *Eph 1:18*
[152] *Matt 5:7*

143

will is not simply "vision" no matter how pure and lucid it be, but rather a "will" that is most "holy," a will of great "strength."

But what is "will"?

True will is "love," "desire," and "act," all at the same time. To will is to love, to desire, to accomplish!

Willing "the good" for others is to love the "good" that is "seen" in them. Just as it is with Me. It means therefore to love Me in others, with a vital, active love that expresses itself in ardent "desire" to see Me in them, to make Me "increase," grow and blossom in them.

That's why there is no true good will without zeal, without this personal, urgent push for my glorification.

Jesus, the supreme Good, has to grow everywhere in everyone.

Wanting the good of others then is to want my Good in them. Oh, how my Heart wishes that this grand "vision" and this grand "willing" of good will would grow in the souls of my consecrated ones. There is often still so much egoistic meagerness in their charity that it makes Me sad, a narrowness there that, alas, is the source of so many actual lapses in charity, and that directly and so painfully affect the inner "quick" of my soul, of my Heart.

Consecrated souls, as "true assistants" who love Redemption, how then are you to help Me show Charity to the world as I have begged it of you?

By mercy, through charity, out of pity for my Heart that overflows with Charity for you, never forgetting to bring this "help" of love to Me, remembering that:

"The beloved is there to help the Spouse!"

Charity of Good Deeds

As I told you, this willing of the good is only genuine when it "turns into action."

That's why good will is only complete when it becomes "good deeds."

Willing the good, in fact, is "doing" the good in an effective way.

"Doing good" is the noble passion of charitable souls, just as it has been my Heart's passion.

He went about doing good.[153]

To work as I have done, for the good of everyone, at every moment, at one's own expense no matter what the cost, is to have grasped the "force" of this veritable love of charity that was asked of my disciples, and that now for the strongest reason is asked of you, my consecrated ones.

But what does it mean to "do good" and how does one go about "doing good"?

The one, true good of the soul, its genuine "well-being," can only be realized when Sovereign Love lives in it, animating, transforming, divinizing all who are in It. It's my Life, therefore, my Growth, my own good in the soul.

It follows from this that "to do good" to a soul is to dispose it, to arouse it, to draw it into the work of resembling Me, which calls for my growth in that soul, a work that the soul alone can do but that it cannot do alone, a work for which the soul needs help, the "help" of other souls.

Yes, such has been the loving plan of my Providence, making you understand that charity is not "supererogatory" but a genuine "duty," a duty "to collaborate with Me," a necessary help in bringing Me into souls.

The greatest "good deed" therefore that a charitable soul can do is to "dispose" souls that it is responsible for "to the good," to lead them to do good!

Consecrated souls, if you wish to be true "helping" spouses to Me, true co-redemptive spouses, shouldn't one be able to say of each of

---

[153] *Acts 10:38*

your lives, each of your days, "It was spent, it's being spent in doing good, in winning others over to the good! Its wake leads straight to my Heart, sweeps up to the Father, the supreme Good, infinite Goodness."

Above all, understand clearly love's total selflessness signified by this word "spend."

And in that regard, ask yourself what would be its opposite? Wouldn't it be to "stop at the self"? What a dangerous stumbling block for souls otherwise dedicated to the exercise of charity:

To believe one is doing good when drawing others to oneself (!), when one is more or less just looking after the self, keeping for self even the shadow of love's purity, the plunder of infinite Treasure.

Selfless charity alone is truly "pure," truly holy, truly strong, for it demands this total renunciation of all egoistic gain. Meditate on my redemptive charity and you will understand! Contemplate my "pierced" Heart from which purifying, divinizing waves flowed and continue to flow upon souls.

Imitate Me! Be sharing!

Make way for love! For its stirring advent!

And if you ask Me how then to "spend" oneself in bringing about the good, I will tell you: Genuine, effective charity, charity that truly works for good is a disposition that condescends, that supports, that gives, that takes delight, that sympathizes, that anticipates, that serves.

"Doing, pleasing, rendering service!"

The two sides of this gold coin that purchases souls after having paid the cost of one's self.

For if Christ has "infinite" value, the value of just one of his members is too great to be able to pay for it with base alloy!

One must have a "pure gold piece," of gold passed through fire, the fire of sacrifice.

Consecrated souls, contemplate, understand this:

When did the infinite Charity of My Heart give to Peter and my brothers its "ultimate service"?

When did I give my Father, my brothers, their "greatest pleasure"?

When did I give them their greatest "happiness"? — glorification in the one case, redemption in the other.

When, if not at the moment of *Consummatum est*; at the moment of the "Supreme Sacrifice"?

The rule is the same for simple acts of charity, whose several forms I have enumerated to you. In their redemptive effectiveness for souls, they are well worth "the price they extol." In the true sense of the word, they are good deeds in the measure that they are "sacrifices of love."

Yes, one must know how to "face evil" in order to "do good" to others. What evils did I Myself not endure in doing good to you?

Remember that "souls live off the death of the apostle," for charity and zeal are not separate matters.

If "sacrifice" — in the image of Christ's Cross — is one of the faces of charity's "coin of pure gold," learn from my Heart that the other face is "joy."

"The heart that turns itself into gift." The "heart" that wants to be my last word, who wants to be first in the matter of charity.

Yes, the heart is the soul of charity. It's the secret of its "gentleness" as well as its "strength." Of its gentleness expressing itself in the joy of giving! Of its strength finding expression in the "sacrifice" of giving!

Only in this measure does a gift made to one's neighbor become true charity, truly a "good deed," a "joy conferred."

Oh! Show Me charity, always!

CHAPTER SIX

THE VIRTUES OF
CO-REDEMPTIVE SOULS

HUMILITY

AND

THE FOUR ENDS OF SACRIFICE

[ADORATION, GRATITUDE, REPARATION, ENTREATY]

Pride is wreaking such havoc in the world at this time that I have a pressing need for its correction.

Listen, consecrated souls, all of you, "If you had been more humble, the world would not be the way it is!" "If you do not hasten to become more humble, the world will keep on running to its ruin."

So that you may be humble, that you may become humble, I begin by giving each of you this simple but infallible means:

"Forget yourself! Care about Me!"

And by way of love's examination, I add, "Are you concerned for Me? Am I your sole concern?"

Yes, I know, I do have a place in your concerns! But to what extent? Can you say that I have the "only place," to the exclusion of all petty, personal, egoistic human concerns?

In order to be able to answer Me, you should know that "to be concerned" means the mind is engrossed and the heart afflicted by the "sole interests" of the One you love, from which it follows that one's own selfish interests are simply forgotten.

So when the activity of your spirit is inspired, dominated by your own interests, or is simply mixed up with them, isn't it "your interests" to the contrary that hold sway and "Mine are forgotten?"

Can you truthfully say then that I am the "sovereign love" of your lives, seeing that I am not its "only interest"?

And that is what pride is at bottom: "love divested of its divine meaning," "love turned away from its celestial center."

Whereas humility, to the contrary, is "love centered on its sacred home," "love flowing back to its divine source"!

If you wish to grow in this virtue, as I ask it of you, develop the habit of viewing it under this aspect of love, for this is its true meaning.

"Love is given justice by a concern that preserves full place for it." And to appreciate that better, consider the humility of my Heart, consider the humility in my Heart!

How many of my Gospel pronouncements reveal this unique concern that everything be "brought back" to my Father, that only his interests be pursued, to the exclusion of my own. *I do not seek my own glory but the glory of the One who has sent me.*[154] Wasn't this the same as saying: "Forget about Me, care about Him"?

"Deep, heartfelt concern solely for the Father's interests" — this truly expresses genuine humility in its most telling form! Its contrast with pride allows you to grasp what humility truly is!

A genuine spirit of humility therefore is a "spirit of justice." "To submit the justice of love to Truth, Truth that identifies itself with Charity!" The infinite Charity of Divine Paternity.

Truth therefore which holds that "Divine Love alone is All" and

---

[154] *Jn 8:50*

because of its infinity, "is entitled to all," from which it follows that "anything that is not this Love is nothing and to this nothing nothing is entitled."

The genuine spirit of "Justice" and therefore of humility lies in the practical recognition of this. "All to All! Nothing to nothing!"

And ideally shouldn't each of your life's breath be able to say to Me, in truth:

"All from You! All to You! All for You, O my Wholly Beloved!

"Nothing from me, nothing to me, nothing for me whom am but nothingness!"

An ideal that calls for: Perfect rectitude in outlook,

                                     Complete purity of heart,

                                     Absolute faithfulness of will!

A three-fold condition whose realization is constantly endangered and hampered. I know this, by the spirit of "duplicity" of the father of pride. That's why, in the trials of your life, "mastering the spirit of humility or of justice takes gradual, never-ending effort."

One is not truly able to attain to this giving "all" to "all" which is what Love is, to allow Him to have "full place," except by giving "less and less to nothing," the egoistic *me*, by giving smaller and smaller place to this *me* until it is entirely banished.

A program so well expressed by my Precursor: *"He must increase and I must decrease."*[155]

Here then is the great, single-minded concern of love, and of true humility and true justice!

Have you never wondered what effect each of your acts has: whether it increases love and diminishes egoism, or instead increases egoism and diminishes love? Any one of your acts could tip the balance either way.

In order to enter more deeply into this love-doctrine about humility,

---

[155] *Jn 3:30*

consider how the spirit of humility forms the very foundation for the great sentiments of love that the four "ends of sacrifice" inspire:

That of the *adoring* Host, of the *grateful* Host, of the *reparative* Host, of the *entreating* Host, the four sublime functions that my Mercy asks you to be associated with as "wholly consecrated hosts."

Recall to mind my "appeal."

Blessed are they who hunger and thirst for righteousness.[156] Have you never thought that this was the proper, most wondrous beatitude of hearts who are truly "humble," hearts that are never "satisfied" except by "giving all to All"! For recognizing with joy that their very being is "received," that they are nothing in themselves, nothing for themselves, they experience an imperious, insatiable need that, "by them, in them," everything be freely given to infinite All-Being from Whom they issued and towards Whom they strive.

The very "soul" of the sentiment and act of **Adoration** is this need for full restitution, this primordial act of justice which is the fitting mindset of the creature.

Mindset of prostration where the "*nothing* takes pleasure in negating itself in order that the All may be exalted," negating itself in the sense of only exercising its feeble life, a life freely received, in order that, of its own free will, it may lose it in homages of praise "offered" to the Life of the *One Who is,*[157] and who in "being" can only be "All" and only be "All Love"!

Tibi soli! Omnis honor et Gloria![158]

Such are *they who adore in spirit and in truth,*[159] who seek the Father! Souls who "hunger and thirst" to disappear so that the infinite Sovereignty of Love might appear more radiant!

"The more you disappear in Me, the more I Myself will appear in you and through you!"

---

[156] *Matt 5:6*

[157] *Exod 3:14*

[158] *Tim 1:17 — To Thee alone, all honor and glory!*

[159] *Jn 4:24*

You recognize here the spirit of my "appeal":

"The true heart of the beloved is the victim of the Spouse."

She has to "lose herself" in Him so as to let herself be taken in.

This "losing" into Love means free and total surrender.

This "being taken" by Love and for Love is the entire essence of that adoration which is defined as:

Life delivered to God, life lost in God, life that breathes for God!

How agreeable to my Father are these adoring souls whose whole life of the heart, by losing themselves, consists in spontaneously, endlessly breathing songs of praise, of felicitation and love's mutual rejoicing:

Tu solus Sanctus, Tu solus Dominus, Tu solus Altissimus.[160]

And isn't this the purest, the fullest and most expressive form that true humility of love can take, a humility which itself is love's justice?

Isn't this the life of the Immaculate Host, *Hostia laudis*[161] in its entirety, a life that offers itself perpetually in *Sacrificium laudis*[162] to the glory of the Holy Trinity?

Consecrated souls, shouldn't your entire life be in close "communion" with this perpetual adoration of My Eucharistic Host, by a generous spirit of sacrifice? A sacrifice of all egoism in a holocaust giving rise to purer and purer waves of love's perfect praise!

Recall what my Church has you sing and pray: *Victimae Paschali laudes immolent.*[163] Yes, only by "immolation" can praise be raised on earth that is truly pure of all human alloys, and alone is thus in accord with the "full restitution" called for by the infinite Justice of divine, most Holy Charity.

Another form that "justice of the heart" takes, and therefore of

---

[160] *Gloria of the Mass —You alone are holy, You alone are Lord, You alone are the Most High.*

[161] *Ps 115:17 — I will offer thee the sacrifice of thanksgiving.*

[162] *Ps 50(49):23 — He who brings thanksgiving as his sacrifice honors me.*

[163] *Gregorian Chant — To the Paschal Victim offer sacrifice and praise.*

"humility," is **gratitude**. This is the second great "end of Eucharistic Sacrifice."

In fact, isn't gratitude, like adoration, basically a most "pure, loving concern to restore everything to its Supreme Owner?

A "grateful" heart, like an "adoring" heart, is a heart that surrenders itself to Love, that "gives up everything" without reservation or expectation of anything in return! (Consider the powerful meaning this "surrendering" has for prayer.)

For if every created heart is pure nothingness in itself, this "living nothing" nonetheless is a "bundle of goods," a "collection of blessings."

That is why adoring praises from this living "nothing" flow up to the ineffable grandeur of the plenitude of Being, flowering naturally in a loving heart under the "blessed actions of grace," flowing back from this "bundle of goods" to the ineffable mercies of the beneficent plenitude of its Creator!

In this regard, meditate on the *Magnificat* of Mary, a veritable outburst of humility from her Heart dazzled by the vision of all the "goods" descending to Her from the Heart of God; *respexit humilitatem.*[164] Inflamed by "justice," her soul "sought satisfaction" in returning everything to this Supreme Source in heartfelt waves of benediction.

"Cultivate gratitude": this loving "habit" of always "thanking God" by everything, for everything, is a most certain way to "cultivate humility"! "Nothing to nothing, all to All!"

And this form of humility in particular also has the great benefit of "stimulating generosity."

Isn't the *Quid retribuam*[165] which extends the *Magnificat*, the most expressive "cry of the heart"? Happy tormenting thorn! "What shall I render? What shall I render to the Lord for all the good things I have received from Him?"

---

[164] *From the Magnificat — He hath regarded the humility of his handmaid.*
[165] *Ps 115:12 — What shall I render to the Lord for all his bounty to me?*

Contemplate this *Quid retribuam* in the works of my Heart as Well-Beloved Son of the Father!

In my Life in the glorious Trinity as uncreated Word, my Holy Spirit is the ineffable, substantial expression of this sublime "return of Love" to the Father, of this marvelous "Love for Love," of the divine Family.

And in my Life as Incarnate Word, Redeemer of the world, "abiding with it until the end of the ages," my divine Eucharistic Host — the on-going Life of Calvary's Victim — is the sublime and merciful expression of this "return of Love," its perfect "actualization"!

Co-redemptive souls, what should the response of your lives be therefore to the *quid retribuam* of your hearts, what if not the *hostia pro Hostia* that my "appeal" asks of you?

"For your sake I made Myself Host." "Be wholly consecrated hosts for Me."

You know this is the only way to "render" love for love, to thus "satisfy the appetite of justice"!

But think about this, that in order for the "reign of justice" to triumph in the world and draw redeeming Mercy down upon it, this reign has to begin by triumphing over you who, in your capacity as "partners of Redemption" don't forget, are "charged with responsibility for the salvation of the world."

May this thought serve to stimulate you ever more strongly and urgently to practice this humility in justice and grateful, magnanimous love.

Yes, for the time is "urgent," truly!

Desolation is spreading over the world!

May your lives as true "co-redemptive spouses" receive from my Father, more abundantly now than ever, an effusion of my Consoling Spirit's graces. You cannot give my Heart any sweeter consolation!

If adoration and thanksgiving are equally "matters of justice" and therefore of humility, how much more is this so of **Reparation**, the third great end of the Host's Sacrifice. For "restitution" is still an issue, not only restitution for the goods freely "received," but for the goods "unjustly stolen"!

If the poor human heart is a nothingness compounded with blessings, this "composite" is also a sinner "laden with debts" to its Benefactor whom it has thanklessly offended. It is "just" therefore that it "restore" the glory that it has in some sense stripped from the Infinite Goodness of its "Father."

"A matter of the heart no less than one of justice!" You know as much! A matter of "filial piety," of filial love, filial honor!

Together let us look at the loving acts of humility that this reparation consists of in the fullest meaning of the word: honest confession, sincere contrition, confident recourse to Mercy, a generous spirit of penance.

"Honest confession of one's unworthiness, of one's culpability." Faced with the infinite Holiness of God as Father and Judge, in light of the sovereign rights of his Love, know your faults, your offenses, "accuse yourself" of them and don't make "excuses" for them, uncover them and do not conceal or disguise them, acknowledge their malice!

Are these not the "failings of love," "love's shortcomings," love's neglect, and as such are they not an "affront" to Infinite Goodness?

Truly declare yourself a "sinner!"

Confiteor! Mea culpa, mea maxima culpa, quia peccavi nimis.[166]

"I have greatly sinned!" Yes, who of you cannot say that?

See how my spouse the Church, during the celebration of the Sacrifice of the Mass, ceaselessly wants to bring you back to this conviction: *Nobis quoque peccatoribus.*[167]

Learn to recognize one's own guilt in the faults of others! Consecrated souls, you understand, don't you, that each of you is "charged

---

[166] *I confess that I have sinned exceedingly, through my fault, through my most grievous fault.*

[167] *To us sinners as well.*

with responsibility" for a world of souls, for the souls of the whole world! And you recognize my "appeal."

"If you had all been better spouses, more abandoned, the world would not be the way it is!"

"The way it is": this dreadful state of desolation of all kinds! — As never before the time has come to reflect deeply on this "responsibility for solidarity"!

Not a single sin in thought, word, deed, or of "omission" (think especially here about these omissions), no matter how isolated, but that it contributes to the sum of sins in the world: a burden borne by the Lamb of God out of mercy!

Does this not profoundly humble you?

A humbling of the mind, yes, but one that must entail a humbling of the heart before "contrition" can arise, the second act of humility in reparation.

"Genuine grief of the heart for having sinned against Love." Against the Crucifix, against the Heart of the Crucifix! The inmost crushing of the soul "filled" with the deepest sorrow, with the keenest "distress" for an ingratitude that has thus so gravely "offended, wounded, transgressed" the infinitely holy and "sensitive" Heart of its God, its Father, its Spouse!

Consecrated souls, remember my loving revelation to my spouse, Margaret Mary: "What affects me the most is. . . ." Isn't there something that plunges you into interior desolation of the most bitter, most moving kind? Your least acts of negligence, the coolness of your love, the "real iniquities" that sadden my Heart the most, are these not your doing, you who are so extraordinarily privileged by Divine Charity?

Allow yourselves then to be filled with extreme grief, with this sorrow of sorrows for having pained Love!

How can one be "loved so tenderly" and then be so cool, so feeble in loving back!

Can there be anything more "humiliating"?! This sorrow alone deserves to sadden and grieve your hearts!

A sorrow that before long translates into "burning regrets of love," both affective and effective, into fervent acts of contrition that truly breaks the heart, as symbolized by Magdalene's brokenness.

Sincere regret expressing itself by the third act of humility in reparation:

"Humble, confident recourse to my Mercy" before the great "pity" of the Infinite Charity of God, Father and Savior! Before the redemptive Host! Before the Blood flowing from my Heart!

Asking for pardon in the name of the infinite merits of my Blood! Blood poured out "for this"! "For the remission of sins." *This is my Blood, poured out for the remission of sins!*[168]

If each soul would say to itself, "Truly, I am the reason Christ had to shed his Blood, because of my offenses and disregard for the glory of his boundless Goodness."

From this would arise profound feelings of contrition. . . .

The soul should also say to itself, "It was all because of me, to atone for my offenses, to forgive me for them, in order that I may be saved."

From this would arise feelings of loving, grateful trust.

Also this "glorifies my Blood by making use of It"! To make use of It by turning to its purifying power, by becoming reconciled, by offering It to the Father! The more you make use of my Blood, the more will you glorify It! The use of love to be made for the souls of the whole world! *"We offer you the Chalice of salvation for our salvation and that of the whole world."*[169]

Reflect for a moment that not to use my Blood in a way is to scorn It, for by so doing one keeps It from bearing all its living fruits!

My spouses, as true helpers of Redemption, be distributors then of my Saving Blood, making use of It for all souls so that, like Mary, you may thus become its "glorifiers," by meditating on the martyred Heart of the Mother of the Savior and of all who are saved!

---

[168] *Matt 26:28*

[169] *Offertory of the Mass.*

Would that humility, trust and zeal might thus be inseparably joined by a like principle of love.

Many sins are forgiven her because she has loved much.[170] — Love much, with a love drawn from its Source, and you will obtain abundant pardon for souls! *No, I do not wish the death of the poor sinful world but rather that it be converted and live.*[171] My Will as Savior is a will for "life," a Will of mercy; but whose power to save is measured by the soul's will to "conversion."

Steadfast willing in a generous "spirit of penitence," as apostolic as it is personal (the fourth act of reparation): *Unless you repent you will all perish.*[172] Here, in this spirit of merciful penitence, we are faced on the one side with the very words of Truth and Sanctity, and on the other with the spotless Lamb who *takes away the sins of the world.*[173]

Faced moreover with a world in peril, with a multitude of souls in distress. Understand the urgency of penitence in a co-redemptive spirit!

Examine yourself! Are you penitent?

For that, two things are necessary:

Know how to accept every suffering with the "appetite" of love of a heart inflamed with justice, with a kind of complacency before suffering and humiliation. For humiliation is a "favor of choice" and should be met with grateful satisfaction as coming from the Goodness of the Father who wants so to love you that He lets you drink some of the drops of that same chalice of opprobrium He gave Me to drink as Redeemer of souls.

Bonum mihi quia humiliasti me.[174]

As co-redeemers, don't you have to drink with Me *the chalice my Father has given Me?*[175]

---

[170] *Lk 7:47*
[171] *Ezek 18:23*
[172] *Lk 13:5*
[173] *Jn 1:29*
[174] *Ps 118:71 — It is good for me that Thou hast humbled me.*

These acts of receptivity are already reparative for they draw others to every generous soul. If you have a little of the flame in your heart, you will understand!

In a spirit of penitence, know how to courageously seek out and seize with avidity all occasions of sacrifice and renunciation, know how to engender these occasions as my Spirit of Love inspires and moves you. Valiantly enlist in the army of Love's volunteers.

Humility moreover, a fervent, loving humility, lies at the root of the fourth great "end of Sacrifice," namely, **Entreaty**.

Isn't it so that entreaty, in effect, arises from the great and "loving concern" of human poverty to glorify divine Opulence, imploring Opulence that poverty be enabled to accomplish the work Opulence has mercifully conferred upon it!

For if every human heart is pure "nothingness," a "living nothingness composed of blessings," and if this nothingness is "burdened with debts" borne of ingratitude, ought it not implore pardon without ceasing?!

Don't forget that this nothingness is also charged with divine affairs, that it has received a mission from God the Father, and that, as such, it must "implore without ceasing for the gifts needed" to fulfill its mandate.

Indeed, the soul that is truly humble of heart understands in one respect that its nothingness is not absolutely "nothing," cannot be absolutely "nothing in and of itself," that the All who is its Creator-Love is absolutely "all," has absolutely "all," can do absolutely "all," such that the soul in another respect understands these two things:

First, that the infinite All wants to be "served by this nothing," even wants to "have need of this nothing," and in some way cannot "do without this nothing" in the consummation of its redemptive work!

Oh, the marvel of divine condescension! As Savior, I say in truth to each of you: "Without you, poor little nothings, I, the infinite All,

---

[175] cf. *Matt 20:22f; Jn 18:11*

159

can do nothing for you, achieve nothing in you, consummate nothing. Without you, I can do nothing through you for your brothers who are my brothers!"

Second, the soul also understands that the "nothing" can only serve the All by making use of the "All," by drawing from the All what it needs to serve It, by imploring from the All the grace needed that its glory may be glorified! For each of you can be heard to echo my Gospel words: "*Without Me*, All-Powerful Love, *you*, poor little nothings, *can do nothing for Me.*"[176]

And the consoling counterpart: "With Me, All-Powerful Love, you, poor little nothing, you can do for Me everything that I ask of you!"

This two-fold conviction is the soul of the prayer of supplication, which soul itself is animated by a love that ardently thirsts for justice, caring only for the glory of the All!

"All for All! All by All! All to All!"

And what a pleasing tribute this entreaty is to my Father. Tribute to my sovereign avidity no less than my sovereign liberality!

Consecrated souls, don't forget that this "entreaty" is essential to the "co-redemptive" office. Hadn't your Redeemer on earth been the great "implorer" of the Father, the merciful Mediator and Intercessor, and does He not perpetuate this incessant intercession in his Host? *Semper vivens ad interrpellandum.*[177]

Unite yourselves with his prayer, commune with his prayer, and enrich his prayer by the example of the great woman of prayer and supplication, the Mother of the Savior and of all who are saved!

Oremus! Imploremus! in unum! It is by this incessant prayer of love that you will serve as ever larger portals to the effusion of my redemptive graces, prayer permeated and made fruitful by sacrifice, prayer permeating and enriching all that you do. It is by this prayer

---

[176] *Jn* 15:5

[177] *Heb* 7:25 — *. . . he always lives to make intercession for them.*

that you will raise the "rampart" of Love without end, that you will feed the fire of its furnace, as victims entirely offered to the grand interests of Redemption!

For right there lies the "great Concern," the divine Concern, the "one Concern" you have been charged with and are responsible for as co-helpers of Redemption!

The more you pray, then, the more will you be "helpers," more loving therefore and of greater consolation.

O my spouses, be humble of heart that you may thereby glorify my Heart!

TRUST

1937

Trust, confidence founded wholly on the infallible, immutable fidelity of my predilection to mercy. Humility formed from an inner, experienced conviction of one's own unreliability and the sincere belief in one's own unworthiness. These are the two sentiments that, blended together and supporting each other, make for genuine, so glorious a trust in my Heart.

To be sure, genuine trust is not some sweet sentiment of the heart where the soul seeks Love's protective covering, selfishly hiding in a corner so disgracefully in these times of turmoil for Love.

No, first and foremost trust is the courage of a will totally surrendered, perpetually, repeatedly giving itself through affirmations of faithfulness, intensifying and increasing them all the more when times are trying.

Genuine trust then is the courage of faithfulness in the face of every hardship, the faithfulness of a beloved who trusts the faithfulness of her Spouse; a firm steady faithfulness responding to infallible Faithfulness.

Just as true love thrives on reciprocity, on proofs of love, so true trust cannot survive without signs that one's trust is being reciprocated.

Could I, your God and Savior, give you any greater sign of trust than to choose you as my co-redemptive partners?

And, in return, what better token of trust ought I to expect from you if not your belief in my trust, in my great confidence in you, with a humble, courageous, grateful belief.

Belief in the gifts no less than in the claims that the grace of your vocation entails.

The more one trusts in my Heart, the more one is tied to It. Each new token of trust is a new and most sweet bond of intimacy. Let us multiply them between us at every instant. This is the ardent desire of my Heart that thirsts so mercifully for love and union.

Real trust is both utmost abandonment and at the same time the most imploring, most assured supplication.

Do you understand the extent to which this abandonment entails courageous detachment of self in order to give one's self over entirely, gently, peacefully to the Will of Infinite Goodness?

Oh, how I love souls who love Me enough to trust in my Love with unshakable conviction, who see Divine Will and Infinite Divine Goodness as one and the same, who spontaneously know how to recognize divine allowances in the way they view events and things.

Such is the deep, personal, growing conviction of genuine trust.

And what does this imploring supplication consist of? How is it exercised if not by ardent entreaties for the triumph of my great redemptive interests. Entreaties that must be mixed with a degree of sacrifice in union with the Host.

Right here then is the true confidence that takes hold of my Heart, for before everything it knows how to take my great, loving interests to heart.

Yet another infallible way to take hold of my Heart is to pass your trust through the Heart of Mary. For then how can I not be irresistibly moved?

And remember that if Mary is the sure wellspring of your trust, she must also then be for you the ideal model of trust most unshakeable.

With what smiling delicacy this Mother of yours and Mine accompanies each one of your acts, with this loving, deep, genuine joy that comes from gentle, peaceful serenity of absolute security in the paternal Goodness of Love.

May your smile also be a veil that conceals your sufferings, a smile you show Me more and more.

May each of you, from the depths of your heart, hear Me say to you: "Entrust to Me what I entrust you with," (the work, the mission, the souls I have made you responsible for). I Myself will take responsibility for these things in the measure that you charge Me with them. Then this will fill Me with confidence.

And may each of you also, from the depths of your heart, say to Me again and again, "I am too certain of Your love to ever doubt Your help."

Here then is the code of genuine trust:

Trust: belief, assurance, security.

Trust: confiding, pouring out, abandonment.

Trust: help, support, filling-in.

Trust: peace, gentleness, serenity.

Trust filled with fidelity and delicacy that calls for: humility, courage, self-sacrifice, and love most of all, all ceaselessly strengthening the bonds of union.

GRATITUDE

1937

How sweet gratitude is to my Heart!

Gushing, spurting up spontaneously from a tender, delicate, vibrant heart, rising to its home, fervent in surrender, in restitution, from a soul wholly given up to its divine Attractor. Jealous defender solicitous for nothing of its own; the imperious need of a consecrated life to return all to its sacred Center.

This is true gratitude, not merely a sentiment of the heart, but true works of mercy expressed by a return of love, returning the gift that comes from a Love one has acknowledged and accepted, for to be grateful is first of all to acknowledge Love's ever thoughtful overtures and gifts. Then having acknowledged these gifts, one thus receives them, welcomes them, and eagerly, generously, warmly opens the soul to them.

My Eucharistic Life, which prolongs my redemptive, evangelical Life, in essence is the perfect, continual life in action of the Father's mercy under the form and circumstance of the Host, which is to say, in and through sacrifice, plenary sacrifice to the point of holocaust.

Enter deeply into my Heart so that you may understand the profound, two-fold meaning of this mystery, that the best graces come from suffering, that to render graces one more than anything has to suffer.

Does your heart understand this?

If only you would remember that the greatest mark of love and the best way to return love is to give one's blood, to give one's life. And that the more my Holy Will crucifies the fuller It is of the Father's love. The cross therefore is at once the most precious matter of mercy and the most perfect means of mercy.

And too, the more that suffering wells up in a loving soul, the more it should lift up, high and pure, its canticle of love's return.

Contemplate the Heart of Mary in her desolation. Do you not hear resonating through her sufferings the ever-mounting canticle of her heroic *Magnificat*?

How could it have been otherwise? Could her Heart ever beat in any other rhythm but Mine? Now, wasn't this rhythm in perfect tune with the love in my Passion, and thereby with the most perfect action of grace?

Here is the simple secret how to tune your hearts to acknowledge love as She did: See everything as waves of grace gushing forth from God the Father's Heart.

Yes, true gratitude basically is absolute trust in the paternal Goodness, in all his Bounties. Think much about this word "all."

Send everything back in rebounds of praise to this divine Heart.

Praise most pure, most humble, most ardent is the natural expression of gratitude.

It is the ebb and flow of love's union, of blessings in exchange. Blessings of merciful graces flowing from my Heart to yours, blessings of praise flowing back from your hearts to Mine.

O consecrated souls, if you want to console my Heart, sing to Me each of you with your whole lives in tune with the action of grace.

As with Mary, may your *Fiat* always be filled with *Magnificat*. This is the choicest gift, or still better, the summit of love in return.

But understand what this "always be filled" means — not merely to thank Me for the things of the past, but also for those of the future and the present as well.

Thank me for all that is past, for the countless considerations and liberalities of love that have formed the fabric of your lives.

Wouldn't each of you have an endless litany of thank-you's to offer up?

Though this gratitude is quite easy and fairly common, because of egoistic preoccupation with self, because of pride, the perfection of gratitude is still very rare.

Now, there is no perfection of gratitude without humility, this virtue dearest to my Heart.

Thank Me for all that is future, with feelings of steadfast, unconditional trust and the assurance that all will come from Love just as it has in the past, and that what comes from Love can only be Love.

Gratitude for the future is already less easy and less common. And for that reason is a delicacy that ravishes my Heart. My thanks to those souls for whom this is a supernatural habit.

Thank Me for the present, with the animated spontaneity that comes from a spirit of faith, with a hearty, eager *Fiat* to my Good Pleasure in this present hour, in the "now," thanking Me all the more that this present hour is more crucifying and therefore occasion for spreading more love.

Now, thanking Me for the present is the most difficult and the rarest of all. And for that very reason, this is where you find true gratitude.

Acts of thanksgiving, spontaneous reactions of a soul truly loving, consecrated, wholly centered on Me, acts of a "co-redemptive spouse" just as my "appeal" asks it of you.

A truly loving soul has such great love for my Will, knows how to thank with *enlightened eyes of the heart,*[178] has such love for my Wishes that at all times it makes as its own my words in the Gospel, *Father, I thank Thee that Thou hast heard me. I know that Thou hearest me always.*[179]

Yes, such a soul knows this and always feels itself heard by Infinite Goodness. It sings its *Magnificat* in the peace and joy of love.

Your gratitude in three dimensions of time: do not forget to have it pass through Mary's Heart that it may reach Me and through Me then attain to the Father.

Also, in a spirit of apostolic generosity, think of expressing gratitude on behalf of others. For alas, there are so many who never do.

MERCY

1940

For the Contentment of my Love as well as your own, help Me to show mercy, help the world to obtain mercy.

Blessed are the merciful for they shall obtain mercy.[180] Yes, I never grow weary of asking you for help, for love's help in all its forms.

---

[178] *Eph 1:18*

[179] *Jn 11:41, 42*

[180] *Matt 5:7*

You who are consecrated, are you not, ought you not be "helpers" by your very consecration, actively loving, actively helping your Spouse?

Do not grow weary of hearing the imploring entreaties of my Heart. Be grateful for them for they contain so much love. All are revelations of mercy no less than of justice.

There are a number who understand this and they console my Heart. But how they grieve Me whose hearts are too small to understand the all-loving intent of my demands. They seem to be amazed that I complain about them.

What an abyss there is between their complaints and my Complaint! Complaint of Infinite Charity on the one hand, complaints of petty egoism on the other.

They complain of small discomforts, little privations, petty annoyances and difficulties.

I complain only of not being able to spread widely enough my outpourings of Mercy, of being hobbled in realizing my desire to save by the lack of cooperation.

Haven't I already told you that my Heart only begs for love because it is bursting with love. Don't forget the commentaries I've already given you on the great complaint of love that my "appeal" represents. Out of divine condescension I remind you of it today.

Grounds for trust. Spur to generosity.

Never separate these two meanings of my great Call. There cannot be genuine trust without generosity no more than there can be genuine generosity without trust.

Absent the union of these in life's experience, the soul loses heart, and can a disheartened soul be helpful, can it be "co-redemptive"?

Examine yourselves in this light: Is there enough generosity in your trust? Is there enough trust in your generosity? For you to be able to draw with confidence from the Mercy of my Heart, don't I have to be able to draw generously from your hearts by the generous offering that you make to Me?

In order that your souls may have the confidence to be open to receiving my merciful graces and to serve Me as "outlets" for spreading these graces over the world, don't you need to be completely open to my divine hold on you, to my most holy Wishes?

My heart is all swollen with treasures of mercy obtained for you from the Father of Mercies, but I need you in order that these treasures may be poured out and my Heart relieved.

I need your generous, confident offerings. I need this increasing alliance of trust and generosity on your part, an alliance lived out in the contentment and agonizing of love.

Without generosity there is no real agony in love.

Without trust, there is no real contentment in love.

And if I won Mercy for you from my Father at the price of all my Blood, shouldn't you as partners pay the same price of blood in order to win outpourings of this divine Mercy that it might now be spread over the world.

All this to convince you that your trust will only be efficacious in the measure that you have the courage of love to mix it with the blood drops of generosity, in total, particularized sacrifice of self. And in that very measure you will be helping Me spread mercy.

In the loving wisdom of my plans for all my brothers on earth, the hour of Justice always announces the hour of mercy close at hand; the heaviness in my arm as Dispenser of Justice always signals the pressing need to pour out my Heart as Savior. The function of my justice is to "clear the way" for mercy. Justice is its herald.

The first step, the primary, indispensable condition for obtaining mercy is to recognize the rights of my justice by wholeheartedly accepting its purifying rigors, going to confession with humility and contrition for one's culpability and blame.

The second step, the second condition is this generous and confident entreaty that I have already spoken of, an entreaty that, if it is to be efficacious, must be accompanied by effective, that is, crucifying reparations. Think of the Host. It entreats by mending, just as it loves by blessing. Four acts and ends of love that are inseparably grounded in Consecrated life to the glory of infinite Charity.

There is another condition to this mission of merciful collaboration, this mission as co-redeemer, one that you are well acquainted with, but do you satisfy it?

Understand in a real way that in order to be able to help Me, it is absolutely necessary that you do as I do. Now, can you say in all truth that you forgive as I forgive, excuse as I excuse? *Father, forgive them!*[181] Can you say that you are all heart for the destitute, as I was, for isn't that what it means to be merciful? Are you all kindness and indulgence as I was, always inclined to pardon? Are you all commiseration and clemency, in thought, word and deed?

To the contrary, aren't you often too severe in your judgments? Think about this, that every harsh judgment about your neighbor is aimed at Me, is a thorn in my Heart, and hinders the outpouring of my mercy on the world.

Hasten to become more indulgent and merciful if you want my justice to give way to my pardon. Yes, in order to open the gates to my mercy, I need the destitute and the merciful, the upright poor, not the proud and rebellious but the humble, the contrite, the repentant, the trusting; those who are truly merciful at heart, compassionate, charitable, in and through whom I can spread the bright treasures of kindness and pity my Heart is filled with, who serve Me as spillways, channels, access points and outlets.

Blessed are the merciful, for having obtained mercy for themselves and their brothers, they shall be worthy *to sing of the Lord's mercies for all eternity.*[182]

GENTLENESS

1937

In accord with the example and lesson of my gentle and humble heart, understand that your love must join gentleness to fervor.

---

[181] *Lk 23:34*
[182] *Ps 138:2*

For if the fervor of hatred is all violence, harshness, brutality, the fervor of love is all gentleness, suavity, charity.

My great thirst for fervor in love is also a great thirst for gentleness.

Yes, I search for, beg for souls that are truly gentle. Only souls such as these are a consolation to Me.

Don't you want to oppose a fervent crusade of loving gentleness to the relentless league of violent hatred?

May your hearts seek to practice this gentleness towards everyone.

Gentleness towards all the things that my Will calls for and that encompass you without let-up in a web of infinite tenderness.

Be such souls then who are gentle to all and to everything, to the duties of one's state, to the rule, to the suffering, to the difficulty, the annoyances, the surprises.

Gentleness towards all who are neighbor to you. Am I not identified with them, and how closely is this not so?

Be gentle at every moment and in every way, in thought, word, conduct, in every respect.

The more gentle a soul becomes, the softer it is, the closer that soul is to my Heart, and the more its own heart deepens to receive the divinizing invasions of my grace.

Yes, gentleness is a most sure indication of my divine Presence, drawing It into the soul so that my Life of love in it may increase.

Listen to this Heart ever ready to have you understand that which gushes forth from its depths.

What is purity of heart if not the absence of all duplicity, of every shadow? What is gentleness of heart if not absence of all stiffness, of all resistance?

With both gentleness and purity then, equally, Love takes full possession and becomes sovereign master of the soul, through the soul's total, absolute, unstinting abandonment and gift of self.

Gentleness and purity therefore are indissolubly, indispensably linked by the bond of love and mutually serve each other as reflection and proof.

Perfect gentleness cannot be without perfect purity; perfect purity cannot be without perfect gentleness.

1939

O consecrated souls, be gentle even to the point of suffering.

The more the cross is kissed with gentleness, the more it eases my own pain. And isn't it the dream of your impassioned hearts to console Me?

Then be gentle to Me, soothing, consoling, more and more.

1940

As the kingdom of brutal force extends its fiery empire throughout the world, my Heart longs to see its Kingdom of gentleness extend itself in your hearts. Are these hearts not kingdoms of grace, and my grace, is it not all gentleness of infinite Charity?

Blessed are the meek for they shall possess the earth.[183]

A gentle heart, following the example of Mine, is a heart that is both "possessed" and "possessing."

Yes, wholly in God's possession, for everything belongs to Him.

In effect, such a heart is all acquiescence, all yes, and all thanks for love, all gift and self-abandonment to the paternal Sovereignty who opens his divine Heart in return.

There is nothing resistant in such a heart, nothing hard that prevents outpouring and mutual possession.

And the more it is "sweetly acquiescent" in this way, the more its sacrifice, united to that of the Host, rises to heaven as a fragrant odor, *in odorem suavitatis.*[184]

---

[183] *Matt 5:4*

[184] *Eph 5:2 — in an odor of sweetness (Douay Rheims).*

From which comes its irresistible, conquering power, both over my Heart and over the hearts of other men, for it breathes forth nothing but charity.

O my consecrated ones, be gentle to Love, be gentle to the infinite gentleness of the Father's Goodness that is in evidence everywhere if you know how to see It.

Believe in It, be in communion with It, in all that It asks and allows. For it is by this spiritual communion that your soul becomes ready to taste the transforming gentleness of Eucharistic Communion. Yes, only then and to that extent will you be able to taste and see how gentle the Lord is. *Gustate et videte.*[185]

Be gentle and you will be gentle to Me, and you will win my Heart.

Be gentle with the gentleness of my Love, and you will win many souls to my Heart.

PEACE

The entire, pathetic world longs for peace but few understand what peace really means. Consecrated souls, come and learn from my Heart what it means.

I want so much for this peace, this seal of the Divine, to reign in you and radiate from you.

Isn't that the great wish of my Gospel?

The soul's inner peace is a presence responding to an absence. Understand this well: my loving, rich, gratifying Presence responding to this absence of you in yourself, of your egoism. An absence both yielding and attracting, yielding you to Me and attracting Me in you.

Withdrawal making room for advances, for the more a soul withdraws from itself, the more that soul attracts Me.

---

[185] *Ps 33:9 — Taste and see.*

What happier, peace-making trade-off could there be!

If the human, that which is created, is always troubling more or less, the Divine, the Eternal, always brings peace.

Don't the most fundamental aspirations of the soul created by a God of Love have some connection to a God of Love?

Only a soul forgetful of itself to the point of being absent from itself truly and effectively understands genuine humility of heart, putting the soul in its proper place which is to let Me takes its place.

Humility therefore is the primary source of peace.

Learn from Me for I am gentle and lowly in heart, and you will find rest for your souls.[186]

Repose of the soul filled with the living, life-giving presence of the infinite, loving Plenitude of its Father God, Presence of the Divine attracted by the absence of the human.

I want to tell you also about the active element of peace. So many souls delude themselves about this subject, thinking it consists of a more or less "sensualist repose," indolent, apathetic, a purely egoistic tranquility, whereas true peace is the repose of a loving heart perpetually giving itself.

In truth, love can only find perfect "repose" in its end, an end which will be union. Repose is gratifying Union, the Eternity of peace in Heaven.

On earth, Love can only find peace, be at rest, when it is on a path that leads to this end. And this path, what is it if not a never-ending movement of giving, bringing about an ever-deepening union.

For love, to be at rest is to give oneself so that one may be united. Now, this giving of oneself, does it not take work?

This activity of self-donation can and even must be an agony for the soul, the agony of an ardent thirst for union, made more acute just in the measure that loves grows stronger.

---

[186] *Matt 11:29*

But this is an agony at peace, a restful, relief-giving agony, never troubling.

Trouble is the enemy of peace, not agony. Trouble is the dissonant agitation of egoism; agony is the ordered activity of love.

But in order to taste the true, spiritual peace of love's agony, this agony has to be commensurate with Love itself. An agony therefore that is wholly, ardently apostolic, embracing all human hearts that they may be won over to my divine Heart.

My Redeemer's Heart is only appeased by pouring Itself out to its last drop. Is your co-redemptive heart appeased in any other way than by pouring itself out, drop by drop until the last drop, by the unstinting gift of self?

Here's another great secret about peace:

A peaceful heart is a heart perfectly ordered to divine contentment, wholly harmonized with every divine preference, a heart for whom I am truly He Who is preferred above everything and Who is contented in everything. A heart therefore that places all its contentment in my contentment, all its preferences in my preferences. Thus a heart that is indifferent to all the rest.

To prefer Me to everything is to take on all my preferences, taking them in mind, heart and deed. Then is my Heart contented in all things. And you are aware of the infallible means for knowing my preferences — obedience, which is the great wellspring of peace.

Obedience whose primary act is to listen to Me, for whether through My Gospel, your Rules, or your Superiors, it is always my Voice that speaks to you and tells you my Wishes and my preferences. *Who hears you hears Me.*[187] Therefore listen to Me with the open mind of faith.

The second act of obedience is to answer Me in a loving spirit, generously agreeing, adhering with abandonment.

---

[187] *Lk 10:16*

Again, trust is one of the sweetest and surest wellsprings of peace. For a consecrated soul who by that fact has been chosen, preferred by Love, what should this trust be if not unshakeable certitude in the unfailing perpetuity of divine preference for that soul.

Preference — the love of predilection recognized through everything, especially through suffering.

My peace I give to you; not as the world gives do I give it to you.[188] *If they persecuted me, they will persecute you.*[189]

The great secret of peace in suffering therefore is trust, confidence in this preferential love, recognized in the sending of trials that most closely match my Redeeming Heart.

The greater the trust, moreover, the deeper the peace. And the more one is abandoned, the greater the trust.

Whatever the sources of peace may be that I have spoken to you about: humility, trust, abandonment, zealous ardor, generosity, notice that in the end peace is always the fruit of a triumph, the triumph of love over egoism.

A battle for life without truce or mercy, a battle no one is exempt from.

Ponder this carefully: there is no middle ground between love and egoism. The least of your acts is either a victory or a defeat of love, and therefore a victory or defeat of egoism as well.

Thus each action, then, has its share, be it help or hindrance, in the great redemptive cause of divine Charity and its triumph in the world, and the Reign of divine peace.

Peace is the true face of happiness on earth. *Blessed are the peacemakers for they shall be called sons of God.*[190] Yes, the great fruit of peace is this beatitude of belonging to the divine Family, of being a child of the Heavenly Father, of being viewed by Him with

---

[188] *Jn 14:27*

[189] *Ibid 15:20*

[190] *Matt 5:9*

full paternal regard, of being loved by Him with full paternal Love, of being led by his paternal hand.

And, in return, of having for Him a heart that is wholly filial, in communion with my Heart.

Peace is the transparency of the divine in the soul, and at the same time the attraction of the divine in this soul and the resonance of the divine round about it.

Meditate on this two-fold fruit and recognize its supernatural alliance: Communion and diffusion.

Yes, peace meditates and this meditation is the welcoming disposition that irresistibly attracts my grace, from whence comes this apostolic fruit.

Peace gives rise to peace, peace communicates itself.

A soul peaceful with my Peace cannot help but radiate peace, a peace that can only be beneficent.

An apostolate that is always most effective, no matter how discreet, and is always possible for everyone.

A small contribution, in accord with the great co-redemptive spirit of my "appeal," to bring to my great work of pacifying the world, this world of souls that has cost Me so much.

For this is genuine Redemption: the re-establishment of peace between souls and God.

Therefore be wellsprings of peace, my consecrated ones, all of you, peace that radiates from your entire being.

ABANDONMENT

August, 1941

What most speeds a soul on its journey to love is this gift of gifts: complete abandonment into the Father's hands.

What is this abandonment? It's a leaping into the deep waters of the divine Ocean, looking neither to the right nor to the left, neither before nor behind. A great plunge of the soul into Love.

Nothing more of earth can henceforth trouble it, unsettle it or fascinate it, for the soul is lost like a drowned person in the ineffable delights of the paternal Will.

But in order to arrive at this point, the soul must grasp well that it has to be out of its depth, that it must have forsaken all earthly support, all human security.

Now, few souls consent to this total detachment, few consent to being out of their own depth. And thus few have the courage to "lose themselves" in Me as the "appeal" asks it of my "true spouses."

To every soul bought back by my Blood, to every consecrated soul in particular, I say with all the tenderness of your Savior: "Be absolutely assured, Soul most beloved, that my Heart will never fail you, if, in order that you not fail Me, you hold on to Me with both your hands.

Don't you recognize in this another image of total abandonment, with the total detachment that it asks for?

In order to hold on to a support with both hands, doesn't one necessarily have to let go of all else, absolutely everything? Now, isn't this the same thing as losing one's footing?

And this courage to let go of everything, what does it amount to practically if not a continually iterated act of dropping all that is purely human, purely personal, egoistic, earthly, to let what happens happen, so that you may hold on, so to speak, to the single fixed point of divine Charity.

May your heart turn toward this positive point, with loving abandonment, so that you might partake of it more generously. And that this expression: "to hold on with both hands" might signify for you the strength of your attachment to my Heart.

The absolute detachment from self that abandonment calls for is an even more absolute commitment to confidence in Me, a confidence so very pleasing to my Heart.

Confidence of Security, Confidence of Safety. This is the

confidence of confidences and is exactly what it means to "hold on with both hands."

Think of a little child, while playing, suddenly frightened by the sight of some animal. What will the child do? Immediately it will leave everything, dropping what it is holding and run for refuge to its father or mother, and with its two little hands will hold on tightly to them. Then it becomes peaceful, for it is sure, certain of the kindness of those it loves. This is the image of a truly trusting soul.

The soul, more or less like the little child, is aware of its weakness, its helplessness, it knows that in and of itself it is nothing but distrust and mediocrity; but humble also, from a humility that comes from genuine self-knowledge and a knowledge of Me, a humility so pleasing to my Heart.

Like the little child, the soul is always running to its Father, a movement all the more fervent the more the soul feels itself besieged by fears and forebodings. For this soul is certain, with a certainty ever more deeply rooted, that the Father in Heaven whose Goodness is without end will come to its aid.

And being certain of that, the soul is perfectly tranquil (like the little child), with a tranquility so completely secure that it is grows stronger the more the times are fraught with human insecurity.

Thus this soul can in all security say and endlessly repeat to Me: "I am totally peaceful because I am so sure of You."

Oh, what delightful music this cry of love is to my Heart, this act of such pure and ardent charity! It is like the other expression I taught you earlier: "I am too certain of your love to doubt your help."

What delights my Heart about an abandoned soul is the aura of peace, calm, and serenity that comes from its trust.

The peace of a soul entirely inserted into the Heart of its God. Plunged thus into the atmosphere of heaven, what can it breathe in if not the fine fragrance of Jesus Christ? What can it breathe out if not the perfume of all his virtues? What can it radiate if not the luminous fire of his infinite Charity?

Consecrated souls, I implore this of you, be radiating souls for Me. Do not forget that all this harkens back to the program of the true spouse — that a spouse can only be spouse by being "mother," by a life of diffusion no less than of communion.

September, 1941

There is no more perfect model of abandonment than my Eucharistic Host. See how, without the least trace of resistance, not even unyieldingness, It lets Itself be touched, carried, given, allowing Itself to be hidden in the back of the Tabernacle as well as exposed in the bright light of the monstrance. And even (oh mystery!) allowing Myself to be profaned by ungrateful hearts.

Yes, truly my Host is but total *laisser-faire* and suppleness, in a spirit of complete, filial obedience; for through the intermediation of human hands, It abandons Itself to the hands of the Father. It is totally handed over into His hands! Continuator of the Crucified one who could truly say, *"Father, into thy hands I commit my spirit!"*[191]

Consecrated souls, you who can only be my "co-redemptive spouses" by becoming "hosts," meditate often on this marvelous attitude of abandonment by the Host, that you may imitate It. Renew again and again this return of your soul, for while it requires courageous abdication of self, its ineffable fruit is an ever deeper divine takeover, a celestial hold on you that transforms you more and more.

The secret of any life that is fruitful in the work of redemption is to put yourself back into the hands of the Father and be taken hold of, transformed, ruled by these paternal hands.

Like my loving Host, always be available to Me, totally available, always ready, totally ready, always and totally free so that my loving Will can be freely grasped, served, lived out by you, "little victim" for the triumph of my work!

This state of total, perpetual availability at the same time is the fruit of true abandonment.

---

[191] *Lk 23:46*

Contemplate how in my mortal Life, prelude to my Eucharistic Life, I practiced to perfection this virtue of abandonment. How I was always at the disposal of my Father, surrendered to his mercy!

Contemplate this and imitate it.

Would that these fervent cries might flow from your hearts in all sincerity, in all circumstances, cries that are genuine gifts to Me: *As You wish, for your pleasure, for your hunger, for your thirst! In gratitude for your love, in gratitude for everything, most beloved Lord!*

Nothing helps my work of redemption more than this life of abandonment understood in this way.

CHAPTER SEVEN

RELIGIOUS LIFE

Who will be able to understand Love, to the point of falling in love with Love, of being the "victim" of Love? The great wish of my "appeal."

Who will be able to understand the divine measure of Love, to the point of rendering back a love without measure?

Who, if not just the one who knows how to lose his or her egoism, imposing silence upon it in order to hear the lessons of love's Master.

For only from Love can you learn love, as it is from Love alone that you draw love.

And to really understand Love, aren't both these things necessary: to learn Love from my Heart and to take Love from my Heart?

Taking Love from Me in order to take It from yourself, by letting yourself be taken by Me. A mutual, unifying appropriation of each other that prayer is made of!

Yes, believe in Love and you will understand Love!

Listen to Love and you will understand Love!

Pray to Love and you will understand Love!

Who will understand the **Extent of Love**! The extent of eternity!

The one who will truly believe that this eternity is Perpetual Charity without end! *In caritate perpetua dilexi.*[192]

---

[192] *Jer 31:3 — I have loved you with an everlasting love.*

The one who will unfailingly believe that this perpetuity is the activity of union in unceasing actuality. *I am with you always to the close of the age.*[193]

Yes, my "eternal always" is a "continual now," a "perpetual present" of love in tireless action! And therefore a continuous outpouring of graces:

"Always greater diffusion for always closer communion."

If it is really true then that my Heart loves you since always and for always, without beginning or end, what is my Love if not a "today at every instant"?

And in return what must your love be if not a succession of acts so uninterrupted as to be permanent.

Permanence of belief and of trust in my Love.

Permanence of response and oblation to my Love.

Here then is the profession that my Heart awaits from each heartbeat of yours: "Right now, right this very moment, I know, I believe that You are loving me, that your Love fills me with gifts, that It wants me all for Itself!

"Right now, right this very moment, You know, You see that I love You, O my Savior, that my heart in all fullness gives itself to You, that it calls You and appeals to You filled with trust."

With each breath of your life, confide to your heavenly Mother the sweet mission of renewing on your behalf this profession of active love in all its actuality, a response to the eternal extent of my infinite Charity that so pleases my Heart.

You too, renew this profession as often as possible: *Et nunc! Et semper! diligo, trado, confido,* echo of *In caritate perpetua.*[194]

Your life will thus be for Me an unbroken succession of praises, a perpetual *Gloria!*

---

[193] *Matt 28:20*

[194] *Now! Always! I love, I surrender, I trust,* echo of *An everlasting love.*

The extent of eternity has this further meaning: Divine "immutability," infinite "plenitude," itself the source of "infallible faithfulness."

In effect, my "always eternal" being an "infinite now" can also only be "always what it is," always the same so that nothing can cause it to vacillate. Yes, truly:

I am always also loving, since my loving is never-ending.

I am always also giving, since my giving is never-ending.

I am always also claiming, since my claiming is never-ending.

The one who will believe this and respond to it will have placed on his or her life a seal of stability, reflection of my Eternity and source of fruitfulness no less than of faithfulness!

If my Heart has to (alas) lovingly complain about so much inconstancy and instability in the faithfulness of my consecrated souls, it's because I have so few of them who truly believe and respond to the infinite immutability of my works of love!

"Believers" with unwavering confidence, an invincible assurance through all the turmoil and vicissitudes!

You who do "respond," listen: Little finite creatures, so infinitely loved, your finitude can only respond to my immutable infinitude by a greater, ever more increasing increase of love added to the *nunc et semper*[195] and repeated with each beat of your heart.

Et nunc! et semper! Et Amplius! diligo, trado, confido!

Indeed, by itself your love is too weak to remain constantly faithful if it is not constantly waxing. May it ask of Me the grace for this: *Fac me Tibi semper magis credere, in Te spem habere, Te diligere.*[196]

I leave it to your heart to put this teaching of my Heart into practice, in accord with my "appeal."

---

[195] *now and always.*

[196] *Make me believe more and more in You, hope in You, and love You. (From the Eucharistic hymn* Adoro Te devote *of St. Thomas.)*

Feast of the Ascension

Who will understand the **Height of Love**? The celestial height of infinite purity?

The one who will raise his eyes that he may believe in it, and who will lift up his heart that he may respond to it.

"Raise your eyes" above all that is fleeting and created and fix them on heaven, the Father's House, dwelling place of immutable, superabundant Goodness from which all things proceed, all the events and deeds of Providence's divine governance!

"Eyes to the heights," that you may see everything coming from the Father, from the Father's Goodness. Is it not from these sublime heights of the purest, most merciful outpouring of love that I Myself descended in order to come and save you? *Exivi a Patre et veni in mundum.*[197]

That I came down to "dwell" and that I continuously dwell by "coming back" under and through the veil of my sacramental Presence.

Sacrament of my Eucharistic Host. "The Father's Sacrificial Victim."

Sacrament of my providential Wishes each detail of which is a gift of the Father and about which it can be said, in truth: *Exivi a Patre.*

But every gift of the Father is also an "appeal of the Father." An appeal to come up, to come back up to the heights of his heavenly dwelling of infinite Charity! *Surge et veni.*[198] And the response to this *surge* is the heart's *Sursum.*[199]

Yes, the "heart to the heights," so that everything be brought back to the Father in a return of love to his loving Goodness.

The *lifting up* (*sursum*) of love by living faith that elevates it.

The *lifting up* of love by humility that brings back everything faithfully to the source of all Goodness.

---

[197] *Jn 16:38 — I came out from the Father and have come into the world.*

[198] *Cant 2:10 — Arise and come.*

[199] *Col 3:1,2 — Seek the things that are above (sursum).*

Look into your rules and into my Gospel for other *Sursum,* and see that their "detachment" is only for the sake of a stronger, higher "attachment," that their "disengagement" from created things, from the contingent, is only for the sake of a purer, deeper engagement with Love, with the Father!

Relinquo mundum et vado ad Patrem.[200]

Ascendo ad Patrem Meum et Patrem vestrum.[201]

Oh, if all of you would truly be able to say "I leave the world and I come. . . ." I'm "going up to the Father"!

Sursum. Pater noster qui es in caelis.[202]

A Patre, Ad Patrem, In sinu Patris.[203]

In this is my entire Life as Well-Beloved Son of the Father!

And shouldn't this be the entire program of my spouses, in loving communion with Me?

Therefore, see the Father's gift in everything, *exivi (I came).*

Hear in everything the Father's call, *surge (arise).*

Make everything a response to the Father, *sursum (upwards).*

See in my "appeal" this gift of the Father, the Father's call.

Live my "appeal" in its entirety so that it becomes a genuine response of love to the Father, a generous *sursum* responding to the *surge* and the *exivi*!

Who will understand the **Breadth of Love**, the endless immensity of its expanse?

The one who will stretch his horizon so that he may believe in it, and who will expand his heart so that he may respond to it.

How does one enlarge his or her heart?

---

[200] *Jn 16:28 — I am leaving the world and going to the Father.*

[201] *Ibid 20:17 — I am ascending to my Father and your Father.*

[202] *Rise up. Our Father who are in heaven. . . .*

[203] *Ibid 1:18 — From the Father, to the Father, in the bosom of the Father.*

Through prayer, prayer that leads to my Heart, to discover in It the adorable perfections of a Charity so especially immense.

An immensity so enveloping, penetrating, overflowing! Weigh these three terms well.

Yes, stretching out to everyone, addressing each, and doing so in infinite ways!

Everything to each therefore just as everything to all!

Love as intimately personal as it is broadly universal. You must remember that my immense Charity signifies both one and the other at the same time, and may this thought help you to enlarge your souls to a life lived always more in truthfulness, to yourselves and to everyone.

Is there any joy more expansive for the heart, for your hearts, for my Heart in yours than this unique, two-sided life?

Intimacy of perpetual communion of wills where the superabundant, divine immensity of my life of Love gives full latitude for your soul's expansion!

Charity of perpetual giving of the self (a self that has become Me insofar as is possible), giving full latitude for the victorious expansion of this same immense superabundance in other souls as well!

This is how you are to respond in truth to the immense breadth of my Love.

A small contribution to the expansion of my redeeming Host!

Never forgetting that progression of love presupposes regression of egoism!

The Gospel word that is most expressive of this full latitude given to Love is the *Adveniat* of the Our Father![204] Oh, say it, live it in communion with my dispositions and intentions, *Adveniat Hostia!*

Who will be able to understand the **Depth of Love**? The depths of the abyss!

---

[204] *Thy kingdom come!*

The one who, in order to believe it, will know how to go deeper into my Heart! And who, that he may respond to it, will allow Me to deepen his own heart!

"To go deeper into my Heart," such is a spouse's ever more alert, more adoring intent — to explore its mysteries, evangelical mysteries, Eucharistic mysteries. . . .

To discover its wonders: the wondrous lights of infinity that flash out from the very incomprehensibility of its love!

So as to "vibrate with its vibrations," vibrations of wishes, vibrations of feelings!

And thus to "sink into its abysses," to "lose oneself" in the depths of transforming life, as "victim" wholly given over to the work of redemption.

Blessed annihilation of the beloved's soul, this loss; a gain for the Spouse, a gain for Love!

Loss of self, in Me, for Me!

You recognize in this my "appeal!"

Feast of the Blessed Sacrament

Feast of the Host's **Irradiation**, of the Host irradiating love, of a love that irradiates souls in order that they in their turn radiate the Host.

Oh, souls so beloved of my Heart, allow yourselves to be irradiated by the love of the Host, so that, to the glory of my Father, you will be able to radiate my redeeming love!

This is your sublime vocation as co-redeemers!

To let yourselves be irradiated is to let yourself be penetrated (and therefore to let your heart be deepened) by the burning rays charged with waves of divinizing life that the host of my present Will contains at every moment. A Will each particular of which is an irradiation from the Father's superabundant Goodness!

An irradiation all the more penetrating as the soul itself becomes more penetrating, and therefore, in a word, more permeable and more receptive to love.

This through a *Fiat* of oblation, of attachment, of entreaty, springing forth from one's inmost depths.

And in order to radiate this Love, if possible, there must only be transparency, the transparency of the host by the radiant serenity that comes from divine possession.

The condition and measure of the radiating, burning attraction that makes all things flow towards the heavenly heights.

Thus the depths join up with the heights in the wondrous unity of love!

In unum! In altum![205]

THE DELICACY OF LOVE

1937

The proper life of a spouse is totally woven with the delicacies of love.

Patterns of thoughtful delicacies from the infinite Love of the Heart of her divine Spouse!

Patterns of thoughtful delicacies from the heart of his beloved!

Yes, delicacy, the most exquisite expression of the heart, should be the distinctive mark of consecrated souls. It isn't a special virtue but rather a perfume of intimacy, a tender blossom that accompanies all the virtues and that has the gift of ravishing my Heart in a very special way.

At bottom such tenderness in a delicate soul is exquisite sensitivity to vibrations that affect it with all that affects Me, most intimately and keenly, and make it insensitive to everything else, sensitive to God's glory alone.

---

[205] *As one. Into the deep.*

Oh, how souls like these have the secret for affecting my Heart, how touching and consoling are these delicate souls who, vibrating with love's least breath, can truly say: "Those things which touch only me, that only pertain to my own little interests, these have no effect on me — I want to be affected only by what affects my Love, and it is Him alone that I wish to touch."

This delicacy of soul, this pure and vibrant harmony, cannot bear the least nuance or dissonance between your heart and Mine and can only persist, you know, by a continuous string of little delicacies (an attitude that cannot persist but by these continuous acts). Little delicacies that, in the language of both divine and human love, can be justly called "little attentions," and which themselves presuppose a great, unique, permanent, absorbing Attentiveness at the center of all the soul's activities.

Attention of the heart that is directed and fixed on my Heart. Don't you recognize the ineffable beauty of this focus? Isn't its attraction enough to be irresistible? How is it then that you allow your attention to wander off to such poor little human trifles? It's because you forget that the first work of prayer is to settle the heart's orientation and attention through daily, ever more intimate contemplation of the attractions of my Heart, attractions to myriad lights that only want to charm and captivate you.

If you want to seed your days with these little attentions that console my Heart, remember then that through all your many occupations, I and I alone must be your sole ardent preoccupation and concern.

This is the great attention of the heart, the great delicacy that will give you eyes to discover all the little tokens to give to Me.

And do not forget that, in this attention, you are being unceasingly, mercifully predisposed by the great Attentiveness of my Heart whose love seeks and pursues your hearts.

To fix the attention of your hearts on my Heart therefore is to encounter the Attention of my Heart fixed on yours!

Could this great Attention of my Heart be so lavish with little attentions if It were not turned towards you? Isn't the course of your days at each step all strewn with little delicacies?

But know this well: One can only gather these delicacies in return for an exchange: this is the great law of love.

In this exchange of delicacies, most important of all should be the constant concern to avoid even the smallest tactlessness, to avoid driving the slightest thorn into my Heart.

Fear and concern that please my Heart, for they are a disavowal of egoism and a protestation of love. Fear and concern being expressed as fidelity to my evangelical councils for vigilance and prayer: *Watch and pray.*[206]

Yes, these are the little delicacies for my Heart, little acts asked of you by your rules and with which you can sow your days.

Little delicacies also of these little repeated acts asking for the help of my Grace, little appeals that are humble, supplicating, and above all confident at times of distress!

Who knows better than Me how feeble you are?

But don't forget that the appeal is what draws the help.

For Me, helping you is to help my own Cause with you, the Cause of Love.

For you, asking Me for help offers Me help, so to speak, and is thus a genuine little delicacy.

Other little delicacies for my Heart are the little returns of love of a soul caught up in the chivalrous need to make amends most expeditiously for all the little indelicacies that escaped from his or her egoistic *me.*

Pained at having pained Me, the soul does not rest until it has in some way avenged my Honor.

How?

First of all, for sure, by a sincere, profound, interior grief completely steeped in humility, regret, and confidence in my Mercy. But also by a restitution twice over and if possible a hundred times over of the glory that his or her egoism has stolen from Me.

---

[206] *Matt 26:41*

This redress alone can console Me.

Thus, two acts of gentleness to repair one act of impatience, two acts of humility to repair one act of pride, two acts of charity for one lapse of charity.

How consoling and glorious for my Heart is this practice of a delicate heart!

This is how these little reparations of love become little exaltations of love.

Marvelous way of using one's faults. A good practice for my coredemptive partners, not only personally but apostolically as well. And how vast the field is here! Think about my "appeal."

Little delicacies most particularly sweet to my Heart like all the little kindnesses to one's neighbor. Little kindnesses so expressive of my spirit, what religious rules generally speak of as "duties."

Don't forget that if the measure of your love as spouse is in your delicacy towards Me, this delicacy towards Me is in the measure of your delicacy towards all who are Mine.

And you know the counterpart now: Every little lack of delicacy, of tenderness towards the neighbor is a painful thorn thrust into my Heart.

Have we to cite some of these charitable ways of behaving in little things?

Offering support, forgiving faults.

Showing interest, sharing in pains or joys.

Providing pleasures, helping others escape tedium, taking it on oneself.

Giving encouragement, showing signs of confidence.

Rendering or asking for a little service. For accepting a service or even asking for it is often one of the most delicate of kindnesses.

In doing these things for others, there's both the "manner" as well as the "matter" of the gift.

And besides, positive acts are always possible, as you know, like little prayers or offerings, so long as the heart is in it.

Isn't it enough to tell you that this touches my Heart to encourage you to strew your days with these little delicacies? — so that the triumphant path of my Love might be strewn with flowers.

The violence of hatred can only be vanquished by the most pure and ardent delicacy of love.

And by other little delicacies that love's little pacts make with my Heart in colloquy with the intimacy of prayer and Communion, aimed at maintaining throughout the day the generosity of a soul resolved to respond with love.

I know your great weakness to be so readily forgetful, to be occupied and drawn into worldly affairs.

But with Me, my Fidelity is not forgetful, it is lovingly attentive. Therefore, if you agree with Me, for example, that each beat of your heart wants to be a burning act of love, do you believe that I will not entertain it as such and that my Heart will not be touched by it, having seen in this agreement a mark of trust, along with an acknowledgement of powerlessness, an act of humility, and a sign of fervor, a desire to love Me all the more.

Renew these little morning pacts in each of your pious exercises, and ask the Holy Virgin to do so often in your name, to remind you of them from time to time during the day so that, with a cry of the heart, you may renew them yourselves.

This way of the interior life is most effective, is it not, so gentle, so easy.

Little delicacies also like these frequent, little consultations, requests for advice addressed directly to my Heart in times of uncertainty, hesitation, or when you are unsure how better to please Me.

Yes, recourse like this, a most pure seeking for my preferences, is particularly pleasing to Me and irresistibly attracts my lights.

I inspire you in the measure that you consult with Me in this affective, spontaneous way, humble and confident at the same time.

I inspire all things in those who consult Me, for everything. And these are always inspirations of "love" responding to your little, loving consultations.

Develop the habit of multiplying them. . . .

Still other little delicacies of intimacy like these little secrets from the heart of a truly smitten spouse who "keeps them for Me alone," and who is drawn to my Heart alone.

Little secrets of love in the form of little confidences about everything, even the most secret, done "in secret" in keeping with the ways of intimacy.

Everything between us. Nothing between us. Nothing but between us.

I keep my secrets for those who keep their secrets for Me. And do not tell love's secrets!

Little delicacies like invocations of praise, of trust, and gratitude, springing all the more urgent and ardent as the soul is more and more caught up in suffering, laid low in helplessness. I am touched deeply by love this pure!

Yes, these little things are most consoling to my Heart: "all the more," "always more," the triumphant retort of love to the solicitations of egoism.

Delicacy of a generosity avid to seize all the little "luxuries" of sacrifice in a "co-redemptive" spirit.

Little delicacies like all the little acts done "through Mary" and "for Mary"; for whatever bears my Mother's seal cannot but delight my Heart.

I leave it to your heart to find on its own still other little delicacies with which to sow your day, delicacies of "charity," of "fidelity," of "trust."

Be one who lives by this delicate love, who is always listening, always lying in wait, always on the look-out for the least signs of my Preferences, of all my Calls, always keeping in mind that these little delicacies from the heart are the most agreeable, most generous and consoling of gifts you can give to my Heart.

Just as the least indelicacy forms the bloodiest wounds.

For one can only be "all spouse" to Me by being "all delicacy."

CONTEMPT FOR THE WORLD

1937

Profound contempt for the world possesses a depth of love that is powerfully attractive to my Heart.

I am not of the world.[207] *You are not of the world.*[208]

Haven't you ever weighed all these words in my Heart?

How greatly has this spirit of the world infiltrated your judgments, your tastes, your attitudes, this antipode of a simple Christian spirit, and even more of the spirit of religious!

Believe my Heart about this:

The more you hate the world (this profound contempt, both affective and effective) the more the world will respect you, recognizing in this the divine mark it expects to find in consecrated souls, and are scandalized when it is lacking.

And moreover, you will conquer hearts in this world for Me. I have such thirst for them, for the hearts of children, the hearts of faithful servants, the hearts of friends, the hearts of apostles. And most especially the hearts of spouses, for only a purely supernatural "radiance" is able to attract others to my Heart.

Recall what I have been telling you: "If you were more spouse, you would attract to Me more spouses, spouses more fervent."

1938

"You must renounce the world in order to save it," renounce its perfidious, insinuating, sacrilegious spirit, and treat it with contempt.

In co-redemptive union with Me, you must "sacrifice yourself" for the world.

---

[207] *Jn 8:23; 17:14*
[208] *Ibid v. 15*

This does not mean you sacrifice to the world, but rather it is the world you must have the courage to sacrifice. You understand the difference.

Consecrated souls, if you do not have this courage to sacrifice the little worldly popularity that Satan perfidiously causes you to judge is sometimes necessary for the good of the apostolate, who will sacrifice it? Who will save the world?

The conviction about this apostolic spirit of contempt for the world is the certain leaven of all apostolic work.

1940

At this grave hour confronting the world, and for its redemptive fate, understand well that in order to help Me as true spouses, in order to save this world, you more than ever have to have, and in magnified fashion, both love and hatred, respect and contempt for it (these in close communion with my feelings).

Yes, respecting and loving in the world all the souls that inhabit it, souls who come from my creative Goodness and whom this Goodness has sent onto the earth as wayfarers, itinerants, as combatants in order that after being tested, they may merit the return to glory and happiness in the Father's House in the heavenly homeland.

Yes, loving this great world of souls as I myself have loved it to the point of my Passion. Passion of gift and sacrifice, as my Father has loved it and never ceases to love it! *God so loved the world.*[209] *I have come to save the world.*[210]

But hating, scorning the earthly spirit, the carnal spirit of pleasure, of pride, cupidity, "the spirit of this world" infused by the prince of darkness, by the prince of this world.

The spirit I came to condemn, combat and conquer. *My kingdom is not of this world.*[211] *I came into the world, but I am not of the world.*[212]

---

[209] *Ibid 3:16*
[210] *Ibid v. 17*
[211] *Ibid 18:36*
[212] *Ibid 9:39 and 17:17*

Be of good cheer, I have overcome the world.[213]

In this light make an examination again and again regarding this contempt for the world as I have taught it to you. Can each of you say truthfully "there is nothing of the world in me"?

You will only save the world in the measure that, on the one hand, you have profound contempt for its spirit, through a life that is truly poor, humbled, crucified (therefore thank Me when, as now, I supply you with more numerous chances for these things), and on the other hand, in the measure that you love the souls of this world more ardently, with a love mingled with passion for my redemptive Reign, in the spirit of my "appeal."

Oportet adveniat Regnuum Tuum![214]

Despite its rush to pleasure, the world is profoundly sad, just because of this relentless pursuit, a sadness, alas, largely culpable for it is a sadness of egoism.

As Savior I am moved to compassion for the world, and by my own free will am sorrowful for it with a sorrow of infinite Charity, mercifully and in holiness sharing all the sufferings their sorrow has brought them that it might be changed into joy.

Listen to the Host reverberate the ever-living words of my Gospel:

My soul is sorrowful even unto death.[215] *Your sorrow shall be turned into joy.*[216]

Don't you on your part want to turn the sorrow of my Heart into joy, by helping Me turn into joy the sorrow of all my brothers on earth?

---

[213] *Ibid 16:33*
[214] *Thy Kingdom must come!*
[215] *Matt 26:38; Mk 14:34 (Douay Rheims).*
[216] *Jn 16:20 (Douay Rheims).*

In truth, I who am King of Happiness, eternal Beatitude of the Father, cannot be sorrowful for any other reason.

Are you asking yourselves how to convert my merciful sadness into joy?

I Myself merited converting the sadness of you poor, pitiful ones into joy by taking part in all the sufferings that cause it, in order that they might be made fruitful unto salvation. Salvation that recovers the divine elation of the Father's Kingdom, promised to all his children and purchased by the Blood of the First-Born Son. Act the same way to Me, by sharing in all my sufferings.

I push my Goodness to the point where I need you in order to make this redemptive Blood fully efficacious in its application to souls. Yes, in the plan of infinite Wisdom, this very thing, infinitely fertile of itself, can only be fruitful in souls by means of your collaboration.

Therefore in the measure that you will truly be my "auxiliaries of Redemption," in accordance with the wish of my "appeal," you will turn the "loving sadness" of my Heart into "loving joy."

POVERTY

1940

The Gospel passage that most expresses my spirit of poverty can be found in the divine doctrinal synthesis of my Priestly Prayer:

Mea omnia Tua sunt et Tua Mea sunt.[217]

My Poverty in essence consists in my belonging to the Father, belonging exclusively and totally. I only exist for Him. I am everything to Him. I am his Good, his Property, his Riches.

Yes, comprehend this marvel:

---

[217] *Ibid 17:10 — . . . all my things are thine, and thine are mine (Douay Rheims).*

My Poverty is to be his Riches, for in possessing Me He possesses in superabundance the infinite Charity He pours out. Therefore it is a mutual belonging, universal and eternal.

And too, what ineffable kindness there is in this unifying possession!

And now, in light of this Gospel, go to your Rules, read them, understand them.

Don't you recognize in them the whole meaning of the Gospel I just spoke to you about?

Be very sure of this, this veritable spirit of poverty, both for you as for Me, is in essence *belonging*. Total, exclusive belonging.

The soul that is truly poor, who is all for Me, nothing but for Me, is my good, my property, my riches.

Yes, marvel of my tenderness, the soul's poverty is riches to Me, just as I am the riches of my Father.

For in possessing this soul, the very superabundance of my merciful Charity nourishes Me and enriches my redemptive Host.

Mutual, perpetual belonging, for if it is said that I leave to themselves any who do not live in poverty, must it not assure those who in fact practice this spirit of poverty that it is I who abandon Myself to them. I am their riches both now and forever.

Blessed are the poor in spirit for theirs is the Kingdom of heaven.[218]

Spouses mutually belonging to each other so as together to belong to the Father, to the sovereignty of his loving and infinitely holy Will, so that his great work of Redemption may be carried out.

That, with the same voice, with the same heart as one, this loving cry might go forth to the Father, *Omnia mea Tua sunt et Omnia Tua mea sunt.*[219]

---

[218] *Matt 5:3*

[219] *Everything of mine is yours, everything of yours is mine.*

You recognize this loving spirit of belonging for the sake of Love's enrichment in these words of my "appeal": "A true spouse's heart is the victim of her Spouse." The victim is the other's good. It lives to lose itself in Him, to be taken and consumed by Him and for Him for the dilation of his loving Host.

For you to remain and grow in this spirit, multiply your acts of losing yourself in Me, of ridding yourself of all that is egoistically personal in order that you may take on all the sentiments of my Heart.

If rampant passion for riches is what's spoiling the world at this moment, if its cupidity is placing it in peril, how shall it be saved if not by the passion for divine riches that is holy poverty.

Know this, my spouses, that if you had all been poorer and thus more conformed to your redemptive Spouse, the world would not be the way it is.

And if you do not hasten to become poorer, the world will continue rushing to its ruin.

For if Redemption entails reparation, all reparation demands compensation, and all compensation of love needs to be superabundant. A simple equivalence won't satisfy it, it has to go beyond. When Satan's hatred intensifies, must not charity increase a hundredfold?

What then does it mean to become poorer?

It means endlessly growing in this spirit of belonging, by continual restitution and self-surrender to the Ruler of all that is good both in heaven and on earth.

Just as I Myself did with my Father, who has delivered all things into my hands: *I commit my spirit into thy hands.*[220]

Mutual surrendering then for the sake of mutual appropriating, mutual compenetrating in conformity with Me.

Isn't the "all to You," "all to Me" of my great Priestly Prayer in fact followed by "all in You," "all in Me."

As Thou, Father, art in Me and I in Thee.[221]

---

[220] *Lk 23:46*

Restitution and compenetration that presuppose perpetual substitutions of the divine I for the human *me*.

Whenever some temptation to egoistic ownership arises, personal views, feelings, personal wishes or satisfactions, develop the habit in this spirit of poverty of belonging to Love, of multiplying these acts of substitution with these words: "Not me but You," as I mercifully exemplified to you when I said to my Father, *Not my Will, but Yours.*[222]

This is the secret of the true interior life, because the permanency of this substitution is what brings about love's unifying consummation. Didn't I go on to say to my Father: *That they may become perfectly one [as We are one]?*[223]

It is precisely by the courageously loving practice of this consummating substitution that the soul becomes host, that, in accord with the great desire of my Heart, my spouses become the living hosts that I incorporate into my Grand Host, as "little co-redemptive continuators" for the expansion of my action in saving the world, to the glory of the Father.

Hostia Laudis.[224]

Adveniat regnum Tuum.[225] Words of the Gospel that, when spoken by a sincere soul, are a sure and efficacious way to appropriate the most precious sentiments of my Heart, keeping silent the egoistic sentiments of human language.

Here are five golden links in the wonderful chain of this belonging of love to Love, which is the true spirit of poverty:

— Restitution of everything to the Heart, source of all good. *Ecce omnia trado.*[226]

---

[221] *Jn 17:21*
[222] *Lk 22:42*
[223] *Jn 17:23*
[224] *The sacrifice of praise.*
[225] *Thy kingdom come.*
[226] *Behold, I give all things.*

— Compenetration of mutual surrender and appropriation. *Tu in me et ego in Te.*[227]

— Substitution of divine ownership in place of the human. *Non mea sed Tua, Fiat.*[228]

— In the unity of the redemptive Host. *In unum ad Patrem.*[229]

— Fruitful expansion of the saving Reign of Love. *Adveniat et Regnet.*[230]

"Take all, be all; by your full rights as Spouse, by my own free will as spouse!" I love this loving invocation so expressive of the true spirit of poverty. When this cry of the soul is truly sincere, it is my pleasure to grant it. I regard the "you be" literally, no less than the "you take." And if the privation is felt more keenly than the parallel, proportional enrichment, this too is brought about no less by my loving faithfulness.

May this assurance stimulate your trust, and your courage too.

Joy in privation, holy and most gentle Joy, privation that brings about dependency and meaningful retrenchment.

In effect, by the spirit of poverty and belonging, the beloved becomes the Spouse's possession. Weigh these terms well. Now, the proprietor alone, as master, is able to dispose of and make use of his own property. That's the right of the one it belongs to.

Belonging is only total if dependence is total. Be faithful to this elementary act of poverty.

Ask as one who is poor, receive as someone poor, use as a poor person. The loss of independence joining up with obedience, such is the primary form of religious poverty.

Another elementary act of this poverty is retrenchment from the superfluous, from superfluous pleasures, superfluous comforts.

---

[227] *You in me and I in You.*
[228] *Not my will but thy will be done.*
[229] *To the Father in unity.*
[230] *Come and Reign.*

Think about this that all privation of egoistic pleasure is a precious gain for love. All retrenchment of human comfort is a strengthening of divine union and thereby an added enrichment of my redemptive glory.

And in this regard understand that all clinging to and chasing after pleasure and comfort is a theft made at the expense of love, a theft made against souls, a theft against my redemptive Host that, as you know now, can only extend itself by the incorporation of other "wholly consecrated hosts," hosts without any speck, any grain of egoistic reservation coming from this spirit of private ownership and pleasure so completely opposed to the true spirit of poverty.

Therefore, keeping yourself poor like the poor, restraining yourself, limiting yourself as someone poor, constitutes a second, essential form of religious poverty.

Still another constant practice needs to be added to this, one especially within your capacity: to work as one who is poor.

Doing so with a well-formed, loving conscience that does not waste time through laziness and laxness, dilettantism, vain curiosity or self-preoccupation.

For understand this well that all waste of time, one way or the other, steals from my redemptive work, which needs all the activity of your life for it to be carried out and completed, without exception, since these are the fully consecrated hosts that my work must have. Oh, do not forget my "appeal"!

Another very pure form of religious poverty is to rejoice at being poor, with little and with less, which means all the shortcomings, needs, bothers, and privations. *Blessed are the poor.*

Rejoicing at the experience of oneself as someone poor, in whatever form this be, whether in strength, talents, capabilities. Blessed indigents who attract the merciful opulence of my grace. Blessed human incapacities that serve divine capacity!

Recall the words of my Apostle: *I will all the more gladly boast of my weakness, that the power of Christ may rest upon me.*[231] Yes, I love this

---

[231] *II Cor 12:9*

cry of praise and trust together, springing from the distress of true poverty.

Rejoicing in being treated by others as a poor person, of being little appreciated, little considered, little esteemed and little valued by them. Privation of esteem and of consideration felt most keenly by self-love, and thereby getting back to the virtue of humility, which is so dear to my Heart.

Examine yourself: are you like this? In all the occasions of privation, and therefore of poverty, do you have this contentment and this most gentle joy?

The gentleness of the true heart of a spouse, beating in union with the Heart of her Spouse, infinite Richness who willingly made Himself poor out of love for her.

The sweetness of union that results from this, and that abandons the soul to the joyful entirety of infinite Goodness.

Truly, can there be any sweeter joy for the heart of a beloved than to be thus totally given over to the enjoyment of the Heart of its divine Spouse?

Now, this is the very heart of the program of poverty that I propose to you and to all, without exception, both in spirit and in form.

That each of you, in order to obtain the grace to be faithful to it, not forget to ask Me for it, praying in the form of the *Fiat* appeal that is so dear to my Heart.

"Poor and crucified divine Spouse, make it so that in the loving, most sweet joy of my heart I may be:

"Wholly and always more completely your belonging." *Ecce.* "Wholly and always more completely your delight." *Fiat.* "Wholly and always more completely your complacency." *Magnificat.*

Yes, "little victims" of my immense redeeming love, may each of you be:

"Always more completely my possession."

"Always more wholly devoted to Me."

"Always more for my glorification alone."

PURITY AND THE CONSECRATED LIFE

1937

To be "consecrated" is to be "set aside."

"To be wholly consecrated" is to be wholly set aside for the service of Love, exclusively set aside with nothing kept back for the self.

Yes, consecrated souls, understand this well that the least personal reservation is a desecration, be this self-love, sensuality, egoism under any of its forms.

It's a portion of the host that remains resistant to total consecration.

Oh! how rare are they whose love is sufficiently pure, sufficiently strong to never show Me the least little reservation! And yet these are the ones who truly understand the meaning of their vocation, who know that one cannot be entirely consecrated to the greater Glory of my Heart if one is not totally "consumed" by the burning fire of my love.

This is the Sacrifice that consecrates the Host. Total Sacrifice to the point of holocaust. The fullness of consecration corresponds to the fullness of oblation.

Understand this too: The unreservedness of virginal consecration is not only ceaseless giving, an everything and an always, but also a *crescendo* of oblation, an always more at every instant with every vibration of the heart, an ever-increasing reciprocity of giving, a *growing into* that magnifies one in the other.

Blessed identification responding to my great desire for consummation in unity.

Truly, the consecrated soul cannot call Me its exclusive, sovereign preference (response to my merciful partiality) if I am not truly its complete sufficiency and its overabundance.

But, alas, such souls are rare, those for whom I am sufficiency, those who have understood that I am not the All unless I am the Only One and where all the rest counts for nothing. Where one finds everything in Me if one looks to Me for everything and therefore seeks nothing elsewhere and nothing more.

For a life that is truly consecrated, isn't my Love compelling enough to fall in love with It alone, and to lose one's attraction to all the rest? Isn't Love's supreme gift its sovereign hold on the soul, always more profound, more transforming as the soul is nourished by the Host Bread of my loving Will (consuming and savoring It)?

Totally in my Possession, totally devoted to Me, such is the program of the consecrated life. Yes, the ideal for the consecrated soul is to be so in the possession of Love, its "little victim," so totally "surrendered" to its divine jealousy that the soul is completely devoted to It, in suppleness, gentleness and in complete dependence, total belonging and abandonment.

The whole devotion of consecrated hearts is to be totally attached to Me in ways always more supple, more gracious, no matter how crucifying my mysterious, loving desires may be.

In everything, always be at God's disposal, at the disposal of Love. Would that my Heart might say of each of you, in all truth, "I do with you whatever I wish. I play on you at my pleasure, as a victim, for the complacency of my Father." Don't you recognize here the sound of my "appeal"? "A true spouse is the victim of her Spouse."

How many are there who, in attachment of complete flexibility, at any moment and in all things are at the disposal of their divine Spouse, wholly at his beck and call, at his discretion, to his liking, as He wishes?

A totally consecrated life is a life of purity. Let us speak then of this virginal virtue that so ravishes my Spouse's Heart.

If purity is indeed an absence of all human admixture, where nothing is to itself, nothing for itself, look at purity rather in its positive sense: Purity is a plenitude of presence, of divine presence, of fulfilling presence.

To be pure is to be entirely engrossed in Me. And doesn't this mean: to be wholly engrossed in all that is Mine, in all of my interests therefore, in all of my loves.

All in my Father, all in my Mother, all in my brothers.

To be truly all in Me therefore is also truly to be in all that is Mine.

1939

A pure soul is a soul made of crystal and like crystal is all transparency and resonance so as to receive and reflect love's brilliant rays.

How I wish that with each tap of my royal scepter, coming from my Will at every moment to strike at your hearts, there would be found in your hearts the immediate resonance of love, which is to say, the spontaneous reaction of grateful adherence.

How do matters stand then? What sound does your soul spontaneously produce? Is it pure? Alas, how numerous are egoism's spontaneities and reflexes, how many outbursts of nature by a sensual *me*! Are such things pardonable on the part of the spouses of a crucified Spouse? Is that how one lives a life of consecration?

If you loved Me with a deep-seated love, a love that is virginally pure, only supernatural outbursts would spring from your heart, only religious reflexes, only spontaneities of a love happy to give itself, and without any reservation and with unalloyed joy one would make whatever sacrifice it might cost you.

1940

O my spouses, help Me in this work of purifying the world that my merciful holiness so pursues! As Immaculate Host, I cannot be served except by partners who are hosts of utmost purity, hosts that are "wholly consecrated," hearts that are endlessly undergoing purification.

For purity alone purifies. A pure heart is a free heart. And the heart is free and liberated when the spirit is steadfast and the senses are kept watch over.

Oh, blessed steadiness of gaze towards the divine horizons that, by attaching the soul entirely to its loving center, detaches it and despoils it of all love's admixtures, of all earthly love, so as to never again love anything except in accord with the Heart of Jesus Christ (meditate well on this "in accord with").

The spirit of perfect purity that draws from my Heart therefore is a spirit of inseparable attachment to God, of growing attachment, of unifying attachment to his holy Will.

Attachment that I myself practiced, I as Savior in attaching myself to the Cross, to be nailed to It, allowing myself to be fastened to It for your Redemption!

Attachment that is to conduct "true co-redeemers" to that same place: "crucified spouses."

Here is the great meaning, the full meaning, the true meaning of the consecrated soul's wholly virginal purity. Virtue proper to the spouse, tied by his or her vocation to a union without end, to its only Love, aspiring only to be joined to It ever more exclusively, to unite all hearts to It.

OBEDIENCE

1940

How does one let oneself become host?

By an uncompromising obedience of love, the watchword for which is found in my "appeal": This *Fiat* that fully welcomes the "consecrating action of my redeeming Will."

Fiat, which consecrated Me as Host for man's salvation, Host for the praise of the Father.

Fiat, which made Me love's perfect Obedient One, obedient unto death, death on the Cross!

Obedience whose spirit, therefore, is essentially a fusion of wills for a service of love. Total, constant, instantaneous fusion, presupposing a fusion of views that lead to a fusion of hearts.

A three-fold fusion then, turning obedience into a communion most intimate, unifying and consuming.

Fusion of wills, for the worship of my Will is the distinctive mark of an obedient soul. Worship not only of my commanding Will, of my

Will as Master, but worship also of my Will's Good Pleasure and preferences as Spouse and Friend.

Worship in adoration of the sovereign Wisdom of this Will. Worship in acts of thanksgiving for the sovereign tenderness of this Will. Worship that places the soul at the complete disposal of my Heart's least desires, causing the soul to cry out at every manifestation it has of my Will:

"Entirely as you please, by my own accord!"

"As you please as Spouse, by my own accord as spouse!"

"As you please as Master, by my own accord as servant!"

"As you please as Love, by my own loving accord!"

Oh, how these invocations so spontaneously, ardently, and so frequently repeated please my Heart! Refreshing pleasure, compensating for all those who, alas, look to withdraw from my Will in order to satisfy their own earthly pleasures.

There is no more intimate and confident participation in my redemptive Cross than in the sacrificial life of fully alive religious obedience.

The worship of my Will in its essence should be "passion," in the two meanings of this word:

The heart's loving fervor, in imitation of Mine.

Sacrifice of one's whole being, sacrifice that is continual and without hesitation. This sacrifice that holds back nothing is the perfect sacrifice of the holocaust.

Don't you recall the forcefully expressive words that reminded you of this in the Letter on obedience you are familiar with:

"The one who obeys becomes a living sacrifice pleasing to the divine Majesty since he holds back absolutely nothing for himself. . . ."

". . . Obedience is an absolute renunciation of one's self . . . where you strip yourself entirely of your own will."

It's the complete detachment from self that is asked of obedient souls, done for the good of God's work that they are helping to realize.

Have you never really meditated and understood that, through your religious obedience, you have the joy and honor, the ability and duty of contributing to the fulfillment of the Father's work and of serving his Glory?

From whence comes the inestimable co-redemptive value of obedience, when this, being what it should be, is truly a sacrifice that consumes the soul as a victim, to consecrate it as pure host and consummate it in unity with Love.

And thus if you really practice this, how great will your help be for Me in the salvation of souls, how greatly you will change into joy the sadness of my Savior's Heart.

But, alas, few are the number of souls who put this into practice to that extent, who practice it "to the extent" that I Myself have done: *unto death on the Cross.*[232] How many can really say that their obedience goes so far as to strip themselves completely of their own will, to the point where all their egoistic preferences are crucified and their wills are fused and identified with Me?

Would that each of you might answer Me in front of the Crucifix where you took your vows.

Search into my Heart for the strength to seek Me and you will surely have the joy of finding Me.

Indeed, the strength to find Me is the strength to follow my path. And the one who follows my path encounters Me at every step.

What is this path?

Traced by merciful divine Justice, my Redeeming path, as you know, is the "way of the Cross," drawing a straight line to Calvary through total, filial submission to my Father's orders.

All of which tells you that the true co-redemptive path is solely the way of the Cross of obedience, to be climbed step by step, without stopping, to the end, to its heights, for it is only from the "summit" of Calvary where the *Consummatum est* was pronounced that the consummation of the Savior's Sacrifice is carried out.

---

[232] *Philipp 11:8*

You will recognize in this "to the end" the total sacrifice that I have been speaking to you about, and how very rare it is. Why is that?

For want of the needed fusion of views. I've spoken to you of this, the perfect fusion of wills. How numerous and frequent are these attachments to one's own judgments, one's own private feelings, all under false pretexts either for the good of some entrusted work or because it was impossible to do otherwise.

Oh, weigh this "I can't" before my Heart; aren't they more or less unconsciously at times simply "I don't want to"?

And then the ways of bending the will of one's superior to order whatever it is one wants oneself! How good self-love and egoism are at that! What you hear said by my saints on this subject is only too true.

Oh yes, alas, too many religious souls still cling to their ideas! And is this not a serious refusal of sacrifice?

Have you not reflected that one is held back by what one holds on to? To hold these ideas, therefore, is to be held captive by them, captive by what is human, captive to creation. This therefore is a grave blundering in the total sacrifice of self, where everything is not consumed in the flames of Charity.

This is not perfect, genuine obedience, therefore; obedience is only co-redemptive when it is totally crucifying, as Mine the Redeemer's had been.

Short of this total abnegation of one's own views, be aware that the true step to sanctity has not yet been taken. One's own spirit, a human spirit, is leading one's soul, not my Holy Spirit of divine Charity.

Ponder this well and understand that one touchstone of this abnegation is the ease with which one willingly enters into the view of others, that their ideas might prevail. And this, not only when it comes to Superiors and primary authorities, but to all one's neighbors.

Is this the case very often? Why isn't it then? Is it for want of a spirit of faith, and a spirit of prayer?

If you were convinced of the truth of this faith that tells you Jesus

Christ is present in the Superior, you would have no trouble conforming your ideas to his or hers. Oh, blessed course of love!

Nothing brings about and strengthens intimacy like obedience. *The one who does the Will of God is my brother, my sister.*[233]

What I said to you was meant for all consecrated souls: "I have enclosed you in my Heart and you will always be there on the one condition that your will remains always enclosed in Mine, so well enclosed as to be buried there in a perpetual act of adherence."

Stay more in the school of my Heart, to learn there, to draw from it this spirit of service, this worship of my Will that obedience represents.

Know that I will be prompt to grant your desires in the measure that you will be prompt to grant Me mine. The more you hasten to answer my entreaties, the more I will hasten to respond to yours.

If then your great wish is to hasten the hour of my Mercy's triumph over the world, hasten to carry out my loving Will by "renewing" a fervent promptness in the observance of your obedience.

May your *Fiat* at every moment be an eager *Fiat* of the heart, immediate, without the least hesitation, without losing a second thinking of yourself and granting the enemy time to wedge his way in.

Oh, how I love this loving fervor, this instantaneousness that comes from it, as I already told you, "to so quickly want what I want that you no longer know whether it is you or Me who wanted it in the first place."

Promptness, which is the best evidence of a total surrender that presupposes the soul's state of loving availability, ready to obey at the least sign. Weigh these expressions well and examine yourselves: Are you truly always ready? Are you able to respond when the least sign is made to you, *"Paratum cor meum. . . . Adsum."*[234] I'm on my way!

Oh, my spouses, be a "live-wire" of Love, always listening, al-

---

[233] *Matt 12:50; Mk 3:35*

[234] *Ps 56:8 and 107:2 — My heart is ready. . . . I am here (Douay Rheims).*

ways at the ready, on the look-out for the least sign, the least call that you may rush to pursue its Good Pleasure, surrounding It with a bulwark of love against the infernal barrages being hurled at It.

Contemplate the good example of my Eucharistic obedience and its fervent promptitude to the words of the priest as I descend at once into the Host.

After that, how could you be distraught at having to obey with all your heart, at having to pronounce this heartfelt *Fiat* that my "appeal" asks of you?

This loving promptitude is nothing other than what the moment precisely calls for, at that very point in time, without delaying for a second once Love has made the sign!

Finally, as its indispensable accompaniment, this fervent promptitude calls for a gentle joy, fruit of the presence of my grace.

I will speak to you further of this loving virtue, joy, this "flower of perfection of all the virtues"; but you already know enough about this to do your joyful best to become, by your ever more generous practice of obedience, my faithful "co-redemptive spouses."

CHAPTER EIGHT

IN THE FLOW OF THE LITURGY

JESUS-JOY

Christmas, 1940

My Heart has Joy for its Name! Urged on by the ardor of my Charity, my Heart is that happy to give happiness to others that I come and lower Myself into the crèche of the Host, as I did into the crèche of the stable.

To lower Myself in order to exalt and raise up!

To raise up my poor, fallen brothers by the peace of reconciliation, joy of the world: *and on earth peace.*[235]

To exalt my Father whose sovereign rights have been offended, by restoring his Glory: Joy of heaven: *Glory in the highest.*

Peace and glory: two-fold gift of the Savior's joyous Coming, of the divine Sun of Justice, which is Sun of love and of mercy! You, my spouses, my intimates, my consecrated ones, understand and taste the distinctive joy of this ever-present mystery of the redemptive Nativity, that you may bring many souls to understand and taste of It.

Joy in giving joy through the sacrifice of self, the only true joy

---

[235] *Lk 2:14*

which consists not of enjoying but of rejoicing. What an abyss there is between these two, the great chasm that separates egoism from love.

To say Jesus-Host is to say Jesus-Joy, for this is Jesus-Love. And to share Jesus' joy is to give joy to his Father, just as He does: the joy of glorification. To give joy to his brothers: the joy of redemption. And doing this by the same plenary act of giving, of loving abasement that is the Life of the consecrated Host.

And, marvel of love, sharing this joy multiplies it. Oh, what love assistance is sweeter than the beloved's multiplication of the Spouse's joy!

Know too that in the very measure that you understand, imitate and thus multiply Jesus' joy, you yourself will taste it, with a delight that is wholly pure and divinizing, that will make Me grow in you, that will make you become Me. Love's blessed union, supreme joy of the Host to work such a marvel!

Jesus is the joy of the soul in the measure that the soul is the joy of Jesus. And the soul is the "joy" of Jesus in the measure that it is the "victim" of Jesus in order to become the "host" of Jesus.

Jesus-Pity, Jesus-Charity, I am and want to be for this desolate world more than ever Jesus-Joy, Jesus-Comforter, Jesus-Happiness. Yes, for even more than Jesus-Hope, even more than Jesus-Savior, I am Jesus-Presence, and Presence of incomparable love, multiplied thousands and thousands of times, renewed over and over again beneath the ineffable veil of the consecrated Host.

Irradiating Presence, overflowing with graces. To say Jesus-Present, isn't it the same as to say Jesus Bread of Life, Jesus who fulfills, Jesus who satisfies! All sorrow invariably comes from some want.

If you wish to give happiness to my Heart, be among those who reveal this secret of joy and resurrection. By your life, above all, be my faithful echo to those near to you.

Tell them that my Host is the Bread of happiness.

Tell them that my Heart is the Home of happiness.

Tell them my Happiness is to gratify by means of Myself so that the superabundant plentitude of the Father's Charity may be exalted and magnified.

In order to help Me to gratify, to gratify with Myself, you have to become Me. You have to become host, host that is fully consecrated, in accord with the ever more lively desire of my "appeal."

Jesus is present with a gratifying presence to those who are present to Him with a gifting presence. He is all gift to those who are all gift to Him, which is why He is Jesus-Happiness.

O my consecrated ones, give Me this ineffable happiness of being able to gratify you most mercifully with Myself. Surrender a place in your soul for the divinizing invasions of the "divine Occupant"!

And then as "auxiliary" lovers also help Me increase my Happiness by making room for Me in the "immense family of souls" that my Goodness has conferred on you and that I so desire to invade and fulfill.

Clear a path for the gift of my Love. Prepare the way for the increasing happiness of my Savior Heart through prayer for the entire world, through self-renunciation and a zeal that is ever more apostolic.

Yes, the supreme happiness that immediately gives access to beatitude is to "die in Me," in the Charity of my Heart, after having courageously spent one's life "dying to self," to one's egoism, to "die for Me," in order to give Me "one's life," deep in one's soul, through a continuous losing of self that offers place, makes room for the divinizing grip of divine possession.

Constantly put into practice by a sincere *Non Mea, sed Tua.*[236] *"Death to me! Life to You!"*

Happy little deaths of your earthly life that have you advance each time further into my Heart, preparing you to come at the moment of your last breath to the same level with Me in the bosom of my Father. Blessed demise!

Truly, the "little victim-host" is then totally "taken and consumed"

---

[236] *Lk 22:42 — Not my will but thine.*

by Me and for Me, as true "co-redemptive spouse" in accord with the vow of my "appeal."

SING TO ME . . . A NEW SONG

1940

My consecrated ones, if you would console my Heart, which needs it so very much, then sing to Me a new Song, so that you may help Me in the work of "renewal" that my Heart wants to accomplish in the world where satanic hatred is amassing the works of death — ruin, devastation, destruction.

For don't forget that *I am the Resurrection and the Life,*[237] and as I revealed to my well-beloved disciple, *Ego nova facio omnia.*[238]

Yes, it is I Myself who wants and is able to renew the face of the earth, make all things new. But it is Me *with you*, friends of Mine, *your* association with Me is indispensable. Recall my "appeal" and the "renewing of fervor" that it seeks from you.

If the hour of suffering is a time for hope, when the creature in distress hurls cries for help to heaven, then the time of greatest suffering is the time of greatest hope, the time most allowed for cries of hope and therefore time of hope's renewal.

Now, you know, hope is a canticle of love, faith's blossoming on earth. A song of destitute love to merciful Love. Indigent love, that is, with the trust of a thankful child as it appeals, as it exalts by invoking, adores by imploring the infinite riches of the loving Goodness of its Father in heaven.

A song where all the loving notes harmonize so agreeably with my Heart: praise, thanksgiving, humility, trust, adherence. A song that only rises, only ascends, only sings on condition that it is ceaselessly repeated in a perpetual *crescendo* of fervor.

For if all life that is not being constantly renewed declines and

---

[237] *Jn 11:25*

[238] *Rev 21:5 — I make all things new.*

wastes away, how is this not the case with Life *par excellence* which is the life of Love? In these times of profound distress and suffering, only by a renewal of hope are you able to sing the new song of love my Heart asks of you as little "co-redemptive helpers."

And yet, know that in order to be renewed in this way, Hope has to be nourished by prayer and patience. Oh, never drop the arms of prayer, this most indispensable element of hope.

My Heart most specially calls for a renewal of fervor in reciting the Divine Office which is the distinctive function of sacerdotal and religious souls.

Have you never noted the beautiful meaning of this word "office" which signifies "duty of service," direct service to Divinity. A tribute to be offered with affection. I invite you to render this service and tribute, to offer it in intimate union with my Heart, in close communion with its sentiments. *Domine, in unione illius divinae intentionis, qua ipse in terris laudes Deo persolvisti.*[239]

Yes, in order to renew yourselves, meditate on this unity of intentions, of divine intentions, which presuppose unity of interests and thus unity of affections along with unity of dispositions. That this be truly so, that with one and the same heart, with one and the same soul, *Cor unum et anima una,* we might together sing the ever fresh canticle of love that all the modulations of hope-filled songs on earth compose.

For that's just what the *Psalms* are, cries of hope with all its ranging notes of love. Psalms always in all things akin to "eternity's actuality."

Therefore make yours all the sentiments expressed there, just as I have made them my Own, with all my merciful affection.

How topical, for example, is the *De Profundis* that you recite so often, and how comforting it is for your soul, and at the same time how glorious it is for my redemptive love to apply it to this poor world and to my dear France in particular. *Israel speret in Domino, Ipse redi-*

---

[239] *From the Divine Office — O Lord, in union with that divine intention by which He Himself paid praise to God for all on earth.*

met.[240] Yes, let her hope in Me simply, without confusion. I Myself will save her. But Me with you, my consecrated ones. I repeat it again and again: For France to be spiritually brought back to life, a perpetual, divinizing rebirth of spirit has to take place in your souls as my partners, through an ever more intimate communion with Me, to Me, in Me.

Omnia in communione. In communione omnium. All things in communion. In communion with all things, which means with intentions, dispositions, views, affection, desires, operations.

In order to sing to Me a song on earth that is always lovingly new, your hope must not only be continually fed by prayer, but it must be continually sustained by patience as well. Patience, this virtue of invincible, loving fidelity by which, in the sufferings and persecutions of this life, as I told you, you would *master your souls and bear fruit.*[241]

But what feeds this virtue? Of what does it consist? As always, look at my Heart and you will understand that patience is made both of gentle acquiescence and strong resistance.

Recall to mind my Passion. Imitate Me: Gentleness of a tireless "yes" from the Heart of infinite Love concealed beneath the ordeal. Strength from the will's tireless "no" to perfidious appeals, be they from a weak ego that would want to capitulate, yield, back off in the face of such suffering, or from an insane pride that wants to take an even harder line.

Your patience therefore has to be the fidelity of your soul believing in and answering to the fidelity of my Heart.

A virile and generous courage is needed in order to endure suffering in this way, in order to bear the Cross actively, to support it with love and not just to drag it along or support it with passive resignation.

There has to be the generosity of adding a share of voluntary sacrifice to the imposed suffering, for whatever the hardship may be, my Heart is too eager for this gift of your heart not to leave room in your love's spontaneity and chivalric *élan* for the addition of a personal

---

[240] *Ps 129: 6,8 — Let Israel hope in the Lord . . . . He shall redeem Israel [from all its iniquities] (Douay-Rheims).*

[241] *Lk 21:19, 8:15*

offering, a little extra immolation. Little luxury without which sensual nature is likely to find its way back again, thus altering the purity of suffering and diminishing thereby even its co-redemptive value.

Would that each of you might search your hearts for what this little voluntary immolation might be (silence, poverty, charity, custody of the eyes) . . . that it might be joined to the painful ordeal of the present time.

Far from making that ordeal more burdensome, this will lighten it since it is love that is being tested, tested more and more, all of which is solace to any truly loving soul.

HOLY WEEK

Holy Thursday, 1939

Listen to these few words about the wonders of the Host whose Nativity feast is today:

The redemptive Host by Itself would only have had to happen on earth to already fully satisfy the Justice of the Father. But out of magnificent, merciful love the Host wanted to remain and to that end made Itself "Eucharistic Host."

But just remaining wasn't enough for this superabundant Goodness. By remaining, the Host wanted to return. Yes, to remain without end and to return without ceasing, to remain in all completeness, to return so as to become always more.

Oh, adore, admire and lose yourself in this mystery, as unfathomable in its all-powerful wisdom as it is dazzling in its love.

For how, you wonder and ask of Me, how can this Host that is divine Plentitude and therefore infinite Plentitude, how can this Host become always more?

The secret of this lies in the very superabundance of this Plentitude, a Plentitude fully sufficient for Itself and its creative work that nevertheless extended its indulgence to the unheard-of degree of not wanting it to be sufficient, as it were, for its redemptive work.

That's why, at every hour of every day, through the unceasing reenactment of Calvary's Sacrifice, I come, I return, in the Eucharistic Host with a fresh, superabundant outpouring of graces, of redemptive power in order to make it actual in the souls of creatures, my Father's children, in order to form and win for Him more host-souls, souls that are more host and that disappear like little particles into the divine Host, for its ever greater extension and dilation until the saving decree of my Father has been accomplished in the world.

That's what it means to return without ceasing, to become always more.

Good Friday, 1940

This is the ineffable mystery of love's consummations that are being renewed and carried out at this moment on earth. Learn how to meditate and understand the marvels of *Consummatum est.*[242]

The consummation of my work is only complete, only satisfied therefore, by your consummation in Me, with Me, in the oneness of the great divine Family.

And by my Father's Holy Will that gave Me this work, your consummation in Me requires that we, you and I, be consumed in sacrifice in the loving flames of his Holy Spirit.

On my part, you know how perfectly and totally I had been consumed, until the last fiber and the last drop of my Blood were spent, and I remain on earth consumed in the sacrifice of the Host. So that nothing was lacking, nothing is lacking on my part in Love's consuming work. But on your part, is there nothing lacking? Has everything been consumed?

Examine yourself in light of my "appeal" which will tell you that to be "consumed" is to be crucified, for that's what it means to be the "victim" of a crucified Savior Spouse. Isn't it so? Are you without any exception the victim of my Love?

And each of you, have you no reservations, are you wholly victim of my redemptive fire? Answer Me.

---

[242] *Jn 19:20*

If it isn't so, it means that everything has not been consumed.

And if everything has not been consumed, everything has not been consummated, for you then are not "wholly consecrated hosts" and the co-redemptive work cannot be wholly accomplished.

And, alas, since you cannot give Me, all of you, a fully satisfactory, affirmative reply, you understand why the *Sitio (I thirst)* of my Calvary remains unsatisfied for so long, and implores so ardently in my Eucharistic Host.

Yes, I thirst for consummation, an ardent thirst of my Great Priestly Prayer to the Father for its realization in each soul, *That they may be consummated.*[243]

But bear in mind that in order to be consummated in the unity of love, one must be consummated in the unity of the Host. Have a thirst for this then, for this consummation, an imploring thirst that agonizes your souls and stimulates your prayers and your generosity.

Send Me too your earnest, urgent, "loving appeal" which asks of Me what I ask of you in my own earnest, urgent "loving appeal."

Holy Saturday, 1940

Yes, help Me to pursue and achieve my consummations of love.

And know that to the extent that you are "victim" of my consummations, you will serve their "outcome" in the immense crowd of souls who depend upon you (weigh well this expression: *who depend upon you*). And at the same time, you become love's living "ramparts" that drive back the infernal assaults of hatred, all by committing yourself to the expansion of my Father's kingdom.

Easter, 1940

Glory to your Glory. Love to your Love, O my triumphant King, with a heart all on fire. Your joy ravishes and fulfills me. May the full achievement of your work of Host be fully consummated, through the graces that flow freely from the Life of your saving Blood.

---

[243] *Ibid 17:23*

Yes, you have understood it well, unworthy "little victim": the crucifixion is but the path to consummation. Its end is the loving marvel of the divinization of my Life, *For I am the Resurrection and the Life,*[244] the great and loving One Who Lives and who *does not wish the death of this poor sinful world, but that it should be converted and live.*[245]

That it might live the great Life of divine Charity, for, prodigy of my mercy, I can only prevent the death of the world by communicating to it my own Life as Savior. I can only save the world by divinizing it. But in order to consummate this prodigy (I tell you this again from the depths of my ineffable Beatitude), I must have your help.

But in order that my consecrated souls be able to truly transmit my Life, isn't it necessary that they be filled with It to the point of overflowing? That their love be overflowing with life, in everlasting deeds of donation, through the fervent multiplication of virtuous acts that prove this love. Now, isn't this so?

Isn't the life of the soul of too many of my consecrated ones lacking in true life because the religious and sacerdotal virtues in them are not sufficiently active, that they regard these virtues defensively, as negatives, and not as something positive, as winning strategies.

All I want is to "renew" the life of love in your souls. This is the great wish of my "appeal," so that you may become its dispensers to many souls.

ENTER INTO THE JOY OF YOUR LORD

Easter, 1941

Dearly beloved souls, you who have undergone my sufferings in order to lighten them for Me, enter this day into my Joy, into the Joy of the Heart of your Glorious Spouse that my Joy may increase.

Understand this well:

---

[244] *Ibid 11:25*
[245] *Ezek 18:23*

The Cross is only a passageway, joy is a dwelling place, the dwelling place of Love. This is the great lesson of the Resurrection.

A necessary passageway, that is true, such was Calvary. — The sole front door to the Dwelling Place of Joy.

I was the first to enter. And my mission as Savior is to be the merciful usher for my brothers, to support them and lead each of them along their way of the Cross, opening a heaven of joy to them. For, though risen from the dead, I am with them still in my Host.

I wanted, by my Eucharistic Presence, to leave oases of joy along earth's painful passageway, oases that would be permanent dwelling places of joy for host-souls.

Happy, blessed are those wholly consecrated souls who have understood, who have tasted that each sacrificial step on the way of my suffering, each *Fiat* to the Cross, is an "entrance to my joy"; an entry all that farther into the dwelling place of Love, a place of countless precincts. *In my Father's House are many rooms.*[246]

Oh, on this great anniversary of my Resurrection, how my beatified, glorified Savior's Heart would like to make the poor, suffering, agonizing, dying world understand that the true palace of happiness, of peace, of life, is the palace of charity, the palace of love, the palace of joy that one can only access through the door of sacrifice.

Then how greatly those who are suffering from this earth of desolation would bless Me for the merciful ordeals I subject them to.

My consecrated ones, don't you want to bless Me for this suffering on their behalf, and on your own behalf at the same time? For don't forget, you are responsible for souls, responsible for the entire world.

Think about my "appeal," and tell yourselves that an avalanche of such pain and sorrow would not have fallen on the world if you, Love's enlightened ones, had not too often deserted the dwelling place of joy, of my great divine Joy (which is the palace of most pure charity), in order to fall back into the sad, dark dwelling place of your ego and its petty little interests.

---

[246] *Jn 14:2*

Now that you have understood, I hope, my great redemptive lesson, don't each of you want to help Me a little to expel from the world this immense, profound sorrow in order that the great joy of peace, the contentment of love might flow over it?

I have such thirst to give happiness, most especially at this hour of such great sorrow! Who will help Me quench my thirst if not all of you whom I wish to be fervent dispensers, possessing my great, loving joy to that end.

In order to spread my joy, commune with my joy. As I have told you, my joy is my Love itself, its great divine Life.

O my consecrated ones, if you were able, if you knew, if you had thus wanted to disappear from this life into this praise, you would have found the secret of communing with my joy in order to spread my joy. Think about this in prayer.

I've already told you, and you've already understood, beloved associates of my Redemption, that in order to bring back a little of the true joy of love into this poor world so weighted down with painful, egoistic sorrow, you yourselves must begin by entering into the joy of your Savior, by advancing there ever more deeply, for otherwise how can you pretend to draw others there ?

But in order to do this, it is absolutely necessary to leave the tight little sphere of your egoistic *me*, its petty little personal interests, escape from the human basement of yourself and take flight to the divine heights.

Oh, blessed *sursum* of a soul that Love alone animates, that Love more and more transports, raises up, attracts, transforms and divinizes!

Blessed ascension of a soul conquered by the Most High, wanting only to soar to Him, to fly to his paternal Heart in order to find there its celestial haven. This joy of *sursum* is the greatest joy of true, loving hearts, of those who, avid to give, know how to see in every obstacle, in every difficulty, an occasion for spreading one's wings, for glancing on high. *Gloria in excelsis!* [247]

Joy of those who know how to recognize in every suffering, every

---

[247] *Lk 19:38*

vexation, in every little sacrifice, fuel for fires of love and therefore for fires of joy, fires with mounting flames that, because they are so pure, soar straight upward towards the heights. *Hosannah in Excelsis.*[248]

Meditate, understand, conquer, savor, spread this joy of the *sursum*, so beneficial to your souls, so contagious to all other souls, so glorious to my Heart. Only in these heights of the *sursum* is the soul able to taste the pure, ineffable joy of divine Beauty.

What I must have in order to purify the poor world of its sordid stains of egoism and hatred is love most pure, charity most pure. My Heart needs the help of purity, of purity's generous amends. But who will grant Me this, from whom will I obtain it if not from you, my "co-redemptive spouses"?

Now, there is no love that is more exalted, more pure than love that is absolutely unselfish, love from a heart that pours out nothing but praise, cries of admiration, glances of kindness, songs of elation, in radiant contemplation before the spectacle of infinite Beauty, the divine Splendor of the Father.

Consecrated souls, in order to make amends for this earth-bound egoism in the poor lives of so many humans at this very moment in this sad world, my Savior's Heart, so wanting at any cost to abduct all to my heaven, needs to have your heavenly joy gushing forth from the loving contemplation of my divine Beauty.

I lack, I don't have enough of these admiring souls, these contemplative souls whose entire interest is "up above," whose entire curiosity is "up above," whose entire complacency is "up above."

Without this total disengagement from the self, without this complete selflessness, there is no pure praise, no pure joy, no pure love; and consequently there are no "true co-redemptive spouses," no "fully consecrated hosts."

While most of mankind at this moment is preoccupied, mired down in purely earthly concerns, how many are there among you, religious souls whose material concerns I relieve a hundred times over,

---

[248] *Mk 11:10*

how many of you are conscious of growth in your souls, who have only heavenly concerns growing in them?

How many are there with enough love in their hearts to have the courage truly to forget themselves, truly to forget all the vain, human curiosities in order to lose themselves in my Beauty, be carried away in my praises, be lost in my Splendor?

How many are there, how many — tell Me. Oh, if you only knew how much your help would hasten the hour of the world's great Redemption.

I have told you these things, all things, so that you may have in you the fullness of my joy.[249]

CONSOLATOR OPTIME

O THOU, OF COMFORTERS THE BEST. . . .[250]

June, 1941

At this moment in the poor world, the most terrible devastations are spreading through the hate-filled machinations of the evil spirit, the spirit of darkness.

But my Savior's Heart that wants so desperately to save all souls from these things, burns more than ever to bring souls redemptive comfort through a new descent, a new outpouring of my Spirit of Love, the Spirit of Holiness. *Consolator Optime.* Oh, yes, Comforter most excellent, surpassing all needs and desires with its gifts.

Divine Illuminator whose Light is Truth, whose Light is always consoling. Isn't the sole purpose of this Light the revelation of Love? *O Lux beatissima.*[251]

Divine Restorer, Spirit who purifies, erases, remakes, who

---

[249] *Jn 17:13*

[250] *From the "Veni Sancte Spiritus" sequence of the Mass for Pentecost.*

[251] *Most blessed Light.*

consoles the soul with the unction of peace. *Peace which passes all understanding.*[252] *Spiritalis unctio.*[253]

Divine Animator, who endows with his power, who transforms in his fire, who penetrates the heart with the ineffable consolations of his charity. *Fons vivus, ignis, caritas.* [254]

The Spirit thus wants to be the great Consoler of all who are afflicted, the supreme Consolation for all sorrows, the great Renewer of the face of the earth.

Oh, consecrated souls, all of you, don't you want to afford my Heart the consolation of consoling your hearts, the hearts of everyone, by a generous outpouring of this Consoling Spirit? Flame from the paternal Heart of your God and my God. What is needed for that to happen?

Two things, that you already know: opening up and calling out.

Opening up, to the point of shedding blood, by offering a *Fiat* of complete surrender to the two-edged sword of Love.

Calling out with the humble, imploring cry, confident of a *Veni* passing through the Heart of Mary and drawing down torrents of love. *Veni, Consolator Optime.*[255]

Can there be sweeter consolation for a loving soul than to console the Heart of the One it loves? Now, learning how to console is the great gift of my Consoling Spirit, his distinctive mission vis-à-vis consecrated souls, the inestimable consolation that He brings them.

To learn, one must first of all understand. Therefore, the Spirit as Divine Illuminator begins by illuminating in the deepest way, *cordis intima,*[256] the soul that sincerely desires to console its crucified Spouse.

To that end the Spirit reminds the soul of the great redemptive re-

---

[252] *Phillip 4:7*

[253] *Spiritual unction.*

[254] *Font of life, fire, love.*

[255] (lit.) *Come, Comforter most excellent.*

[256] *in the inmost heart.*

alities paid for at the price of his Blood, and of the cry his Blood utters: *He will teach you all things and bring to your remembrance all that I have said to you.*[257]

The price of my Blood, its purifying and divinizing action. *This is my Blood poured out for the remission of sins.*[258] *He who drinks my Blood has life eternal.*[259] From whence comes the supreme consolation for all those who receive my Blood and by It quench their thirst, as It gushes forth from the Source of all consolation which is the Sanctuary of my Heart.

O Consolator optime. The cry of my Blood, its thirst, its call. My Holy Spirit, Tongue of fire from the Trinity, makes you resonate with It and ceaselessly to proclaim It from the depths of your heart. Listen to It: Offer Me chalices with which to receive Me, living chalices of hearts that are pure, open, ardent, filled with desire.

Yes, my Heart is a Chalice that seeks chalices. A Chalice overflowing with divine Blood seeking human chalices, the hearts of men and women, in order to divinize them by the purifying and transforming effusion of this Blood in merciful torrents. The Chalice of eternal Salvation.

But, alas, I find few souls like this, souls who are for Me true, living chalices of my Blood, and yet only these merit the title of "true co-redemptive spouses." Few souls therefore into whom I can pour out the treasures of my consolation, and this is what causes the great desolation of my Savior's Heart: my great suffering is having to hold Myself back in pouring out my Blood.

Yes, if my Heart has so great a need to be consoled, it's because It has such need to console the hearts of others, and to be unable to do what my Heart so wants is an immense affliction for It. My Heart is truly desolate at not being able to console as the Love of my Heart would like. It can't, you know, because too many hearts are closed to It or are half-closed.

---

[257] *Jn 14:26*

[258] *Matt 26:28*

[259] *Jn 6:54*

You understand now what has to be done in order to console my Heart, what has to be. You will be chalices of consolation to Me in the measure that you will be and will form chalices of my Blood, which means hearts ever more widely opened, through trust and generosity, to my outpourings as Savior. This is the great loving lesson of the Spirit Who Consoles.

It is also as divine Redeemer that my Holy Spirit is the *Consolator Optime* for the soul. Indeed, what is it, loving souls, that causes you the greatest suffering if not the awareness of weaknesses and deficiencies in your love response to my Heart, of your lack of correspondence to all the advances of my grace, of your pilfering and your cowardice in my Father's service. For you see, don't you, that you have thus more or less deformed, effaced my Image in you, thwarting, hindering the divine work.

This awareness gets transformed in you as feelings of interior distress, of trouble and anxiety, each stain on your soul being a wound to my Heart. Personal distress heightened by an apostolic distress at the thought of the numberless wounds that the stains of souls inflict on my Heart. Yet it was to console you in this deep, inner distress that I assigned to my Divine Spirit the mission of applying to you the healing power of my Blood. As most Holy and Merciful Artist, *Right Hand of my Father,* not only does He cleanse but, in accord with the divine ideal, He redraws my Image.

He cleanses the deformed traits of egoism with my Blood. By that same Blood He redraws the divine traits of my Love. A work that He performs in the measure that the soul cooperates humbly and courageously: *lava, sana, riga.*[260] In thus pouring out my Blood into the soul, the Spirit pours into it the Spiritual unction of Peace, his Peace, the true consolation of heaven.

Therefore, souls most beloved, if you want to console my Heart, constantly have yourself restored and be endlessly consoled by my divine Spirit. Yes, constantly, for through Satan's endless solicitations your egoism is inclined to despoil your soul. Would that at the end of every day, or even better after every action, you might cultivate the

---

[260] *be cleansed, be healed, be firm.*

habit by my Holy Spirit of turning to the restorative power of my Blood: Divine Restorer, deign to restore me by the consolation of your redemptive Blood. Thus will your soul be a chalice of consolation for Me.

The excellence of my Consoling Spirit is not only that He restores what has come undone, but that He renders it more beautiful. He perfects the masterpiece conceived in the Mind of the Father. And so, as France falls apart, He wants to restore her and make her more beautiful. For the Spirit, to restore is to perfect. It was in order to complete and bring to perfection my work as Savior that I sent the Spirit into the world and am continually sending Him. He is the Divine Illuminator and the Divine Restorer only so that He may be the Divine Animator. Such is the distinctive mission of the Spirit of Holiness, the Sanctifying Spirit.

To animate means to transform, to transfigure. The Spirit comes as a reformer to work on all that is deformed and disfigured in the soul, by conforming and configuring it to the Image of the Incarnate Word, and thereby effecting a marvelous, divine transfiguration. Transfiguration that is the ultimate ideal of perfection to which every consecrated soul is specially called.

Consolator Optime, this is the work of consoling that my Heart intends for the Feast [of Pentecost] fast approaching. Listen therefore to what is addressed to each and every one of you, that you may keep it more closely in the depths of your hearts: *Venite ad me, omnes qui laboratis . . . Et Ego reficiam vos.*[261]

Souls, you who more or less feel yourselves a failure, overcome with egoism, come quickly to my Heart that wants to restore you to greater beauty through my Holy Spirit, that, by having you pass through the fire of love, wants to make you more pure, more divine.

Yes, remake you, which means to recast you in the burning crucible of infinite Charity.

---

[261] *Matt 11:28 — Come unto me all who labor . . . and I will give you rest.*

Feast of the Sacred Heart

1938

Feast of my Heart: Feast of my "appeal." Stream of fire rising up from its thirsty depths to flow into the hearts of my consecrated ones, that I may consume them, consecrate them, consummate them as one with the "co-redemptive Host," to the praise and glory of my Father.

Yes, feast of my "appeal," because the feast of my Heart is the feast of my fire and the feast of my fire is the feast of my Thirst, just as it is simultaneously the feast of my overflowing waves of love.

To celebrate my Heart, then, give It this day an abundance of trust and praise in the most pure joy of wholly surrendered love, of a wholly consecrated heart, one that is wholly victim therefore. For whoever says *feast* means jubilation and sumptuous abundance, as in the lover's gift to his beloved, the beloved's to her lover. And isn't the most generous gift the one that gives up the most, with a joyful heart that delights in the giving, the *Fiat* full of *Magnificat,* no matter how austere may be the faith and the cross along the way.

I Myself become joy and feast most sweet in making you generous, by giving you a festive heart, by pouring out these dispositions of generous love, for you sense well enough that they only come from Me, and that my most ardent Wish is that they become permanent, efficacious realities in you.

That is why I tell you: Remain and live with a festive heart. Isn't each of the feast days of my Heart for my spouses? Just as for Me, your Savior, each day was my Father's Feast Day, and my Heart never ceased to throb and beat with joy as I delivered my Being to the Father's redemptive Will. *Voluntarie sacrificabo tibi et confitebor.*[262]

On each page of my Gospel you find this delight in generosity of giving, giving to the point of holocaust. Delight therefore that not only can co-exist with suffering, but finds in suffering cause for a more

---

[262] Ps 53:8 — *I will freely sacrifice to thee and will give praise (Douay Rheims).*

ardent, more profound and purer outpouring; not necessarily felt but lived, in a wholly spiritual way.

Exsultavit spiritus meus in Deo.[263]

1939

This feast of my Heart is the feast of the Irradiation of my immense Love. There is no more radiant, irradiating focal point than the wounds of my Heart made crimson by fire and blood, as perpetual outpouring of redemptive Charity.

Irradiation that penetrates deeply: consuming, consecrating, consummating, fecundating.

Be all "prey" for Me, ever more "consumed," by the *Ecce* that is ever more given-over in a poverty that is ever more open-minded and generous.

Be all "host" for Me, ever more consecrated, by the *Fiat* that is ever more acquiescent and obedient, even unto holocaust.

Be all "spouse" for Me, ever more consummated as one life, by the *Magnificat* that rises ever higher from a chastity that is ever more virginal.

Be all "co-redeemer" for Me, mother ever more fruitful of souls, by the *Adveniat* that ever more conquers through an apostolic dedication that is ever more zealous and selfless.

Then each of you will be a true child, wholly child of the Father, whose only life is to join in Goodness's great work with all your heart and soul and strength.

This is what it comes down to practically: with each new breath that creative Love accords you, to lose your life in Me more completely, to increase, spread the Life of the redemptive Host until It entirely covers the world and through the triumphant effusion of his Mercies, the Father's complacency is entirely satisfied.

---

[263] *Lk 1:47 — My spirit rejoices in God.*

Hic est Calix Sanguinis mei, novi testamenti, qui pro vobis et pro multis effundetur in remissionem peccatorum. . . . Bibite ex Hoc omnes. . . . Gratias agens.[264]

Hic, this, my Heart, is the Chalice of the Blood of redemptive Love, purifying, pardoning, saving Blood for the remission of sins. Divinizing, uniting, life-giving Blood of the new union.

The consolation, the joy, the triumph of the feast of my Heart is to pour out the Blood of this Chalice upon you, consecrated souls, upon many, upon the greatest number possible, upon the entire world of souls. So that thanks be rendered to the Father, grace be given to the world, and that the union be sealed this time forever.

The present to make to my Heart for this feast, therefore, is to offer It hearts that are open and free, so that they may receive this redemptive Blood and shed It in their turn. Now, cannot such hearts, ought not such hearts be called chalices, called to be living chalices completely consecrated to the work of redemption?

Yes, my Heart is a Chalice that needs chalices for It to be poured out, chalices of hearts that are totally given over to It, and you have understood now what this means, that chalice for Chalice, as host for Host, signifies blood for Blood.

In order to collect the divine Blood, the primary use of the Chalice, mustn't there in fact be an opening in the heart? Now, when one says opening, isn't one saying wound, and therefore an effusion of blood?

In order to pass on the divine Blood, which is the second use of the chalice, isn't the same thing necessary, that the heart must be open and even pierced so that its own blood might gush forth?

Consequently it's only in the measure that one has a spirit of sacrifice that a soul merits the signal honor of serving Me as co-redemptive

---

[264] *Canon of the Holy Mass — This is the Cup of my Blood of the new testament, which will be shed for you and for many for the forgiveness of sins. . . . All of you, drink from It. . . . Giving thanks.*

chalice. The spirit of sacrifice whose practical form is nothing more than whole-hearted *Fiat* to my consecrating action. And this *Fiat* itself is just the generous response to the urgent invitation of the *Bibite ex Hoc omnes.*[265]

To quench one's thirst with Me, your Redeemer, in the Chalice of the divine Will, doing so at every instant, with all one's being, in large gulps, right to the bottom if necessary, so as to really be my "true co-redemptive spouses."

And, by this more intimate deepening of union that each drop of exchanged Blood produces (with each beat of the heart, if possible), to help make it happen that a new Alliance of merciful Redemption between the Heavenly Father and humanity be concluded and sealed.

This is the great work that my Heart pursues at this moment, and for which sake It pursues you with its supplications.

Become my feast, celebrating with a triple offering of the chalice: two to Me, one of Me. First, a chalice offering of your heart by the generous effusion of all its blood, which is to say, all that it contains in order that it might quench its thirst in the Chalice of my Heart, with all that It contains, allowing Me to pour in you and by you my redemptive Blood and in this way, by your partaking of it, sweeten my Chalice's bitterness.

Then, a chalice offering the hearts of all people (hearts you are charged with and are responsible for), so that you may give them what they don't know and don't want for themselves, and that this offering may contribute to open their hearts, allowing Me to pour my Savior Blood on them and in them.

Offering to my Father the Chalice of Salvation which is my Heart, *Offerimus Tibi Calicem salutaris.*[266]

Triple offering to be made through the mediation of the incomparable Chalice of the Immaculate Heart of Mary.

Do not forget that I am counting on you to renew France, to renew

---

[265] *All of you, drink from it.*
[266] *We offer You the Chalice of salvation.*

Christianity: The sovereign reign of Christ over the world, by my Blood, by my Host.

The Hearts of Jesus and Mary

1937

Perfectly conformed in all things, both wounded by love, these two Hearts are inseparable. You know this, but do you live by it? Are the two of Us both inseparably united in your life?

And in the first place, is my Heart inseparable from yours to the point of being the One you can't get along without? The Indispensable One?

For that to be the case, wouldn't you have to separate yourself from everything else, from all that encumbers you, and do without the little earthly objects, the little human, mundane pleasures that are incompatible with my divine Heart?

And isn't the Heart of my Mother as inseparable from yours as it is from Mine, with a tender maternal presence indispensable to the heart of every true child?

Isn't everything that comes from a treasure a treasure? And when this Treasure is a Heart filled with infinite fervor, what can come from It if not treasures of love? May its fiery waves be poured out on you, my consecrated ones, beginning with the priceless treasure of the Immaculate Heart of Mary. Thank Me for Her! Thank Her!

And then, don't you recognize that my "appeal" is one of these choice treasures sprung forth from the emblazing depths of the treasures of my Heart, to rekindle the flame in the hearts of my consecrated ones. That flame is burning there, I know, but I want it purer, more alive, more ardent, more radiant.

Oh, do not bury this treasure. You would deprive yourself of so many graces, and you would cause Me so much pain! But let it show as much as possible, I implore you! The time has come when this treasure of my "appeal" has to sparkle in souls more and more, so that my great Kingdom may spread. I count most especially on you for this. Do not let Me down.

October 20

Is not my Admirable Mother my Masterpiece of love! All adoration! All radiance! All the more radiant as She profoundly adores, prostrate, recollected, in most intimate communion with Me of views, of heart, of will, for the complacency of the Father: such is the true life of the spouse wholly surrendered to the hand of Love.

Such is Mary, your model and also your treasure, your second treasure, inseparable from my Heart, your first Treasure.

If my mission as Christ Mediator has Me be the "great Substitute" and "great Supplicant" on your behalf before the Father, the mediating mission of Mary constitutes this very thing for you before Me her Son — the great Substitute and great Supplicant. Therefore have pass through her maternal Heart the ardent supplications that my Heart implores that you make to Her. She will purify and embrace them.

My Heart is entirely open because It gives entirely, no less than It claims entirely, for It loves entirely. Entirely open in order to reveal Itself and to spread Itself. Entirely open in order to gather and take in. The same two-fold rhythm of love's unitive movement. What is it that opens my Heart? The burning two-edged sword of redemptive Mercy.

I seek vibrant hearts whom I can have keep my supplicating appeals, whom I can have feel my loving thirst. To whom should I turn if not to my consecrated ones? May they gaze at the Immaculate Heart of Mary for the model of an entirely vibrant soul.

Yes, she entirely resonated in her Heart with all that affected Me. Her Heart vibrated only for Me and always for Me, always in unison with my Heart for the complacency of the Father.

This vibrating in unison is the indispensable condition of the unity and union that I desire for all consecrated souls.

My Mother and I were all heart One to Another. Learn from Us that to be all heart is to be at one and the same time all overflowing and all yearning, both burning with the most pure love.

236

Strive to become "all heart," which is to say all fire and flame for Me alone, for the interests of my Father, for his Will taken in, savored, satisfied and glorified.

1938

My true spouses are not only spouses *of* my Heart but *in accord with* my Heart. That is, whose hearts are in tune with Mine, whose hearts beat in unison with Mine, with a burning love, beating in the two-fold rhythm of divine Charity: towards the Father and towards souls. Communion and diffusion!

And what Heart had been more and in better accord with my Heart than the Heart of Mary: wellspring and immaculate sanctuary.

Honor her Heart by imitating It, and by turning to It, so that Mine may be more and better glorified, by responding more generously to the wishes of my "appeal."

"CONSECRATED SOULS, BE SAINTS"

All Saints Day, 1940

Shouldn't the beloved bear the same distinguishing marks as her Spouse, if she really wants to do honor to his Name, be one of his household, enter into his privacy. Now, what are the distinguishing signs of Jesus, your Spouse? Was there anything more glorious than his blood-soaked marks, blood-soaked with love, divinely glorious?

Imitate my saints. What are they? What do they do?

All saints are martyrs of love. The measure, the very essence of their sanctity, is their blood mixed with Mine. Blood that is mixed meaning blood that is shed and lost in Mine, blood changed into my Blood in order to spread its redemptive effusions over the world.

And the more generous this mixing, the stronger the covenant of transforming intimacy between their hearts and Mine. And now we have the definition of the saint: An intimate of my Heart changed into Me through martyrdom. The blood marks of martyrdom's great love therefore are the distinguishing marks proper to sanctity.

Be my holy spouses, O consecrated souls, bearing the marks of your crucified Spouse with humble pride, courageous in your faithfulness.

For the most Holy Host to be able to expand its sanctifying action to the glory of the Holy Trinity, It must have holy hosts.

These are "the living, wholly given-over hosts" that my "appeal" speaks of in its quest for "little co-redemptive continuators." Oh, I implore you, do not forget my precious "appeal."

Don't forget, chosen souls, that you are consecrated to the Saint of all Saints, that you are the spouses of the Saint of all Saints.

Do you comprehend the obligation of sanctity that follows from this for you?

Yes, the Will of my most Holy Father is that you become saints and that you form saints of others. These two sides of your sublime vocation, both personal and apostolic, are inseparable.

No soul is holy who does not work to form saints for Me. No soul can form real saints for Me who does not work to become a real saint.

But what is a saint? A saint is one who is in perfect harmony with God, one therefore who is divinized, by a gradual substitution of the divine for the human in all one's activities of thought, heart and will. One divinized by love, divinized in love. A heart freely lost in the divinizing fires of my Heart's Charity.

Love's marvelous synonymy between this divinization, this harmonization, this sanctification.

Of all the sanctuaries of my religious families, can I really say that they are "Holy Places" as they should be by their very definition, can I say that from each of them there rises to heaven a harmony of love that glorifies my Father and consoles my Heart? A harmony ever more pure, more melodious, more sonorous, without a discordant note, without dissonance in charity, humility, poverty, obedience? How will you answer this?

What distorts everything, as you know, is egoism, egoism in all its forms, in all its deviations from Charity's great love that alone is in harmony with God, that alone is truly holy.

Recall to mind what I told you: To be sanctified in Truth is to be sacrificed in Charity, which means to perpetually immolate in the flames of my Heart those endlessly renewed solicitations of the egoistic *me*. In this consists love's great work of saintliness.

Oh, place yourselves there. Never cease returning to it. For I know how woefully fragile your hearts are, whose every failure to love brings a false note into the choir of my spouses.

Would that each of your pious exercises, being in collocation with my Heart, might be occasions for reestablishing harmony, for restoring closer accord with It and by It. For remember that a soul is in harmony with God, is agreeable and glorious to the Love of its heavenly Father, only to the extent that the soul is in harmony with my Heart as Savior and Spouse, united and divinized in Me, and to the extent, too, that the soul puts Me in harmony with the hearts of others.

Nothing chills my Heart, nothing disturbs the choir's harmony like discord of charity among my spouses. May they think about this by pondering the consoling counterpart as well.

November 21

What waves of delightfully pure and vibrant harmony came endlessly from the most tender childhood of Mary's Immaculate Heart! A Heart with its two-fold movement of love for the Father and for souls that harmonized so perfectly with Mine.

Yes, learn this great secret of saintliness from Mary, the Mother and Queen of all saints, that it is love alone that sanctifies, for love alone harmonizes and thereby divinizes. And understand from Her that the love word that harmonizes with everything is this heartfelt *Fiat* that my "appeal" speaks about. Always the same loving lesson that my Heart cannot help but repeat to you, so thirsty is It for your loving response.

You have understood, and my "appeal" tells you this, that this divinizing harmony with my Heart, which is what saintliness consists of, is a "harmony of hosts," of hosts fully consecrated to the work of redemption, from which it gets its indispensable apostolic character.

Yes, the Will of my Father is that you work with Him to form saints, which means not only to conform and harmonize your own hearts with Mine, but also to bring all those into harmony with Me that I have conferred upon you, to confront them, to put them in tune with Me, making my Priestly Prayer your own: *For their sake I consecrate myself, that they may be consecrated in truth.*[267]

Forming other Jesuses, prolongations of Jesus, souls transformed into Jesus, making for Me other Myselves, this is the main maternal function of my spouses. Would that they might remember what I said: In every baptized soul there is a latent Jesus, a Jesus aspiring to be realized, to be formed.

Would that your unique, motherly concern might be working therefore to give each day a little more of Jesus, as much Jesus as possible, this most precious trust that my Love has conferred upon each apostle for souls that have cost Me so dearly. Have souls take on the form of Jesus, remembering that for this transformation into Jesus there has to be conformity to Jesus. Have them enter deeply into the intelligence of Jesus' Spirit. Have then enter deeply into the heart of Jesus' affections, enter deeply into the will of all that Jesus wills.

To that end, be filled with all this yourselves, to the point of overflowing.

OTHER THOUGHTS

— Only my crucified spouses can aspire to the consoling honor of being able to lighten the wounds of the Crucified One, above all the wounds of my Heart from which has sprung (with what loving vehemence) every word of my "appeal."

— A genuine life consecrated to love cannot be a sheltered life but must be an exposed life.

But to what? Meditate on my Life as Christ Redeemer and you will understand what your life as redemptive co-redeemers must reproduce: an extension of Mine.

---

[267] *Jn 17:19*

240

— Know that love does not live on ideas, however noble they may be, but on actions performed at every moment with all one's being.

A *Fiat* that merely exists in the mind is sterile. Only a *Fiat* that is enacted engenders a co-redemptive life. Only *Fiats* that are carried out can capture the moment.

— If to *be* is to *act*, then to be truly religious is to act as a religious; to be truly consecrated is to act as someone consecrated; to truly be spouse is to act as spouse.

Do you act that way and therefore are you that way?

— Don't you have to oppose satanic fury with saintly folly?

The foolishness of the Cross is the foolishness of love. And the foolishness of love, isn't that the wisdom of the heart?

— For love undergoing a test, there is no true service without sacrifice.

— Offer Me hosts. Offer yourselves as hosts. That is my imploring refrain of love. When will it touch your hearts?

Who will take away my chill? Who will quench my thirst? Where will I find an oasis and a hearth if not in the sanctuary of each consecrated soul?

Isn't my Heart Itself oasis and hearth for you, One so divinely loving?!

— Love does not improvise its works. It prepares them. Has not Love conceived them in the unchanging Council of its Eternity?

And as regards redemption, Cross and Blood are its preparations, the exclusive and indispensable path of its triumph.

Look at my Heart and you will understand.

Let us unite our hearts as hosts, and together we will prepare the triumph of Love.

— Don't forget that if prayer in and of itself directly supplicates, suffering can do so even more. Suffering suffered well (that is, well-offered, in union with my redemptive suffering), isn't this in effect prayer *par excellence?*

Prayer *par excellence* in its effectiveness. Prayer *par excellence* in its perpetuity as well, for under any of its multiple forms every moment's lot is prayer. Whether this be physical pain, heartbreak, anxiety or helplessness, separation and privation, or simply abnegation of the will demanded by the duties of one's state.

Now, under each of these forms, prayer can and should be a "prayer" in union of heart with Me.

— Wouldn't a spouse's heart that has truly understood my great redemptive Thirst want more than ever to pour out to my Heart, from its depths, repeated waves of the purest and most ardent praise, blessings and acts of gratitude?

Oh, what sweet compensation this would be for my love, this supernatural spontaneity of your hearts on every occasion of suffering! (Don't wait for big ones.)

— I need and am searching for souls who welcome Love, who wholly welcome Me at every moment, in all the forms my thirsty tenderness takes, who know how to open to Me willingly, cordially, as soon as I knock. And isn't every moment under my Will?

The more you welcome Me with affection, the more will I divinely invade and fulfill you.

— Just as I was "at home" in "my Mother's house," and as I would truly like to be "at home" in the houses of my spouses, complete Master there to act as I please!

— I beg you, be religious to the core, be souls that are supernatural to the core. Oh, no, this life of a spouse-host won't be nice and easy, it will be deeply serious. Reflect on this and truly open yourselves up to this depth of soul that my love so covets, that It may penetrate it, to the point of this blessed holocaust of your entire being.

— How can a soul that is consecrated to Me hesitate for a single instant loving all that I love, desiring all that I desire, preferring all that I prefer, believing all that I affirm? The elementary formulas of love: are they being lived out?

— Let Me love you in a divine way, which is to fulfill you with love.

Give Me the joy of fulfilling you with Myself, but don't forget that allowing yourself to be fulfilled begins by allowing yourself to be taken *in toto*, allowing yourself to be stripped down to the last thread, consumed to the last fiber.

— A true spouse ought to let herself be literally taken by the Spouse she has given herself to, to rejoice in being taken. And doesn't He Himself take his Fidelity to heart, with a superabundance beyond all desire.

— Would that sacerdotal and religious souls by their total consecration might be fiery lightning rods for this poor world so furiously shaken by hell.

— Without the heart's mutual, on-going effusion, there is no real life of intimacy. To communicate Christ completely and unceasingly, as true apostles, you must completely and unceasingly commune with Christ. Commune with Him by being always of one mind with his views, his feelings, his wishes.

— Understand the loving secret of the detachments that I permit and multiply in your lives: I cannot be truly "Presence for the soul," living, permanent, absorbing Presence in the way that I desire except through the absence in you of everything else.

— I can only become your heart's Plenitude in the solitude of complete detachment. But then, the more that nothing hampers It, I am Plenitude overflowing, transforming and intimately consuming by a divinizing compenetration.

— These are the strippings that prepare for the incursions.

— The humiliations and self-denials are prelude to being raised up and transported to the Father's dwelling place.

— Just be flexible in my divine hands so that you may just be "victim" of my blazing Heart. That's the loving program of the spouse who is "all spouse."

— What is needed to disarm the satanic legions, to parry the blows hurled against Love, if not hearts that are burning, weapons of heroism, in order to serve as target?

Consecrated souls, all of you, accept this post of choice. A defensive post where one can only hold out by conducting an offensive of love. For the only way to effectively parry the blows of hatred is to turn the blows against the egoism that, at bottom, is but a pet name for hatred's principle.

— Joy and the cross: inseparable factors of love on earth. Without the cross, joy is but ephemeral pleasure, devoid of love. Without joy, the cross is but sterile suffering, it too devoid of love.

— It is from the host that the *Hosanna* of love gushes forth.

— For my disciples, and even with more reason for my spouses, not to follow Me to Calvary is to flee from Me. Not to serve Me to the point of suffering is to betray Me. To not be crucified with Me is to have a hand in my Crucifixion, to crucify Me in some way.

— The more I cause you to suffer, the more you should strive to smile. A "thank you" smile to Love.

The more I cause you to feel the rigors of love, the gentler should your *Fiat* be.

— Smiles and gentleness are the buds of delicacy and, without these, the gifts from my consecrated souls always lack something, no matter what they cost.

— The more I associate you with my sufferings, the more I deepen the capacity of your soul. And the more you embrace this suffering with love, the more I invade this capacity, filling it to overflowing so that you overflow into the souls I have given you.

I help you, help Me. Let us help one another to carry the Cross of redemption.

— Transfixion, being pierced, is the condition for the transmission of crucified love.

❖

Made in the USA
Columbia, SC
19 February 2020